Lynn Mitchell
Cocoa Beach, FL
2005

Elegant Irish Cooking

Elegant Irish Cooking

Recipes from the World's Foremost Irish Chefs

Noel C. Cullen,
Ed.D, CMC, AAC

Photography by Ron Manville

LEBHAR-FRIEDMAN BOOKS
New York Chicago Los Angeles London Paris Tokyo

LEBHAR-FRIEDMAN BOOKS
425 Park Avenue
New York, NY 10022

Published by Lebhar-Friedman Books
Lebhar-Friedman Books is a company of Lebhar-Friedman, Inc.

Printed in the United States of America

LIBRARY OF CONGRESS CATALOGING-IN-PUBLICATION DATA
Cullen, Noel C.
Elegant Irish cooking/Noel C. Cullen
     p.cm.
Includes index
ISBN: 0-86730-839-7 (alk. paper)
     1. Cookery, Irish. 2. Food habits Ireland. I. Title.
TX717.5.C845 2001
641.59417-dc21   00-058359
Fc.

Designed and composed by Richard Oriolo

Visit our Web site at lfbooks.com

Dedicated in Linda's memory to Concern Worldwide,

the epitome of Irish hospitality in its greatest form . . . feeding and helping those in need.

On behalf of all Irish and American chefs, I dedicate this book to their great work.

Concern Worldwide
104 East 40th Street
Room 903
New York, NY 10016
212. 557. 8000

Concern Worldwide
Camden Street
Dublin 2
Ireland
011. 353. 1 475 4162

Acknowledgments

Sincere thanks to:

Dr. Lewis J. Minor

Bord Failte (The Irish Tourist Board)

Geert & Marie Maes, Gaby's Restaurant Killarney

Great Southern Hotels (Galway)

Mr. Oliver Kehelly and Shannon Development

Mount Juliet House Hotel

Magherabuoy House Hotel, Portrush, N.I.

Northern Ireland Tourist Board

for their generous sponsorships and assistance with the site photography in Ireland.

Contents

Appetizers & Light Meals

Molly Malone Smokies

Warm Oysters in Guinness Sauce with Puff-Pastry Leaves

Oysters with Red Onion, Balsamic Vinegar, and Home Dried Plum Tomato

Galway Bay Oyster Casserole

Baked Carlingford Oysters with Herb Butter

Baked Egg with Smoked Irish Salmon

Smoked Salmon and Crab Parcel, Kilakee House

Smoked Salmon and Jerusalem Artichoke Soufflé on a Tarragon Butter Sauce

Tartare of Salmon, Wrapped in a Parcel of Smoked Salmon

Mussels with Garlic, Chives, Butter, and Crushed Hazelnuts

Crab Tart with Roast Prawn Tails and Ribbons of Spring Vegetables

Pan-Roasted Quail with Kildare Boxty

Bacon-and-Leek Flan

Slasher O' Reilly's Roasted Garlic Chive Royale with Wild Mushrooms

Baked Stuffed Mushrooms Shelbourne

Tomato Mousse on a Bed of Black Olives and Balsamic Vinegar

Avocado King Sitric Style

Cashel Irish Blue Cheese Seafood Bake

Soups

Mussel and Ham Bisque

Jackeen's Cockle and Mussel Soup

Dublin Bay Prawn Bisque

Galway Oyster Broth with Dill and Tomato

Connaught Coast Seafood Chowder

Arklow Fish Stew Baked in a Pastry Crust

Ulster Cream of Potato Soup with Smoked Salmon and Chives

Tipperary Creamy Mushroom Soup

Celeriac Soup with Smoked Bacon and Potato Bread

Potato and Cabbage Soup

Lentil and Coriander Soup

Cream of Watercress Soup with Warm Herbal Drop Scones

Lettuce and Nutmeg Soup

Chilled Armagh Apples and Apricot Soup

Potato and Sorrel Soup

Leek and Irish Cashel Blue Cheese Soup

Fish & Seafood Dishes

Nuggets of Salmon with Mushrooms, Connemara Style

Baked Liffey Salmon Filled with an Herbed Lobster and Cream Stuffing, *Grainne Ni Mhaille*

Roasted Peppered Salmon with a Tomato-and-Basil Relish

Pan-Fried Salmon with Sorrel, Apple, and Scallion Relish

Pan-Seared Fillet of Salmon with Roasted Peppers and Pineapple Compote

Gratin of Cod with Tomatoes, Bacon, and Dill

Grilled Halibut Steak with Parsley Butter

Deirdre's Seafood and Saffron Shell

Roast Fillet of Hake with Potato and Black-Olive Sauce

Steamed Fillet of Hake Kenure House

Fillet of Sea Bass and Shrimp with Wild Mushrooms and Nettle Butter

Turbot Fillets with a Savory Herb-and-Tomato Crumble

Baked Fillets of Flounder with Cabbage, Smoked Bacon, Roasted Potatoes, and a Grain Mustard Sauce

Poached Sole Fillets in a Clonmel Cider Sauce

Poached Fillets of Sole and Oysters with Spinach and Gratine Riesling Sauce

Roast Pike with Lovage, Bacon and Chicken Sauce

Bay Scallops in White Wine and Butter Sauce

Portrush Scallops with Baby Leeks in a Citrus Vinaigrette

Baked Stuffed Lobster, *Uisce Beahta*

Ballyferriter Lobster Gaby

Mullaghmore Lobster Soufflé, *Classiebawn*

Salads, Dressings & Cold Sauces

Vinaigrettes

Balsamic Vinaigrette

Sherry Vinaigrette

Orange Vinaigrette

Limantour Vinaigrette

Hazelnut Vinaigrette

Tarragon Citrus Dressing

Homemade Mayonnaise

Aioli

Cashel Blue Cheese Dressing

Honey Mustard Dressing

Morrin's Summer Salad

Warm Smoked Chicken Salad with Creamed Lentils and Roasted Garlic

Lobster and Vegetable Salad

Warm Salad of Emyvale Duck with Orange and Balsamic Dressing

Warm Rabbit Salad with Thyme Vinaigrette

Corned Beef and Cabbage Salad

Noel's Mushroom Salad

Traditional Cold Irish Potato Salad

Beef, Lamb & Pork Dishes

Layered Slices of Top Round of Beef Braised in Smithwicks Ale

Medallions of Beef with Madeira Sauce and Traditional Ulster Champ

Maggie Kerrigan's Beef Stew

Mullingar Beef Tenderloin Steaks on a Bed of Spinach with a Red-Wine Sauce

Roasted Sirloin of Beef Crusted with Peppercorns & Fresh Herbs, Served with a Tarragon Butter Sauce

Pinwheel of Beef and Colcannon *Niamh Chinn Oir*

Grilled Guinness-Marinated Sirloin Steaks with Chived Potato and Tomatoes

Ballymaloe Steak-and-Oyster Pie

Traditional Irish Lamb Stew

Traditional Killorglin Lamb Pie with Thyme and Roasted Parsnips

Peppered Leg of Lamb with a Ginger, Red-currant and Vinegar Glaze

Braised Lamb Shanks, with Roasted-Garlic Mashed Potatoes

Roasted Rack of Wicklow Lamb with an Herbed Crust and Mint Butter Sauce

Traditional Dublin Coddle

Lamb Cutlets (Chops) with a Basil Crêpe and Braised Vegetables

Traditional Cork Crubeens

Pan-Seared Loin of Pork with Derry Apple Relish

Cured Boneless Pork Cutlets with Barley-Stuffed Cabbage Parcels

Boyne Valley Honey-Braised Pork Tenderloin with Snowpeas and Grapes

Boiled Limerick Ham Shanks with Mustard-Grain Cream and Crisp Cabbage

Veal, Poultry & Game Dishes

Baked Spinach-and-Cheese-Stuffed Veal Cutlets with Oven Roasted Potatoes

Veal Escalopes with Orange Butter and a Roasted Vegetable Salad

Lady Linda's Veal Pinwheel with Garlic-Butter-Crumb Tomatoes

Kiwi-and-Gin Sauced Tenderloin of Veal with Asparagus Soufflé

Honey-Glazed Breast of Duck with Peppercorn Dressing on a Bed of Spiced Celeriac

Roast Templenoe Duck with Rhubarb-and-Honey Sauce

Roasted Chicken with Walnuts and Tarragon

Braised Young Chicken with Cabbage, Bacon, and Rosemary

Crab-Stuffed Chicken Breast with Broccoli–Cream-Cheese Mousse

Arbutus Lodge Chicken Hibernia with Leek Pilaf

Venison Sausage with Rutabaga Puree, Red Cabbage, and Apple

Pan-Seared Loin of Venison, Carden's Folly

Muckross Park Venison-and-Mushroom Pie Puree with Basil and Jameson Irish Whiskey

Braised Center Cut of Rabbit with Pearl Onions in a Broth of Red Lentils

Roast Mount Juliet Pheasant with a Potato-and-Parsnip Puree and Apple-and-Grape Sauce

Vegetable & Potato Dishes

Lemon Cauliflower and Broccoli

Pureed Rutabagas with Garlic

Minted White Turnips

Braised White Cabbage

Green Beans with Roasted Red Bell Peppers

Creamed Spinach with Garlic

Carrots in Orange Sauce

Double-Baked Westmeath Potatoes with Shrimp and Scallions

Parsnip Puree with Sesame Seed

Moore Street Vegetable Tart

Bird Flanagan Potato Pancakes

Bella Cullen's Colcannon

Traditional Ulster Champ

Roasted Dublin-Style Potatoes

Linenhall Boxty

Sligo Glazed Potatoes

Donegal Twice-Baked Potatoes

Preface

THIS BOOK IS A LABOR OF LOVE. IT IS NOT INTENDED TO BE A CULINARY textbook or solely an ethnic cookbook, but a celebration of elegant cooking that reflects the current excellence of Irish culinary ingenuity. It is a collection of recipes bound not only by my own culinary perspective, but a desire shared by my colleagues to demonstrate that Irish chefs have finally taken their place in the world of *haute cuisine*. The excellence of modern Irish cooking, and those master chefs responsible for this high quality, have (until now) been one of the culinary world's best-kept secrets.

There is now a discernible pride and confidence associated with Irish cuisine. Modern Irish culinary masters have developed a progressive and uniquely Irish style of cooking, with the legendary form of Irish hospitality and the finest raw ingredients, dining in Ireland's restaurants has truly become a joy.

While simple and delicious home cooking and baking have always been first rate in Ireland, great changes have taken place in the professional cooking arena, there never has been a more exciting or appropriate time to write about these changes in Irish cuisine. Difficult as it may be for some to imagine, Ireland has evolved into a haven for the discerning diner.

To my Irish chef colleagues and teachers, particularly Jim Kilbride, my inspirational mentor and friend, and to my former students, apprentices, culinary competition teammates, and my fellow Panel of Chefs of Ireland members—my friends, sincere thanks for sharing your recipes with me and for keeping my dream alive. To Ron Manville, my friend and photographer, whose camera captured such beautiful images of Ireland and her food, and who shared the adventure of traveling through Ireland with me in Geert's fish van—many thanks. To the many Irish culinary educators, hoteliers, and restaurateurs, who for so long strove to raise standards and professionalize the Irish culinary world, much appreciation to you all.

Without the loving encouragement and guidance of my wife Linda, who is my gastronomic colleague, Irish chef extraordinaire, my pal, and the love of my life, this book would never seen the light of day. Her special insight into my culinary Irishness armed me with the fortitude to write an Irish cookbook, rather than taking the safe and mediocre culinary path of writing a general cookbook. Without her drive, this book would have remained a dream.

Special thanks and appreciation also to my excellent Boston University colleagues, the School of Hospitality teaching assistants; Scott Wickie, Christine McDermott, Dale Chick, and Jason Beecher, and, finally, a very special thanks to Mary Donlon who graciously Americanized my manuscript and, thus, made it infinitely more readable.

NOEL C. CULLEN
Boston University

Introduction

DRAMATIC CHANGES HAVE TAKEN PLACE IN IRELAND'S KITCHENS AND restaurants.

Over the years, Irish food and cooking in the United States has called to mind images such as corned beef and cabbage, potatoes, and boiled bacon—all usually overcooked and greasy.

While this may be the case some of the time in the United States, the opposite is true in Ireland's professional kitchens. Ireland's kitchens are now populated by enthusiastic, skilled culinarians eager to prepare, cook, and present the finest dishes prepared from the freshest native products.

. . . and the real beauty of Ireland is much more than skin-deep. And it can hide itself. And I truly think that Ireland at its best is still a secret for connoisseurs

—KATE O' BRIEN,
My Ireland, 1962

Kenmare is a small town in County Kerry, Kinsale is a tiny seaport town steeped in Irish history and lore, located in adjacent County Cork. Both have many award-winning restaurants. Collectively, they have been called the birthplace of Ireland's current gastronomic revival.

Kinsale's reputation as a culinary center grew in the early 1980s, when a profusion of talented people opened superb restaurants. The number and high quality of these restaurants in this small town was amazing. Restaurants such as the Spinnaker, The Man Friday, Gino's, and, later, The Vintage, The Bistro, Bacchus, The Blue Haven, and others led to the establishment of the Kinsale Good Food Circle. This was the first time local tourism in Ireland was built

Culinary Renaissance

Kenmare and Kinsale: Irish Culinary Jewels

upon a center for good food and restaurants. These small beginnings led a new breed of Irish chefs and restaurateurs to a new confidence, and raised the standard of restaurants and fine dining which many others have since emulated.

Close to the most southerly point in Ireland, Kenmare Bay etches its way inland to form a divide between the Bere and Ring of Kerry Peninsulas. Located in the Kingdom of Kerry (Kerry natives refer to their County as the Kingdom), Kenmare dates from 1775. It is one of the few planned towns in Ireland, and is set at the beautiful foothills of the MacGillcuddy Reeks, one of the most scenic areas in Ireland. In addition to its beauty and location, the town has enjoyed a reputation for hospitality and good food for over a hundred years.

Kenmare's first gastronomic golden age occurred in 1897, when a railhead hotel was opened for wealthy English tourists en route to subtropical Parknasilla, the Irish Riviera. This hotel continued to operate as the core of the local tourism industry, until falling business and the demise of the railway line in 1976 forced its closure. In 1980, the hotel was purchased and elaborately refurbished. More important, it brought to Kenmare an influx of highly talented young hotel and restaurant titans.

So began Kenmare's second golden age; only, this time, emphasis was placed on high quality cuisine. Indeed, Kenmare boasts a number of Michelin star establishments (Michelin stars are the Oscars of the restaurant industry). Enthusiastic locals point out that the tiny town has more award-winning restaurants per capita than Paris.

Both towns continue to be a centers for the culinary revolution currently sweeping Ireland.

IRISH HOSPITALITY

Over the decades, Irish hospitality has impressed visitors by its scale and spontaneity. The famed Irish patriot and statesman Daniel O' Connell wrote: "The hospitality of an Irishman is not the running account of posted ledgered courtesies, as in other countries; it springs like all his qualities, his faults, his virtues, directly from his heart."

Irish people are famous for being unusually friendly to outsiders, but the incredibly generous reception given to visitors in earlier times had a cultural source that was not tied up with simple friendliness. Hospitality was seen as a basic duty; a warm welcome and warm food were basic rights of any traveler. Any caller could not be turned away without bringing bad luck and a bad name to the household. The Christian belief that a stranger calling might be the Savior coming to test the goodwill of the household also played a part. Travelers to Ireland, from the Norsemen on, all commented on the unusual extent of Irish hospitality.

The fifth century Brehon laws insisted that relatively well-off households were bound to entertain guests. The effects of this unique form of Irish hospitality continue to this day: It is quite common for a restaurant's chef to be seen in the dining room welcoming guests and discussing menu selections with diners. Great hospitality helps make Ireland truly memorable.

ANCIENT IRISH COOKING

Irish cuisine, like most others, is based upon the evolution of one-pot cookery, Irish stew is perhaps the best example of the Celtic version of one-pot cooking. Peasant dishes that are the product of a single source of heat contained in one pot. Some present-day Irish food habits go back to prehistoric times.

The building of the *fulachata fiadha* involved pits with an arc-shaped hearth at each end. The pit was filled with water, then heated stones were added to bring the water to a boil in a short time. Large joints of meat were wrapped in either straw or hide, tied with a straw rope, then lowered into the pits. Indeed, anthropological and archaeological data suggests that crude ovens were also constructed by the ancient Irish, which would partially explain why the culinary principles of boiling and roasting in Irish cuisine arose simultaneously.

Ireland has always had great cooks. Under the clan system, cooks were important members. The Brehon Laws (highly advanced, civilized rules, and edicts of the Irish clan system) laid down strict rules about food and hospitality. From forty-gallon communal bronze caldrons, cooks provided daily sustenance for the entire clan. This tradition of inventive and creative cooking continued, from the days of the high kings of Ireland through the age of the great houses of the landed gentry to the beginning of the modern commercial hotel and restaurant industry.

Curiously, in ancient times Ireland's most recognizable emblem, the shamrock, was actually not what we think of as shamrocks, but watercress. It was regarded in ancient Ireland as having sacred and magical qualities. It was said those who ate it gained the power to see fairies, and, in earlier times, the plant appears to have been described as a female aphrodisiac. Modern shamrock is actually a type of clover.

THE ISOLATED ISLAND

Ireland has lived isolated from the world through long stretches of its history. Being in the North Atlantic played its part, but other factors were involved. In the second century A.D., Ptolemy made a fairly detailed map of Ireland based on contacts that had been made through trade. Tacticus wrote from Rome that Ireland's harbors and sea approaches were well known to contemporary sailors; although the Romans never conquered Ireland they certainly knew were it was. From prehistoric times through the middle ages it could be said that Ireland fought with Britain and traded with Gaul (later France), from which Ireland imported wine, salt, and iron and to which Ireland exported hides and wool.

Many countries have had a period they call their *golden age*. In Ireland, *golden age* refers to the time between the seventh and ninth centuries when Ireland was known as the land of saints and scholars. It was a time when the cultural currents of Christianity blended with the Celtic traditions to produce great results in the intellectual and artistic spheres. It was also a time of relative peace. Ireland was converted to Christianity in the fifth century by St. Patrick the patron saint of Ireland. By the seventh century, the Irish church was centered around a number of important monasteries.

Celtic society had come to terms with the idea of Christianity by seeing the monks as a family, and the leaders of their clans. It was from this period we get a glimpse of the recipes and menu items from the daily diet of the clans. It was innovative; vegetables, herbs, and garlic and the occasional animal were boiled in a forty-gallon cauldron, and a curious large implement known as a *flesh fork* was used to extract the whole cooked animals from the cauldron.

Because monks were the educated people of the golden age, it was they who recorded recipes and described what people ate. Monks introduced the notion of hospitality. The *bruidne* which, when translated, means hostel, comes from this period (perhaps the first inn). All were welcome. A great cauldron maintained in each *bruidne* would feed everyone, no matter how many, and a general warmth of hospitality was provided. Irish monks brought their religion and culture to mainland Europe from the seventh century, including their culinary skills, (this predates Catherine de Medici's introduction of Italian chefs and their culinary talents to France in the sixteenth century).

Irish eating habits have been largely influenced by climate, geography, industry, and immigration. The introduction of new foods to Ireland is due mostly to immigrants. Irish culture and eating habits stem mainly from the Celts; however, since Celtic times Ireland has for the most part been left to itself to develop and nurture its own culture and cuisine. Ireland has often been outside the mainstreams of European history, therefore, it has developed a distinct cuisine of its own over the centuries. Contributing to this unique cuisine is Ireland's splendid island isolation, separating it from the cultural and culinary innovations of the continent of Europe.

Other cultures and cuisines, such as Italian, French, or German, did not influence Irish kitchen as they have American cuisine. Indeed, Ireland is not, and never was, a melting pot of cultures. Historically, emigration has been the norm in Ireland. The only immigration or colonization has been through invasion. Such was the case with the coming of the Vikings, the English, and the Scots. Generally, the invaders colored Irish culture and cuisine without seriously altering it. As a primarily agrarian nation, Irish cuisine has grown and developed from the rich bounty of its land and waters.

*A plague-wind blew across
the land,
Fever was in the air,
Fields were black that once
were green,
And death was everywhere.*

—M.J. MACMANUS, 1849

With the nineteenth century came the beginnings of great hardship, famine, and despair. The great potato famine of 1845–50 decimated Ireland, reducing its population by half, through starvation, disease, and emigration. Over one million people perished, and a further million left Ireland as refugees and immigrants, many of them settling in the United States. Understandably, memories of those tragic times have left an indelible mark on the Irish people which, in turn, shaped their culinary heritage.

The potato is the one food that most people associate with Irish cooking. It was introduced into Ireland in the seventeenth century; many credit Sir Walter Raleigh with its introduction, but historians disagree. The theory that he planted it first in Youghal, County Cork, following his return from the colony of Virginia is rejected for the reason that when this was supposed to have happened he was dead. There is also speculation that the potato arrived accidentally, as a result of a Spanish ship that foundered off the west coast of Ireland following the ill-fated Armada of 1588.

How the potato got to Ireland may not be that important; what is certain is that it was a major crop by 1610 and it served to feed the burgeoning Irish populace. Although not immediately a staple, the poor depended on it increasingly throughout the following century. The potato, which provided very good nutrition, was not labor intensive—a small plot could produce a very high yield. The small amount of time needed to tend the crop meant that a peasant could cultivate it and at the same time work, as a laborer for the large farmer. The nutritious potato became the mainstay of the agricultural laborers and tenant farmers, and it dominated the diets of at least one-third of the Irish population.

The consequences of this new dependence were to produce the greatest tragedy ever to befall the Irish nation. More and more land was cleared of its plant and animal life in a search for arable soil. Furthermore, the potato was normally boiled, and this meant a fire, which further contributed to stripping the land for fuel.

In less than a day, and with no warning, blossoming potato plants were reduced to withering black stalks. It was Benjamin Disraeli who later noted how a "single root" had changed the history of the world. Ireland, by the eighteenth century, had become a one-crop country. In 1842, potato crops in the Eastern part of the United States and Canada began to fail. The blight that caused this failure eventually traveled to Europe. It reached Ireland in the summer of 1845.

At that time, out of an Irish population of eight million, it is estimated that more than five million of the population depended entirely upon potatoes to survive. The average Irish person at that time consumed between ten and twelve pounds of potatoes daily, and often ate little else. The great potato famine was a watershed in Irish history.

Sadly, this period is also remembered for the needless cycle of starvation and poverty that led to the ultimate tragedy of the Great Famine, because, at that time, great quantities of Irish produce were going for export while people continued to starve.

During this time, the ruling British government consulted with the famous French chef of the Reform Club in London, Alexis Soyer. His brief was to concoct a palatable, low cost and nutritious soup. French cuisine had come to aid Ireland's hungry. The story ended sadly, with public resentment at such an hysterical level, that the well meaning M. Soyer had to leave Ireland secretly to avoid being lynched.

The Spud

Although it carries both blessings and curses for its role in Irish history, the potato still enjoys an honored place in Irish cuisine. The humble spuds, also affectionately referred to as murphys or praties, are still an important and essential part of the Irish diet. Indeed, most Irish people consider a dining experience without the potato incomplete. The Irish make them into soups, pancakes, pastry, and breads.

New potatoes are much anticipated by the Irish. These potatoes are cooked in boiling salted water, and served with fresh mint leaves and butter. The delectable ideal of the new spud is when they are described as "balls of flour" by the natives. One may confidently expect potatoes to be featured at the main meal in an Irish home as well as on the menus of elegant restaurants in Ireland.

Traditional Irish food has evolved from a wholesome, if limited, range of peasant dishes that has represented traditional Irish culinary fare for centuries. While these foods are still prevalent on menus, the range and creative adaption of these traditional dishes has developed and expanded spectacularly over the past twenty years.

Irish people eat a lot, perhaps because of a famine psyche. The average Irish person consumes 163 percent of recommended daily calorie intake. Although many might believe that the Irish are great meat eaters, statistics show they lag behind other European nations. Vegetables are not enormously popular, and a great deal of vegetable intake is made up of potatoes, cabbage, and root vegetables like carrots and turnips. Surprisingly, as an island nation, the Irish do not eat as much fish as their European counterparts. While eating habits have evolved through the centuries, one thing remains constant—a love of dairy products. Milk and its derivatives, particularly butter, were the favorites of old Ireland and are still eaten more than any other foods.

Bacon and ham have always been popular meats in Ireland. The leg of the pig is called *ham*, everything else is termed *bacon*. Pig meat has been eaten in Ireland since the earliest times. Limerick bacon and hams remain, to this day, a superior-quality meat because of its distinctive, juniper-smoked flavor.

Traditional Irish bacon is salty, and requires soaking in cold water overnight to remove the salt. It is almost a given that at least one meal per week in Irish households will be shoulder of bacon, potatoes, and cabbage, with the cabbage cooked in the water used to boil the bacon. It is from the loin and the belly of bacon that the indispensable part of a traditional Irish breakfast is produced— the *back and streaky rasher*, thin slices of bacon. The back rasher has the eye of the loin, some fat, and a tail piece, and the streaky rasher is similar to the bacon served in the United States.

Beef became part of the Irish diet in the eighteenth century when new colonist eating habits were introduced. The native Irish tended to use cattle as a source of dairy produce. Corned beef, long considered quintessentially Irish, was introduced more recently, as a way of utilizing secondary cuts of beef. More American than Irish, it is traditionally served with cabbage on St. Patricks's Day (March 17th). However, spiced beef is an Irish specialty. This dish was usually served cold the day after Christmas (St. Stephen's Day), but can now be found all year 'round. It is basically corned beef with a mixture of allspice, cloves, cinnamon, and nutmeg rubbed into it. Ireland produces seven times more beef than it consumes.

It has been said that mutton and lamb are to Ireland what beef is to England. The Celts did not prize cattle for their meat, generally relying on sheep or pigs. Sheep farming was one of the only ways of life in the barren mountain areas of Ireland (and still is). These lands were unfit for farming, tillage, or cattle. The meat of sheep is the main ingredient of Irish stew. Irish lamb has a distinctive flavor, much commented upon by visitors to Ireland. It is generally roasted, the rack, or *fairend*, as it is called in Ireland being the most popular. Goats, like sheep, are natural mountain animals and are making a comeback to the Irish table. Goats' milk is farmed commercially and is used in the thriving Irish farmhouse-cheese industry. All things organic are being revisited, and goat's meat is becoming popular again. Goats have a long association with the colorful Puck Fair in Killorglin County Kerry where, each year, a wild goat is captured and crowned king.

The Hearty
Irish Breakfast

Famous the world over, the hearty Irish breakfast is as varied and full of flavor and character as Ireland itself. From the northern reaches of Donegal to the rolling green hills of Kerry, a distinctive variation of breakfast has evolved over centuries. The Irish breakfast originated in the nineteenth century and was called a *fry*. Traditionally, the fry included a combination of pork, potatoes, grains, and dairy products, along with a pint of ale. Today the basic ingredients remain the same, minus the ale.

Breakfast has always been an important meal in Ireland and, today, usually includes the elements of the fry: rashers, black-and-white puddings, sausages, eggs, and even lamb's liver. One visitor to Ireland once suggested that the heartiness of the Irish breakfast was the modern day revenge of the Irish on the great potato famine.

Uniquely Irish, black pudding is a type of sausage made of pigs' blood mixed with salt and lard, oatmeal, onions, and spices. White pudding is a variety made without the blood, using minced liver and other organ meats. Both puddings are usually fried. Black pudding has become one of those traditional foods that has been gentrified, and can be seen on upscale menus as an appetizer served with apple sauce.

Drisheen, Crubeens, and Coddle

Drisheen, mostly associated with Cork, in the south of Ireland, is a form of black pudding made from the blood of sheep, but without the variety of ingredients in black pudding. Other organ meats continue to remain popular, most notably liver, kidneys, tripe, and sweetbreads. Although not strictly organ meat, *crubeens*, the hind feet of pigs, are still found in Irish homes and indeed one of Ireland's foremost restaurants, The Arbutus Lodge in Cork rekindled an interest in crubeens in a modern style and feature them as a starter course, indeed, the cover of the menu at the Arbutus features a reproduction of a painting called "The Crubeeen Eaters" by the renowned Irish artist Pauline Bewick. Crubeens are boiled with onions, carrots, and seasonings for two hours and are gnawed on like corn on the cob.

Coddle is a Dublin dish, beloved by Jonathan Swift. It is made by boiling together sausages, onions, bacon, herbs, and potatoes. Coddle was, and still is, a Saturday evening dish, usually following the consumption of a few pints. Dubliners are quite proud of their individual recipes for this dish. To make a great coddle, some swear by a particular brand of sausage, while others insist that tomatoes should be added, and others suggest coddle only comes into its own when it is reheated after it has been cooled.

Fish and Seafood

Ireland has been working hard in recent years to increase the landing and consumption of fish. Comparatively speaking, for an island race, Irish people are not great fish eaters. However, there is a great variety of fish off the Irish coast. The Gulf Stream brings warm water fish, and the colder waters to the north brings Arctic species. Among the most larger popular fish catches are: cod, hake, haddock, ling, plaice, black sole, and whiting. In earlier times, herrings and mackerel made up a very important part of the diet of the poorer people of Dublin. Shellfish, such as cockles, mussels, scallops, oysters, prawns, lobsters, and crabs continue to be plentiful.

Ireland is criss-crossed with lakes and rivers. Fed by both mountain springs and frequent rain, these rivers and lakes are host to a variety of fish, most notably salmon and trout. Salmon, of course has always been *the* Irish fish with oak-smoked Irish salmon cited as among the best in the world. Other freshwater fish include pike, bream, and perch. Lough Neagh (the largest lake in the British Isles) has long been famous for its eels, which never really found favor in Ireland, but are much sought after by our European neighbors.

In many Irish coastal areas, seaweed is still used in cooking, particularly soups (indeed it was those who lived near the coast who survived the famine best). *Carrageen moss* is the best known of the edible algae. It's a branching greenish or purple weed, normally sold dried. It is very bland-tasting, and widely used as a setting agent instead of gelatin. Carrageen is rich in iron and minerals and is considered a traditional Irish health food. Many Irish chefs passionately believe in its culinary and healthful properties. Other seaweed varieties used in Irish cooking include dulse or dillisk, a reddish-brown seaweed found on all coasts of Ireland. It, too, is usually sold dried. It may be added to fish or vegetables soups. Like carrageen moss it is soaked in cold water prior to use.

Colcannon and Other Potato Dishes

Colcannon is a traditional dish still common in Ireland, indeed, in these days of comfort foods, it has grown in popularity as an integral part of many menus. It consists of kale (cabbage is often substituted), potatoes, onions, seasonings, milk, and the ubiquitous part of almost all Irish recipes—butter. My Uncle Jim liked to have two lightly fried eggs on top of his colcannon, as a dressing. Like barm brack, colcannon was mostly made at Halloween, when it also contained a ring, a coin, a thimble, and a button, all wrapped, and each with its own significance. Tradition or superstition decreed whoever got the ring in their serving would be married within a year, the coin stood for wealth, the button for bachelorhood, and the thimble for spinsterhood.

Potatoes form the basis of many Irish dishes, including *boxty*, which are potato pancakes. Another dish called *champ*, or *bruitin*, is a mashed-potato dish made with milk, seasonings, and scallions, topped with butter. There are numerous versions of this traditional Irish dish and, apart from the potatoes, ingredients vary from region to region. These old dishes have been revitalized by many Irish chefs.

HONEY AND GARLIC

Honey was, and still is, a very important part of Irish cuisine. Salmon was normally eaten with honey, and side dishes of honey were served with many foods. Indeed, one of the most famous legends in Irish mythology concerns the warrior Finn MacCool, who burned his finger from the honey coating on the salmon of knowledge. The Brehon laws of Gaelic Ireland, dating from the fifth century, regulated the production of honey, and was used as a form of currency.

Contrary to contemporary thought, garlic, together with a great number of other herbs, have been used in Ireland since prehistoric times. Garlic was cultivated by the monks during the golden age, and was eaten with bread as a relish instead. The healthful and other aspects of eating garlic are well known worldwide. Garlic butter remains, to this day, a popular accompaniment to steaks and fish.

BAKING

Another of Ireland's great strengths is traditional baking. Baking has long been an integral part of Irish cuisine and, if there is anything distinctive about Irish bread, it is the widespread use of milk, particularly buttermilk, as a primary ingredient. The most widely baked bread, and the item which most Irish bakers will tend to pride themselves on, is the brown soda bread. This modern variety only appeared in the nineteenth century, when bread soda was introduced as a raising agent. It is generally made using a moist wholemeal-wheat flour, and usually includes buttermilk or sour milk as one of its ingredients.

Brown bread (without soda) has been made in Irish homes for centuries. The tradition has never lapsed and dates from the time when people lived too far from towns to go to bakeries. In cottages and small farmhouses, bread and fruit loaves were made in a skillet or pot oven, over an open turf fire. Burning embers were place on top of the lid to allow the bread to cook on top as well.

A variety of other breads are baked in Ireland, including variations of sourdough, and breads containing apple and even potato. In Northern Ireland, for example, white soda breads with fruit added are quite common, and are known as *soda farls*. Griddle bread, the most popular northern Irish bread, is quite thin and fried on both sides and is part of the Ulster fry, the traditional breakfast.

In Irish, barm brack is *barin breac*, fruit bread; it is the traditional bread for Halloween. Barm brack is also associated with other festivals, most notably St. Brigid's day, February 1st. Symbolic objects intended to divine the future are often included in bracks.

Most historians agree that the secret of distillation was brought to Ireland, probably from the Middle East, by missionary monks, around the sixth century. They discovered the alembic that the Arabs used for distilling perfume could be put to better use, and adapted it into a pot still. They found that if a mash of barley and water was fermented with yeast, then heated in a pot still, the alcohol could be separated and transformed into a spirit with wondrous powers. The monks called it *uisce beatha,* Irish for water of life. Over the centuries the Irish words were corrupted into the anglized *whiskey*.

For centuries, the fashion for Irish whiskey was widespread. Queen Elizabeth I was said to be very partial to it, almost certainly acquiring the taste from Sir Walter Raleigh, who had a huge estate in County Cork. Raleigh's

Poitin is the most mysterious word in the country places of Ireland. It is never spoken: it is always whispered. This illicit firewater, which is distilled in the dead of night, or on misty days which hide the smoke from the still, has always been made in lonely hills of Ireland.

—H.V. MORTON,
In Search of Ireland, 1930

records indicate that he stopped off in Cork to pick up a present of a thirty-two-gallon cask of home distilled *uisce beatha* to bring to Queen Elizabeth. It was Czar Peter the Great who endorsed Irish whiskey with the acclamation, "of all wines, the Irish spirit is the best."

The difference between the highland variety Scotch whisky and Irish whiskey is far greater than the spelling. While both are based on barley, part of which is malted, the malt for the Irish variety is dried in a closed kiln and not over open fires, which gives the smokey flavor to Scotch whiskey.

The oldest distillery in the world is Bushmills in County Antrim in Northern Ireland. Situated on the banks of the River Bush, it was granted its license by King James 1 in 1608, although distilling on this site goes back to 1276. The water from the River Bush tributary, St. Columb's Rill, is still used to this day to make the whiskey. Other old and famous Irish whiskeys include Jameson, Paddy, and John Power. An American commentator, having sampled the barley delights of the golden Irish amber for the first time, was overheard to say . . . "it's like a torchlight procession marching down your throat."

Another product used widely in cuisine worldwide that has Irish roots is Hennessy brandy. It was first distilled by Richard Hennessy, who was born in 1720 in Killavullen in County Cork. Hennessy went to France to become an officer in the French Army, where he fought in many battles. After being wounded, he retired and settled in Cognac and established his now world famous distillery.

These wonderful combinations that have evolved over centuries to produce the unmistakable subtle taste of these Irish distillations is responsible for a wide array of flavors and, when combined with different foods, they give recipes a unique Irishness.

Poitin (often spelled *potchein*) dates back to the seventeenth century, when duties were first imposed on the distillation of spirits. It is a drink of many names; some call it the Connemara doctor," or "Irish moonshine." Poitin is a clear distillation of barley, sugar, and pure mountain water. The manufacture of this fiery brew always takes place up in the hills close to the source of

Ireland's crystal clear streams. Poitin was sometimes sold in *shebeens*, or shops, which were no more than private houses that advertised their function by hanging a wedge of turf over the door. Shebeens doubled as pubs and illegal liquor stores.

Despite the many admirable qualities attributed to it, from its use as a marinated for tough meats, as a flavoring agent in braised items, to its reported medicinal value, it remains illegal. However, it is not unusual to encounter its use in Irish cooking.

Wine is not used in cooking for its alcoholic content, but as a seasoning that enhances the natural flavors of foods with only a suggestion of its presence. Through the years Irish chefs have used wines and other alcoholic beverages imaginatively to marinate, baste, tenderize, flambe, and deglaze. Alcoholic beverages have always enjoyed an alliance with food in Irish kitchens.

Since ancient times in Ireland, wine has been seen as a food. It is one of the great gifts from yeast that also includes cheese, bread, and brewing. Cooking with wine is as old as wine itself.

Whether working acts of magic in the cooking process or serving as an accompanying beverage, wine can bring out the flavor of foods. Used correctly and wisely, it can raise the normal dish to an exceptional level. Irish chefs have always been aware of this.

For centuries, the marriage of wine and food has been a happy one. Wine flowed freely in ancient Ireland. However, most people have always associated Ireland with the pub, and visitors forever extol the pleasures of the fare on sale. Indeed, the Irish pub is the center of Irish life and the place where an estimated two million pints of stout are consumed daily; however, more and more Irish pubs feature menus with creative and imaginative dishes.

Generally not associated with Ireland, wine has many Irish connections. Within the Bordeaux vineyards for example, there has been a prevalence of Irish names for over two centuries. Bordeaux was a long established partner in trade in wool and beef in return for wine. The Barton, Johnston, Lynch, Burke, Dillon, Morgan, and McCarthy families were the most successful, and their names still adorn the finest wines of Bordeaux.

In the early eighteenth century, more wine was consumed in Ireland, England, Germany, and Holland than in France, where it was relatively rare. Dublin and Leith, in Scotland, were importing more wine from mainland Europe than London. The thirst for wine in Ireland at the time is evident in widely used round-bottomed glasses that did not allow the drinker to rest his glass on the table. The drinking habits of satirist Dean Jonathan Swift, a connoisseur of fine clarets, were not unique. Many contemporary visitors to Dublin remarked on the sheer volume of wine consumed by the citizens of all social classes.

LIQUEURS, MEAD, AND IRISH CREAMS

Liqueurs were originally used as medicines, love potions, aphrodisiacs, and cure-alls in Ireland. This is easy to understand, because many herbs, roots, and seeds that were used to make liqueurs are still used in pharmacology today. Irish liqueurs are traditionally made by mixing or redistilling spirits with flavoring substances such as fruits, flowers, herbs, juices, and other natural flavors. Among the best known is Irish Mist. Irish Mist is one of the oldest of the Irish liqueurs which is still used extensively in Irish cooking. The recipe for this Irish liqueur consists of four great Irish spirits, blended with the honeys of heather and clover and a dozen hand-picked aromatic herbs. From Tullamore (*tulach mhor*), the recipe was lost during the The Flight of the Wild Geese (the exodus of Irish warriors in 1692). It was eventually located in Austria and returned to Ireland. Its perfect balance of potency, good taste, and aroma makes it an ideal accompaniment to many recipes.

In 1974 R&A Baileys Gilleys launched Original Irish Cream. They discovered the secret that would allow milk to be separated into double cream and blended with natural flavors, Irish whiskey, and neutral spirits. Steeped in history and lore, it was named after one of Dublin's most famous pubs, The Bailey.

Soon to follow Baileys into the market place were several other excellent cream-based liqueurs, including Carolans and St. Brendan's. For the Irish chef, these new cream liqueurs spawned a whole host of opportunities to utilize these products in desserts and other recipes.

Debate continues on which is the oldest—grape wine or a liqueur called *mead*. Mead is a fermentation of honey, water, and herbs. History has recorded its use in Ireland before the fifth century, where it was made secretly by monks. Mead came to be the chief drink of the Irish, and is often mentioned in Gaelic poetry. This honey wine was also believed to have the powers of virility and fertility, and it became the custom at weddings for the bride and groom to be toasted with special goblets full of mead, which they would use for one full moon after the wedding. This tradition is the origin of the word *honeymoon*. Mead is equally pleasant as an ingredient. Irish chefs give it high praise for its mellow taste, which adds a subtle sweetness to meats, poultry, and even vegetables.

In eighteenth-century Ireland, almost every town had its own brewery. In 1750, the first Arthur Guinness had a brewery in Leixlip, County Kildare. His brew was so much appreciated by Dr. Price, Archbishop of Cashel, that he left a legacy to his favorite brewer. With this legacy, Arthur Guinness bought a disused brewery at St. James Gate in Dublin with a lease for nine thousand years. Since then, Guinness has probably become the best known Irish export.

Irish Brews

Arthur Guinness began brewing at St. James's Gate In Dublin in 1759; it is still brewed there today. Guinness began by making traditional Irish ale. He soon changed to a new drink made from roasted barley—the new drink was called *porter*. Initially, the drink was unpopular with Dubliners. Later Guinness produced a "stronger extra stout," shortened over the years to *stout*.

By the beginning of the twentieth century, Guinness was the largest brewery in the world. Guinness still uses the same strain of yeast pioneered by Arthur Guinness, and the brewing process—involving roasted Irish-grown barley, soft water, hops, and yeast—remains the same.

In addition to Guinness there are several other excellent Irish stouts, including Murphy's and Beamish and Crawfords, both brewed in Cork for over 150 years. The special association with stout and food is a long standing one. In fact, many aficionados believe oysters and Guinness are a perfect partnership. Stout is used as a tenderizer for beef, a flavor enhancer for fish, and a sweetener in dessert puddings, pies, and cakes. Indeed, the traditional Christmas pudding served by my mother would not have been complete without the addition of Guinness Stout.

While many Irish brewers saw the new value in brewing stout rather than ale, the Kilkenny brewery of Smithwicks continued to brew their own distinctive ale. Smithwicks was first brewed in 1710 on the site of the fourteenth century abbey of St. Francis in the heart of the medieval city of Kilkenny (which for a short time was the Capital City of Ireland). Smithwicks' qualities, with its light, delicate flavor and its rich golden color make it perfect for batters, and cakes, as well as for braised or stewed items.

Cider is one of Ireland's traditional beverages. The process of pressing apples, and extracting and fermenting the juice goes back to ancient Celtic times. Irish cider benefitted from the Anglo-Norman influence and, by the seventeenth century, a time known as the first golden age of cider, there were over 350 varieties of cider apples growing in Ireland. Clonmel came to be the home of cider production and remains so to this day. In Ireland, cider emerged as a truly sophisticated beverage, which many regard as an alternative to wine, as both undergo a similar process. Irish chefs consider it to be as flavorsome as wine in recipes.

THE CULINARY TRAIL OF AN IRISH CHEF

As long as I can remember, I have always had a passion for, and a love of, food and good cooking. This passion has been with me since I began my career as a very young apprentice, under the tutelage of Chef Willy Widmer, a wonderful Swiss culinary taskmaster at the old Jury's Hotel in Dublin. Over these past thirty years of involvement with the culinary arts, I have witnessed many happy, and much welcomed, improvements and changes affecting the Irish culinary world.

I recall reading many cookbooks at an early age. It struck me that most of the authors recalled the culinary influences of mothers and grandmothers. Some were from the homes where the father was a chef or a restaurateur, and most had discovered their cooking roots there. For me, reading cookbooks was more enjoyable than reading thrillers or westerns. Although I grew up in a family where food played a central part, none of my family had any formal connections with the restaurant business, except Nanny.

Early on, our family moved away from Moore Street in Dublin, where I was born, but I continued to live there for period with my Aunt Maggie, known to us children in pure, family Dublinese dialect as Nanny. She prepared and cooked some of the most wonderful stews and breads, and served these to the street vendors of Moore Street. (Moore Street is a very old open-air fruit, vegetable, fish market in the center of Dublin City, famous not only for its foods, but also for its colorful street vendors, and their equally famous brand of razorsharp wit and reparte.) I would bring Maggies' stews to these wonderful characters, whom I remember as being very generous and kind to a young boy.

"What is a *commis chef*"? inquired my puzzled and concerned mother.

"It is an apprentice chef," I confidently answered, "and that's what I want to be.

"But how do you know that's what you want to be?" she asked.

"Because I can cook all day and sample the food I cook," I innocently replied.

This exchange took place some thirty years ago in our Dublin home. So, I became a *commis chef*. One thing was certain, I immediately liked everything associated with being in a large commercial kitchen—the noise, the smells, the hurried activity of all the chefs. It was pure excitement and fascination for an impressionable thirteen year old. However, like most thirteen-year-old boys I truly did not know what I wanted to do. I was lucky. Now, after all these years, I can honestly say that the wonderment of the kitchen I experienced then is still with me to this day in all its fullness, and I have never regretted my decision to make cooking my career.

However, the first day of my apprenticeship was anything but pleasant, and could easily have turned me against continuing in the culinary arts. It will remain with me forever. As an innocent young apprentice chef, filled with expectations of my future in the culinary profession, and armed with my new chef uniforms and my meager set of chef's knives, I began my orientation. However, my first day on the job, as an apprentice chef in Jury's Hotel in Dublin, was almost my last. I reported to the back office for a time card and was then directed to the male changing room. After considerable effort, I eventually found this room. When I got there, there was no available locker to store my street clothes after I had changed into my uniform. I reported to the head chef and introduced myself to him. He barely acknowledged my presence, and with a gruntlike sound waved me toward the *sous* chef who assigned me to the *garde manger* department (in Ireland and England this department is known simply as the larder department where essentially the same functions are carried out).

This particular chef *garde manger's* method of induction and orientation was to give nicknames to new apprentices and, with sarcasm, constantly ridicule them. At the end of my first period that day, I returned to the locker room to discover that my street clothes had disappeared. I had to cycle home that afternoon in my chef uniform. My parents were furious; they wanted me to remain at home and to consider some other profession. After considerable soul searching, I eventually did go back to the hotel that evening.

Back then, apprentices were not permitted to express themselves in any way. It was very much a controlled environment, consisting of a combination of school-based studies and working next to a chef *de parti*. And, depending on the individual, he might or might not show and explain to you what it was he was creating. I was lucky—apart from my first awful day in the kitchens of Jury's Hotel, I got to work with wonderfully skilled craftsmen. They taught me discipline and an appreciation of the fundamental skills of cuisine. These old masters believed that before a chef could begin to create individual dishes or develop a particular culinary philosophy, at least ten years had to be spent learning the basics. They believed that only when these were understood and mastered, was it possible to create different dishes.

My apprenticeship took five years. During the first year, I was not allowed to work at the stove. I do remember chopping a lot of parsley and onions, and cleaning the stoves. Back then apprentices did not question the chef's instructions, they just did what they were told. The basic unwritten philosophy for apprentices was, to let them do hard and dirty work for one year and, if they are still here then, they will make it. If you made it after the first year it got better. That's the way I learned and it had its merits and advantages—repeat and repeat until your hands know how to move without your having to think about it.

Cooking was very organized and disciplined, and rarely deviated from the classic preparations. Improvisations or personal interpretations were not permitted; chefs simply did not think that way. Menus were classically French and very predictable. *Nouvelle cuisine* and other innovations were later to open the floodgates of culinary creativity. However, I still get a thrill when I look back at my apprenticeship in Jury's Hotel—especially, the preparation and decoration of the cold display platters for the buffets.

While the apprentice workdays were hard and demanding, they were not without humor. Being the new apprentice with little experience, I was a prime candidate for induction ceremonies which, I later found out, took place in almost every kitchen with every apprentice. The first week I remember being sent by the chef *garde manger* to the *sous* chef for the lobster gun. After inquiring how big the lobsters were, the *sous* chef indicated the large lobster gun would be necessary, and gave me a set of fire extinguishers to bring back. I returned, to the laughs and howls of those who witnessed what I had just done. From that moment on, I was adopted into the kitchen brigade and no longer felt an outsider. Rightly or wrongly, this was part of passing through the gate to the inner circle of acceptance in the world of the Jury's chef apprentices.

During the summer, students from the local culinary school were assigned to Jury's kitchens. A popular sport for the hardened apprentices was to play jokes on these students; my own personal favorites included assigning to one of these hapless victims the chore of chopping flour with the heavy cleaver until it creamed, sending them to fetch a bucket of steam, and asking them to separate eggs—the brown from white.

On another occasion at Christmas, Mr. Gray, the *maître d' hotel* lined up the chef apprentices in the pantry. Each apprentice had a traditional Christmas pudding with a sparkler stuck in the top. What we were expected to do was to follow Mr. Gray around the dining room singing "Jingle Bells" in chorus. At the count of three, Mr. Gray pushed open the door to the dining room began singing, but we stayed back, he was committed and he had to do a solo around the room singing "Jingle Bells." Of course, we apprentices disappeared before he returned.

In the pressured world of apprenticeship in Jury's kitchens, humor was a must. It was a necessary part of building morale, and to laugh together allowed us to perform together and to depend on each other.

Upon completing a required five-year apprenticeship, it was expected that new apprentice graduates would complete their training abroad and, in Ireland, this usually meant Germany, Switzerland, or France. I chose England, not because I had concluded that English cuisine had suddenly become celebrated, but because I was offered a position at the world famous Cafe Royale in London as a first *commis* to the chef *saucier*. It was the swinging late sixties, and London, to a nineteen-year-old, was the center of the universe.

Within the traditional pecking order of the *parti* system, the sauce chef was long considered the aristocrat of the brigade. Sadly, this was not the case at the Cafe Royale. I soon discovered that I knew more than this aristocrat and had a stronger passion for good food. This man was the laziest person I have ever met. He was a tyrant in my eyes. He called me Paddy, in a voice laden with superiority and venom. While it was common for English people to call Irish people Paddy, usually it was a kindly recognition of Irishness in the same way that Scottish and Welsh people were referred to as Jock and Taffy, but this gentleman meant something else. It was my first introduction to racism. I learned nothing from him other than unprofessional shortcuts in sauce-making. He was the only chef I have ever known who could make one pot of what I describe as *jack*—a sauce which was a jack of all trades. From this pot of white sauce he could make all the other sauces required for the menu—*demi-glace*, tomato, fish, and chicken *Veloute*. He would simply change the color. I was the happiest first *commis* in London the day this culinary genius announced his impending departure.

The greatest lesson I learned from that experience were all the negative aspects of cooking—*what not to do*. I also remember making a lot of sauce *chasseur*. *Contrefilet de Boeuf Chasseur* was the most popular menu item, with *Supreme de Volaille Princess* a close second. Rather than leave to find a more challenging job, I decided to approach Chef Metivier—the mercurial *grosse bonnet*, of the Cafe Royale's banquet kitchen—and brazenly asked for the saucier's position. Schooled in the classic traditions of Escoffier, Metivier was taken aback by my temerity. I had just turned twenty and was much too young in his view for such an important assignment. I persisted and asked for a six-week trial period. If he was dissatisfied after this period I would gladly return to my old position as first *commis*. He agreed.

This was a great challenge and opportunity for a young chef. Now, for the first time, I could allow my creativity and passion for good food and cooking to come forward. It was not very difficult to achieve this. By simply applying the tenets of the great fundamentals that I had learned during my apprenticeship days, together with flair, passion, and professionalism, it was relatively easy to make improvements.

Following the six week period—success! I was appointed the chef *saucier*. I had arrived, and I became a minor star in Chef Metivier's brigade. My culinary arrival in this very traditional French kitchen occurred when I was invited to prepare and cook the *coq au vin* for the weekly Saturday morning meeting of some of London's most famous French culinary icons. This meeting was tradition at the Cafe Royale, going back to the Escoffier era in London. I was honored, and this signaled to me the bestowing of a culinary knighthood of a sort but, more important to a young enthusiastic chef, it was a recognition and acceptance of my cooking skills by these great old masters. Incidentally, the recipe I used for

We may live without poetry,
music and art;
We may live without conscience
and live without heart;
We may live without friends;
We may live without books;
But civilized man cannot live
without cooks.

—EARL OF LYTTON, 1860

the *coq au vin* required it to be thickened with the blood of the chicken. It was directly from Escoffier's *Guide to Modern Cooking*, which is still my culinary bible—for me, pages one to one hundred represent the eternal verities of the culinary arts.

At the Cafe Royale, I developed as a chef, acquiring not only new recipes, but learning modern methods of production and the essentials of high-quality catering for large and small parties (the Cafe Royale catered many parties that often included members of the British Royal family). I marveled at the speed and skills of all the chef *de parties*—the interplay of the departments choreographed by the chef *de cuisine* and the *maître d' hotel* as the entire guest dining experience came together.

I also gained a tremendous appreciation for the taste, flavor, and presentation of food. The true measure of a chef in my view is when they taste the food and satisfy themselves it is correctly cooked, seasoned, and garnished before it goes to the guest. As a chef, I was not conscious of any major food influences on me at the Cafe Royale; these would come later.

I returned to Ireland following my stint at the Cafe Royale, first to Jury's, my apprenticeship *alma mater*. I was offered a position as the head chef in the newly opened Skelligs Hotel in the small fishing port of Dingle, located in County Kerry in the furthermost southerly reaches of Ireland. Dingle, to a native of Dublin, was almost akin to going to the dark side of the moon. The town was located in a *Gaeltacht* area (regions within Ireland where Irish was still the everyday spoken language). Shamefully, I did not speak my own language. However, I accepted the challenge because there was a glamorous side to the assignment. At that time a large international film was being made in Dingle—*Ryan's Daughter*—and with all the films celebrities staying at the hotel, I looked forward to this with great expectations. After all I had just returned from the great Cafe Royale in London, so the Skelligs would be a breeze. Was I wrong! Dingle was somewhat isolated to easily get supplies and, indeed, trained help was very difficult.

The film stars and international crew all had a gastronomic sophistication beyond the limitations of my menu and the culinary capabilities of my kitchen staff. Very quickly, I learned not to compete with my guests' superior repertoire of international culinary experiences, but rather to concentrate on what I could prepare and cook from the local fish, vegetables, and produce. I revisited old traditional local Irish recipes and modernized them. I discovered a wealth of great dishes made from local seafood and vegetables, and, thanks to the wonderful people of Dingle, I learned how to cook them. I also learned to speak Gaelic.

These dishes were uncomplicated and simple in their approach, they needed only the freshest local ingredients and required an elegant simplicity, love, and gentleness. This is when and where I believe I learned the nature of good cooking. I also discovered the single most important ingredient in good cooking is the quality of the basic ingredients, and that the less the chef does to it the better. It is critical to allow the natural flavors to emerge by delicate cooking, and by using sauces that compliment, rather than cloak, the flavors. Good food beautifully and simply cooked is the essence of a great dining experience. My sophisticated international hotel guests loved it. Before this, I had always believed to be a great chef one needed to know all the classic dishes and be able replicate them exactly every time.

The Skelligs Hotel was a watershed for me; it's where I unashamedly discovered my true Irish culinary roots. It is also when I abandoned the strict tenets of French classical cuisine and began to amalgamate and blend my new-found culinary freedom into a definitive Irishness. It gave me a confidence and pride in true Irish cooking that I had not experienced before.

I still remember the first culinary competition I entered. It was when I was an apprentice at the Irish Salon Culinaire in 1967. I cooked and prepared six rainbow trout, removed the skins and decorated them with flowers made from cucumber skin and tomato roses; I thought it was the most beautiful display in the world. It was also my first introduction to aspic jelly. Sadly, I did not win any awards on my first outing. However, the amount of new knowledge I got from that effort propelled me to further research and study and, apart from the competitive aspect, it provided me with a vehicle for artistic culinary endeavor. The next competition I entered, I won a Certificate of Merit. My mother had it

Foodshows and Competitions

framed, and it hung proudly over the fireplace in our family home for many years. Despite many accolades and awards received over the years, that certificate still means most to me, including my culinary Olympic medals.

Food shows and competitions, whether individual or at the national team level, serve important functions in culinary development. At the individual level, they can inspire chefs to new professional heights and they can provide an outlet for artistic expression which, in most cases, serves to raise the individual chef to a higher sense of professional worth, which permeates all other aspects of their work. All the training and discipline needed to succeed can lead to becoming a celebrated chef which, ultimately, assuring success as a restaurateur.

At the international level, competitions can serve to make a culinary statement about a national cuisine and the skill level of a nation's chefs. These events can also provide an arena for making philosophical statements about national food trends. Over recent years, the successes of Irish chef teams in international competitions contributed to instilling a new confidence within the Irish culinary world.

In my case, food-show displays became a stepping stone to artistic expression. I loved to prepare and decorate cold display platters, from the concept to all that shinyaspic, the neatness of the layouts, the garnishes, the great color combinations, and, of course, winning awards. I had some success, winning many gold medals. After ten years of doing cold food displays I eventually lost all interest in them; the reason being that I realized they were totally impracticable from a customer standpoint and made no statement about my cooking skills. The true professional chef, in my view, is the one who recognizes the impermanence of the art. The chef's customer is the most important final arbitrator of a chefs' cooking skills. Food is cooked to be eaten, not shown.

However, over the years, creating new recipes from new products or combinations of new and old recipe items remains exciting to me. I once discussed this with Phil Coulter, the renowned Irish composer, who is also a great gourmet. Cooking, according to Coulter, is very much like music. Simple or difficult, pleasing to some, and not to others.

Maestro Coulter pointed out that there are only a limited number of musical notes available to the composer. It is how the are brought together, arranged, and assigned to different instruments, and played by professionals which makes the music truly exceptional. In culinary art, there are only a number of true cooking principles; however, there are no limits to the variations which can be arranged in various orders with certain ingredients that are then cooked with love and care. This analogy, I believe to be a perfect description of a true chef's calling: Write the recipe and execute it to perfection every time. It is an impermanent art. What sustains me from that analogy is that a chef's reputation depends on the last meal served, not on the last gold medal won.

Dublin Institute of Technology is the oldest culinary school in Ireland. Indeed at one time it was the *only* one. In 1977, an advanced two-year cooking program for industry chefs was launched. While it was a program of study under the banner of the world famous City and Guilds of London Institute, it was taught at DIT. Its numerical course designation was 706/3, and this is how most student members referred to it. Beyond the class members, it became known as the Tuesday Club, because it met on Tuesdays. I was lucky to have been selected as a member of the first class of twelve chefs of the Tuesday Club. This splendid program was launched under the direction of a great inspirational Irish culinary guru, James Kilbride. Since its beginnings, this program has graduated more than 150 master chefs. As chef Kilbride often pointed out, the nationality of the chef makes no difference, what matters is that he or she shall be blessed with a fair share of imagination and creativity.

This program raised my appreciation of the wonderful history associated with culinary art and hospitality in general. Kilbride gave me a new pride as a chef. Not only did he apply the rigorous culinary requirements of the City & Guilds, but he also believed chefs should be cultured people who are schooled in communication, science, technology, art, and personal development, along with an appreciation of the marriage of food and wine. It is my belief that this two-year course and, later, a similar two-year pastry program made a significant contribution in raising the consciousness of the Irish chef.

In the past two decades, no one can doubt that the Irish hospitality industry and, more significantly, the restaurant industry and cuisine, have undergone dramatic changes. Ireland is a wonderfully productive island, boasting outstanding beef, lamb, pork, and vegetables. Its waters furnish the finest fish and shellfish, and the quality of its dairy produce is legendary. Many innovative foods have been generated from excellent growing and farm-related enterprises, including venison, organic meats, vegetables, mushrooms, superb farmhouse cheese. Specialty cheeses are made in most areas of Ireland. Irish baking, too, is legendary; it's a rare thing to find an Irish restaurant where they don't take pride in their home-baked breads. Even the most sophisticated restaurants have their own particular variation on the traditional crusty brown bread.

As the value of tourism to Ireland became evident in the late sixties, much infrastructure was developed to accommodate the expected visitors. Up to this time, there was only one college engaged in culinary education and, along with chef apprenticeships under the auspices of trade unions and some individual hotels conducting limited training, this was the extent of chef education in Ireland.

In 1964, the Irish government set up an agency which became known as CERT, the council for recruitment and training for the hotel and tourism industry. This combined agency of industry professionals, educators, and civil servants developed training programs and acquired modern training facilities for the implementation of culinary education. This far-sighted initiative succeeded in recruiting and training hundreds of chefs over the years. In fact, what was once a chef-trainee recruitment program has now become highly selective for these much-sought-after training positions.

Despite setbacks, the Irish hotel and restaurant industry has grown. Like other countries in which fine dining in hotel restaurants has declined, Ireland has provided opportunities for the chef/owner to flourish. Concurrent with this development was both an increase in local diner sophistication, and in international diners seeking to explore native Irish cooking.

To further propel this rebirth of cuisine, some important culinary developments occurred simultaneously. The Irish Panel of Chefs, a professional chefs' organization dedicated to improving the culinary art in Ireland, was rejuvenated. This organization set about organizing and competing in cooking competitions. Under their auspices, international competitions were entered. Outstanding successes ensued, contributing to the prestige of Irish chefs. Indeed, the travels and exposure by these chefs to other international cuisines also played an important role in the upgrading of Irish cuisine.

In addition, outstanding cooks such as Myrtle Allen, Declan Ryan, John Howard, Colin O' Daly, Terry Mc Coy, and Gerry Galvin received international accolades for their restaurants and cooking styles. Traditional Irish cooking was revisited and classical French cuisine was abandoned for what has become known as *progressive Irish cuisine*—the adaptation of classical cooking to first-class food products.

NOEL C. CULLEN
Boston University
April 2000

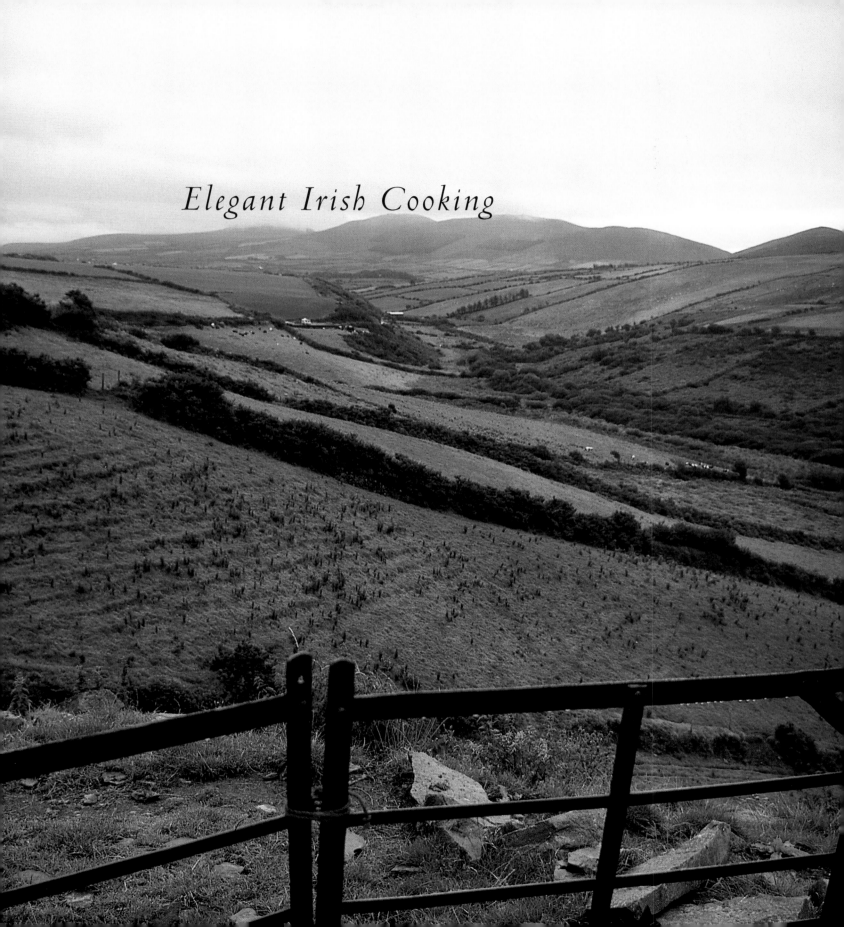

Elegant Irish Cooking

Appetizers & Light Meals

THE TERM *APPETIZER* **AND** *HORS D'OEUVRE* **OFTEN CAUSE CONFUSION.** *HORS D'OEUVRE* **IS**

used to describe small portions of food served either before the main meal or as the

first course of a meal. *Hors d'oeuvre* means "outside the work." Originally, they were

served as a first course, in a room separate from the dining room.

Appetizer, on the other hand, is an American term that describes a small portion

of a very flavorful food or drink used to stimulate the appetite at the beginning of a

meal. The words *starter* and *appetizer* are often used interchangeably to describe the

meal's first course. In recent times, because of our health and diet consciousness, this

section of the menu has become a popular area from which to choose light meals.

Appetizer courses are relatively new to Irish menus. The ubiquitous soup had long been the traditional *entree* to the main meal and, up until recent times, the selection of appetizers on Irish menus was considered boring and limited in inventiveness. These menu items usually consisted of: egg mayonnaise, chicken liver pâté, chilled slice of melon, smoked salmon, and, perhaps in some places, adventurous items consisting of a plated variety of food known as *hors d'oeuvre varies.*

Irish chefs have long since abandoned this limited fare. This section on Irish menus has become more innovative. The old menu items have been replaced by selections of new, creative, exciting appetizers and light meals, ranging from different combinations of smoked fish and eggs, to pasta, savory flans, potato pâtés, quail, boxty, vegetarian tarts, tomato mousses, and many others, all brought together to provide diverse and interesting culinary creations of the best traditional Irish foods.

Molly Malone Smokies

1 shallot, dice fine

1 clove garlic, crushed

8 medium shrimp, shelled and deveined

1 teaspoon chopped parsley

1 tablespoon butter

1 tablespoon white wine

juice of ½ lemon

2 ounces smoked haddock, diced

2 ounces smoked trout, diced

1 ounce smoked salmon, diced

⅛ teaspoon sweet paprika

2 peeled and seeded tomatoes

⅔ cup heavy cream

1 tablespoon mixed grated Swiss and Parmesan cheese

1. Preheat oven to 425°F.

2. Cook shallots, garlic, shrimp, and parsley in butter in sauté pan, 1 minute.

3. Add white wine and lemon juice.

4. Place the diced and smoked fish with other ingredients in the pan, and cook for 30 seconds.

5. Season with paprika, mix in tomatoes, and cover with cream.

6. Fill individual 4-ounce earthenware ovenproof ramekins with fish mixture, top with cheese and bake in preheated oven, 6 to 10 minutes, until bubbling and golden brown on top.

SERVES 4

Paprika is made of powdered dried sweet and red peppers grown in Hungary. It is used in sauces, stews, salad dressings, tomato dishes, and with fish and shellfish. To shell shrimp (either before or after cooking) start at the large end and peel away the shell. In the United States, jumbo shrimp are sometimes erroneously referred to as *prawns*. Prawns are a different species of shellfish, and are quite common in Ireland, with Dublin Bay Prawns being the best known.

PRESENTATION

SERVE IMMEDIATELY, PLACING EACH RAMEKIN ON A BASE PLATE WITH A FOLDED NAPKIN UNDERLINER.

Warm Oysters in Guinness Sauce with Puff-Pastry Leaves

To open oysters: Hold the oyster firmly, with a cloth in one hand, hinged end towards you. Insert oyster knife in the area where top and bottom shell meet, and prise open with a twisting movement. Slide knife blade along inside edge of upper shell to sever the muscle holding the shells together. Remove any pieces of broken shell. Cut muscle attachment to lower shell.

Note: The oysters for this dish should be cooked only until their edges curl; their bodies should be plump. Oysters become tough when they are overcooked.

PRESENTATION

PLACE OYSTERS ON BOTTOM HALF OF PASTRY LEAVES. COAT WITH GUINNESS-AND-HOLLANDAISE MIXTURE. PLACE PASTRY LID ON TOP.

OYSTERS AND PASTRY LEAVES

1 sheet prepared puff pastry cut into 6 by 12 inch squares

egg wash (1 egg mixed with 2 tablespoons of milk)

6 tablespoons prepared hollandaise sauce (see recipe that follows)

2 shallots, finely diced

2 tablespoons butter

³/₄ cup Guinness, divided

1¹/₂ cups heavy cream

36 shucked oysters (reserve oyster liquor)

HOLLANDAISE SAUCE

3 tablespoon malt vinegar

1 teaspoon finely diced shallots

1 bay leaf

¹/₂ teaspoon crushed black peppercorns

3 egg yolks

1 cup clarified butter, hot

juice of ¹/₂ lemon

¹/₈ teaspoon cayenne pepper

PASTRY AND OYSTERS

1. Preheat oven to 400°F.

2. Roll puff pastry to ¹/₄ inch thickness and cut into ¹/₂ inch squares. Place on greased cookie sheet and brush with egg wash.

3. Pierce the pastry with a fork and bake in preheated oven until golden brown (about 8–10 minutes).

4. Allow to cool slightly, then split the squares horizontally to form a top and bottom half. Hold in a warm place.

5. Prepare hollandaise sauce and hold in warm place. Do not expose to direct heat.

6. Sauté the diced shallots in butter over low heat for 2 minutes.

7. Add 6 tablespoons Guinness and oyster liquor. Reduce further until you have approximately 2 tablespoons liquid.

8. Add cream. Simmer until it coats the back of a spoon. Strain.

9. Add 6 tablespoons hollandaise (reserve remainder) to the cream and Guinness reduction. Hold in a warm place.

10. In a saucepan, poach the oysters gently in the remaining Guinness. Do not overcook. See *Note*.

HOLLANDAISE SAUCE

1. In a medium saucepan, over high heat, reduce vinegar with shallots, bay leaf, and peppercorns to approximately 1 tablespoon liquid.

2. When reduced, add 3 tablespoons water. Strain, reserving the liquid.

3. In a food processor fitted with a steel blade, combine the warm reduction and egg yolks. Blend 15 seconds, at high speed, or until the mixture thickens slightly.

4. While the food processor is running; slowly pour in the hot clarified butter over a 15-second period, in a think stream. Butter must be hot [120 F] to cook the egg yolks. Use an instant-read thermometer. If the butter is too hot, egg yolks may curdle.

5. Add lemon juice and cayenne.

Oysters with Red-Onion Balsamic Vinegar, and Home-Dried Plum Tomato

Oysters are considered by many in Ireland to be the perfect appetizer. They are delicious, yet more than a dozen can be eaten without exceeding the food value of an egg. According to Jonathan Swift, the famous Irish writer and satirist, who was Dean of St. Patrick's Cathedral in Dublin: "He was a bold man who first ate an oyster."

PRESENTATION

PLACE THE ONION MIXTURE ON A PLATE. TOP WITH TOMATO. PLACE OYSTER ON TOP. ALLOW THREE TOMATOES AND THREE OYSTERS PER SERVING.

GUEST CHEF

Fergus Moore, Chef, Sheen Falls Lodge, Kenmare, Co. Kerry

HOME-DRIED PLUM TOMATO

12 plum tomatoes

½ teaspoon sugar

salt to taste

2 cloves garlic, crushed

2 sprigs fresh rosemary, chopped

2 sprigs fresh basil, chopped

2 tablespoons olive oil

OYSTERS AND RED ONION BALSAMIC VINEGAR

1 red onion, finely diced

1 teaspoon chopped chives

2 tablespoons olive oil

1 tablespoon balsamic vinegar

12 raw, shucked oysters

1. Preheat oven to 125°–150°F.

2. Sprinkle the plum tomatoes with sugar and salt. Dry on a sheet pan in preheated oven overnight.

3. Remove and marinate for 1 hour in olive oil, garlic, rosemary, and basil. Drain.

4. Mix red onion and chives with olive oil and balsamic vinegar just before serving, to prevent discoloring.

Galway Bay Oyster Casserole

1 tablespoon finely diced onion

½ cup sliced mushrooms

4 tablespoons butter

3 tablespoons all-purpose flour

5 tablespoons milk

5 tablespoons cream

2 teaspoons sherry

⅛ teaspoon cayenne pepper, optional

½ teaspoon chopped parsley

salt, to taste

20 oysters, shucked, liquor reserved

½ cup fresh white breadcrumbs (to prepare fresh breadcrumbs, remove crust from any white bread and pulse in a food processor)

1. Preheat oven to 400°F.

2. Sauté onions, and mushrooms lightly in the butter. Add flour and cook gently, 2 minutes. Consistency should resemble wet sand.

3. Combine the milk and cream. Add to the onion-and-mushroom mixture. Bring to a boil, stirring frequently.

4. Add the sherry, cayenne pepper (optional), parsley, and oyster liquor to the sauce.

5. Arrange opened oysters in individual cassoulets (or other suitable ovenproof dishes), pour over the sauce and sprinkle the top with the fresh white breadcrumbs.

6. Bake in a preheated oven, 14 minutes, or until golden brown.

SERVES 4

Ireland produces two types of oysters—*native* or *flat*, and *gigas* also known as *Pacific* or *rock* oysters (distinguished by their frilly shells). Native oysters are seasonal, spawning during the summer months only. Gigas are available year around.

PRESENTATION

PLACE OVENPROOF DISHES ON PLATES WITH NAPKIN UNDER-LINERS.

Baked Carlingford Oysters with Herb Butter

SERVES 2

Carlingford Lough in Co. Louth is famous for the quality of its oysters. Live oysters should be as fresh as possible. Reject any oysters with broken shells, that don't have tightly closed shells, or that have shells that don't snap shut when tapped. The smaller an oyster is for its particular species, the younger and more tender it will be.

PRESENTATION

SERVE ON A ROUND PLATTER, ACCOMPANIED BY A GLASS OF GUINNESS.

GUEST CHEF

Pat Kerley, Chef/Proprietor, Quaglinos Restaurant, Dundalk, Co. Louth

2 cups red wine

1 small shallot, finely diced

½ clove garlic, crushed

salt to taste

⅛ teaspoon chopped tarragon

⅛ teaspoon chopped parsley

8 tablespoons unsalted butter, softened

1 cup fresh white breadcrumbs

6 Carlingford oysters

1. Preheat oven to 375°F.

2. In a small saucepan boil red wine and shallot until reduced by ⅔ to approximately ½ cup.

3. Add garlic, salt, and herbs.

4. Whisk in softened butter and add just enough breadcrumbs to bind the mixture.

5. Open oysters and reserve in the deep shell. Place on baking sheet.

6. Cover oysters with herb butter and bake in the preheated oven, 7–10 minutes.

Baked Egg with Smoked Irish Salmon

1 egg

¼ cup cream

1 tablespoon diced smoked salmon

salt and freshly ground pepper

1. Preheat oven to 350°F.

2. Separate egg. Put egg white and cream into bowl and whisk.

3. Season with salt and pepper. Add smoked salmon.

4. Lightly butter a ramekin dish and pour in mixture.

5. Place whole egg yolk in ramekin with mixture. Place in a deep baking pan. Pour boiling water halfway up the side of the ramekin. Bake in preheated oven; 10 to 15 minutes, or until risen.

SERVES 1

Generally, cooking this egg dish over gentle heat for a longer period, (rather than over high heat for a brief period) allows for even heat penetration and helps to bring the texture of this dish to a thickened, rather than a hard, stage.

Smoked salmon is one of Ireland's most renowned foods. It is often served accompanied by lemon and traditional brown bread and butter.

Typically, ramekins resemble scaled-down souffle dishes, are porcelain or earthenware, and hold about 4 ounces.

PRESENTATION

SERVE IN THE RAMEKIN DISH ON A PLATE WITH A NAPKIN UNDERLINER.

GUEST CHEF

Stella Doyle, Chef/Owner, Doyle's Seafood Bar, Dingle, Co. Kerry.

Smoked Salmon and Crab Parcel, Kilakee House

Prepared crab is available in cans, as lump or claw meat. Once opened, refrigerate and use within one day.

Kilakee House is set in the scenic foothills of the Wicklow mountains overlooking the City of Dublin. The building that houses the restaurant enjoys a colorful historic past. Built in the eighteenth century, it was supposedly haunted until 1977 by a mysterious black cat.

PRESENTATION

PREHEAT OVEN TO 425°F. PLACE THE PARCEL, FOLDED EDGES DOWN, ONTO A LIGHTLY BUTTERED OVENPROOF DISH. SPOON THE CHEESE SAUCE OVER THE PARCEL. PLACE IN PREHEATED OVEN UNTIL GOLDEN BROWN ON TOP, ABOUT 1 MINUTE. SERVE IMMEDIATELY ON A LARGER PLATE ON A NAPKIN UNDERLINER.

GUEST CHEF

David Edwards, Kilakee House Restaurant, Co. Dublin

SAVORY PANCAKE

1 egg white

½ teaspoon finely chopped parsley

½ teaspoon finely chopped tarragon

½ teaspoon finely chopped thyme

1 clove garlic, crushed

1 cup all-purpose flour

¼ cup milk

salt and freshly ground pepper to taste

oil, for greasing

FILLING

1 shallot, diced finely

1 teaspoon butter

¼ cup dry white wine

juice of ½ lemon

1 cup heavy cream

¼ cup smoked salmon strips

¼ cup crabmeat

2 tablespoons grated cheddar cheese

SAVORY PANCAKE

1. In a standing mixer, whisk egg white until fluffy.

2. Gradually add herbs, garlic, flour, and milk to egg white. Mix at low speed.

3. Slowly add water while increasing the speed of the machine, until the mixture is smooth and the consistency of heavy cream.

4. Remove from machine and season with salt and pepper.

5. Ladle batter onto a heated and oiled crêpe pan, swirling the batter

around the pan quickly and evenly to lightly cover the pan's base. Cook evenly, with as little color as possible on both sides. Keep the crêpes warm (stack and cover) while the filling is being prepared.

FILLING

1. Place shallot in a saucepan with butter. Cook over a low heat, without browning, approximately 1 minute.

2. Add wine and lemon juice; reduce by half.

3. Add cream to the saucepan; heat until mixture becomes slightly thick.

4. Mix in the smoked salmon and crabmeat and heat for 30 to 50 seconds.

5. Remove the salmon and crabmeat mixture from the sauce using a slotted spoon. Place on the center of the pancake. Fold over the edges of the pancake and shape into a parcel.

6. Mix the cheddar cheese with the remaining sauce.

Smoked Salmon and Jerusalem Artichoke Soufflé on a Tarragon Butter Sauce

SERVES 4

The most common variety of the Jerusalem artichoke resembles a potato. It contains inulin, a carbohydrate, which is beneficial to diabetics and others on a low-starch diet. These artichokes are normally prepared in the same manner as potatoes, although the cooking time is shorter.

PRESENTATION

UNMOLD THE RAMEKIN ONTO WARMED PLATES AND SURROUND WITH TARRAGON BUTTER SAUCE.

GUEST CHEF

Kevin Arundel, Chef, Marlfield House, Gorey, Co. Wexford

SOUFFLE FILLING

4 slices smoked salmon (approximately ½ ounce each)

salt

½ pound Jerusalem Artichokes

1 medium egg

1 egg yolk

2 tablespoons melted butter

4 tablespoons heavy cream

BUTTER SAUCE

2 tablespoons white-wine vinegar

2 tablespoons dry white wine

1 shallot, finely diced

2–3 teaspoons cold water

8 tablespoons butter, cut into small pieces

1 tablespoon tarragon leaves, finely chopped

salt and freshly ground pepper, to taste

1. Preheat oven to 350°F.

2. Mold the slices of smoked salmon into four ramekins. Chill. Allow the smoked salmon to overhang the top of the ramekin molds.

3. Boil artichokes in salted water, until soft, (15 to 20 minutes). Drain. Place onto a baking sheet and dry in a preheated oven, 3 minutes. Cool slightly.

4. Lower oven to 325°F.

5. In a food processor fitted with a steel blade, blend the cooled artichokes with whole egg and yolk. Add melted butter, then cream, slowly, for 30 seconds.

6. Pour the mix into the smoked-salmon-lined ramekin molds. Fold smoked salmon overhang and seal top, pressing down slightly.

7. Place into a water bath and bake in a preheated oven, for 20 minutes. Remove from oven, and let rest, 10 minutes.

SAUCE

1. Reduce vinegar and wine with shallots in a small saucepan over high heat until 1 tablespoonful liquid remains.

2. Add 2–3 teaspoons cold water. Slowly whisk in the pieces of butter.

3. Add chopped tarragon. Season to taste.

Tartare of Salmon, Wrapped in a Parcel of Smoked Salmon

Chives are members of the onion family and are used extensively in Irish cooking. Although normally associated with tenderloin of beef, tartare is now a term that generally denotes the chopped raw flesh that has been marinated or flavored with herbs or seasonings.

PRESENTATION

PLACE TWO PARCELS ON EACH COLD PLATE. GARNISH WITH LETTUCE AND LEMON WEDGES.

8 ounces fresh salmon

¼ teaspoon salt

½ teaspoon sugar

Zest of ½ lemon

1 tablespoon chopped chives

1 tablespoon lemon juice

8 slices smoked salmon (approximately ½ ounce each)

1 head curly endive lettuce

1 lemon, cut into wedges

1. Sprinkle fresh salmon with salt, sugar, lemon zest, and chopped chives. Sprinkle with lemon juice and marinate. Refrigerate 12–24 hours.

2. Finely chop the fresh salmon with a sharp knife (do not use a food processor).

3. Place 1 ounce of the salmon tartare on each slice of smoked salmon.

4. Fold into the shape of a small parcel and tie with a chive string. Allow 2 per portion.

Mussels with Garlic, Chives, Butter, and Crushed Hazelnuts

32 large mussels, well scrubbed

¼ cup white wine

juice of 1 lemon

½ pound lightly salted butter

2 tablespoons chives, chopped

¼ cup chopped hazelnuts

⅛ teaspoon salt

⅛ teaspoon milled black peppercorns

½ cup fresh white breadcrumbs (to prepare fresh breadcrumbs, remove crust from white bread and pulse in a food processor)

1 teaspoon paprika

1. Cook mussels in white wine and lemon juice in a 3-quart stock pot until mussels open, about 1 minute. Remove from heat and let cool.

2. Remove one shell half from each mussel. Discard, reserving the remaining shell half, containing mussel "meat" for service.

3. Pulse butter, chives, hazelnuts, salt and pepper in a food processor until smooth, approximately 30–60 seconds.

4. Spoon the prepared butter onto the mussels in the half shell.

5. Combine breadcrumbs and paprika and sprinkle over the butter.

6. Place mussels onto ovenproof serving dishes and bake in preheated oven at 375°F, approximately 5 minutes.

SERVES 4

To remove the hazelnut's bitter outer skin, roast the whole nuts in a 275 F preheated oven for 12–15 minutes. They should give off a good aroma and just begin to darken. While still hot, rub in a dry towel to remove the skin.

PRESENTATION

SERVE OVENPROOF DISHES ON LARGER PLATE ON A NAPKIN UNDERLINER.

Crab Tart with Roast Prawn Tails and Ribbons of Spring Vegetables

SERVES 6

Dariole molds are usually 2 to 2½ inches in diameter and about 3 inches tall. These round, flat-based molds have straight sides sloping slightly outward to an open end.

Safflower oil is a flavorless cooking oil that can be heated to high temperature, making it an excellent oil for frying and roasting.

PRESENTATION

REMOVE THE PRAWN TAILS FROM OVEN. REMOVE SHELLS AND DISCARD PRAWNS. KEEP PRAWNS WARM. POUR THE SAUCE ONTO WARMED PLATES. REMOVE THE TARTS FROM THE MOLDS AND PLACE IN THE CENTER OF THE PLATE. GARNISH WITH THE PRAWN TAILS, A MOUND OF VEGETABLES, AND SOME FRESH DILL LEAVES.

CRAB
1 cup white fish such as cod or hake

1 cup crabmeat

½ cup heavy cream

3 medium egg whites

2 tablespoons butter, to grease molds

Salt and freshly ground pepper, to taste

SAUCE
2 cups fish stock

¼ cup dry white wine

⅔ cup heavy cream

GARNISH
12 prawn or shrimp tails, shell on

¼ cup each carrot, leek, celery, and onion, cut in thin strips

1 tablespoon of safflower oil

2 tablespoons butter

6 dill sprigs

CRAB

1. Preheat oven to 350°F.

2. In a food processor fitted with a steel blade, blend white fish until smooth.

3. In a medium bowl, flake the crabmeat. Add to the blended fish and mix.

4. Partially whip cream and mix with crabmeat mixture.

5. Beat the egg whites until stiff.

6. Fold in the egg whites and correct seasoning with salt and pepper.

7. Divide the mix between 6 lightly buttered dariole molds.

8. Cover tops with buttered parchment paper and plastic wrap. Poach in water bath and bake for approximately 17 to 20 minutes.

SAUCE

1. Place fish stock in a medium saucepan and reduce by ½.

2. Add wine and reduce by ⅓.

3. Add cream, and simmer until sauce is creamy. Check seasoning.

GARNISH

1. Preheat oven to 400°F.

2. Place vegetable strips into water and bring to a boil, 30 seconds. Strain. Place the vegetables immediately in iced water. This procedure is known as *blanching* and *shocking*.

3. In a separate pan reheat vegetables in butter.

4. Brush the prawn tails with safflower oil, set to roast on a baking sheet in oven, 2 minutes.

Pan Roasted Quail with Kildare Boxty

Blanching means to cook foods, most often vegetables, briefly in boiling water, then shocking briefly in cold water until cool. Watercress is blanched to enhance its color and to remove bitterness.

Quail flesh is firm, white, and delicately flavored. Although it is customary to hang some game birds, this is not true of quail. Quail is usually eaten fresh and prepared simply.

PRESENTATION

HEAT THE SAUCE. ADD WATERCRESS AND PARSLEY. PLACE BOXTY IN THE CENTER OF A WARMED PLATE. PLACE THE RIBS OF CELERY AND CARROT ON TOP OF THE BOXTY. ARRANGE THE QUAIL ON TOP, GARNISH WITH THE BUTTON ONIONS. POUR THE SAUCE AROUND THE QUAIL AND POTATO.

QUAIL
1 boneless whole quail

1 tablespoon olive oil

1 rib celery, cut into 3-inch long pieces

1 small carrot, cut into 3-inch long pieces

6 sprigs watercress

1 sprig rosemary

1 slice smoked bacon

1 tablespoon butter

¼ cup tawny port

¾ cup chicken stock

½ cup heavy cream

BOXTY
4 button onions (also known as boiling onions)

1 large all purpose potato (skin on)

salt and freshly milled pepper

1 tablespoon chopped parsley

QUAIL

1. Sauté quail in olive oil with celery and carrot. Roast vegetables and quail together at 375°F in small pan or dish, 12–15 minutes. Reserve pan juices and vegetables.

2. Pick the leaves from the watercress and blanch in boiling salted water, 30 seconds. Remove and shock in ice water, which stops the cooking process and preserves the vivid color of the watercress. Drain well and chop.

3. Chop rosemary and smoked bacon. Simmer gently in butter, 1 minute. Add port and boil down until almost no liquid remains. Add chicken stock and reduce further by ⅔. Finally, add the cream. Stir over medium-high heat until mixture thickens, about 30–40 seconds.

BOXTY

1.   Preheat oven to 350°F.

2.   Blanch the button onions and set aside.

3.   Wash and peel the potato. Grate into a bowl. (The grated potatoes should be used immediately.) Season the grated potatoes with salt and milled peppercorns. Place into a 6-inch-diameter lightly buttered ovenproof sauté pan, approximately 1 inch deep, and fry until golden brown.

4.   Turn boxty in pan to cook evenly on both sides. Place pan containing potatoes in preheated oven and bake, approximately 6–8 minutes. Set aside and keep warm.

Bacon-and-Leek Flan

SERVES 6

Leeks are one of the oldest known vegetables in Ireland. They form the basis of many flavorings in soups, sauces, and stews, as well as being served as a vegetable itself.

To prepare leeks, split the trimmed leek from top to bottom and wash thoroughly under cold running water to remove all the trapped dirt between the leaves

PASTRY

scant 1 cup whole-wheat flour

1 teaspoon baking powder

1 teaspoon salt

1 teaspoon brown sugar

2 tablespoons shortening

2 tablespoons butter

3 tablespoons cold water

1 tablespoon oil

FILLING

1½ cups leeks, diced (white part only)

4 slices Canadian bacon, cut into julienne

4 tablespoons butter

4 eggs

2½ cups milk

3 tablespoons heavy cream

¼ teaspoon each salt and freshly ground pepper

¼ teaspoon paprika

PASTRY

1. Preheat oven to 400°F.

2. In a small bowl, combine flour, baking powder, and salt.

3. Add shortening and butter, cut into small pieces, and rub gently until mixture resembles fine breadcrumbs.

4. Dissolve sugar in 3 tablespoons of cold water and oil. Add enough liquid until the mixture comes cleanly away from the sides of the bowl.

5. Turn onto a lightly floured work surface and knead gently, 1 minute. Allow pastry to rest (covered) in the refrigerator, 15 minutes.

6. Roll out pastry and line an 8 or 9 inch greased tart pan. Pinch the base of the dough all over with a fork and bake blind (line the pastry with parchment paper and fill with rice or dried beans) in preheated oven, for 5 minutes. Remove the parchment paper and dry filling, and bake, 5 minutes.

FILLING

1. Preheat oven to 375°F.

2. Place bacon into a small saucepan of boiling water. Boil 1 minute, pour into strainer. Run cold water over bacon.

3. Cook bacon in dry pan until brown and crispy. Strain off excess fat.

4. To the same pan, add the butter; sauté leeks quickly over medium /high heat.

5. Beat together eggs, milk, heavy cream, and seasoning. Add leeks and bacon.

6. Pour into pastry shell and dust with paprika. Bake in a preheated oven, 35 minutes, or until the flan feels firm in the center.

GUEST CHEF
Matt Dowling, CERT

Slasher O'Reilly's Roasted Garlic Chive Royale with Wild Mushrooms

SERVES 4

Slasher O' Reilly and his comrade Gunner Magee are heroic figures associated with the battle of Ballinamuck in 1798. Their mastery of the Irish guns at this battle was decisive. It was during this period of Irish history that the French general, Humbert, along with a small army, came to Ireland to support Wolfe Tone's United Irishmen movement.

PRESENTATION

RUN THE TIP OF A KNIFE AROUND THE MOLDS TO FREE THE SIDES OF THE ROYALE. UNMOLD THE ROYALE ONTO THE CENTER OF A WARMED PLATE. SPOON THE MUSHROOMS AROUND THE ROYALE AND GARNISH WITH SLICED SCALLIONS.

ROASTED GARLIC CHIVE ROYALE

1 whole head garlic

1 tablespoon olive oil

1 tablespoon chopped chives

salt and freshly ground pepper, to taste

2 cups heavy cream

¼ teaspoon nutmeg

4 medium eggs

1 tablespoon butter, plus additional, for greasing

pinch cayenne pepper

MUSHROOMS

1 pound wild mushrooms (chanterelles, morels, shiitake, and oyster)

2 shallots, sliced

2 tablespoons extra-virgin olive oil

salt and freshly ground pepper

8 fresh basil leaves, shredded

1 teaspoon chopped parsley

4 medium scallions, sliced lengthwise

ROASTED GARLIC CHIVE ROYALE

1. Preheat oven to 350°F.

2. Using sharp knife, cut about ½ inch from the top of garlic.

3. Arrange in shallow baking dish and drizzle oil evenly over top.

4. Bake in oven uncovered 45–60 minutes or until soft, brushing often with oil (roasted garlic should be soft, mellow, and buttery when cooked).

5. When cooled, separate garlic cloves, squeeze from skins and chop. Place in a medium saucepan with chives and cream, simmer, 3 minutes, over medium heat. Strain through a fine-mesh sieve; season with salt, nutmeg, and pepper.

6. Lightly butter 4 ramekins or dariole molds.

7. In a bowl, whisk eggs; stir in cayenne garlic cream. Divide equally among molds.

8. Place on a deep baking pan. Pour in boiling water until it reaches halfway up the side of the molds.

9. Bake in preheated oven, 20 minutes, or until firm to the touch. Remove from oven, allow to cool slightly.

MUSHROOMS

1. Wash mushrooms and trim stems. Depending on size, leave whole or cut into large pieces.

2. In a skillet, over medium heat, saute the shallots in olive oil. Add mushrooms and sauté, 2–3 minutes. Season with salt and milled peppercorns. When cooked, toss with basil leaves and parsley.

Baked Stuffed Mushrooms Shelbourne

The common cultivated mushroom (ranging from white to brown) is recommended for this recipe. However, wild mushrooms such as portabello or shiitake may also be used. When choosing common cultivated mushrooms, look for those that are firm and evenly colored with tightly closed cups. For this recipe, select larger mushrooms of equal size so that they will cook evenly.

This dish was a popular appetizer at Dublin's famous Shelbourne Hotel.

PRESENTATION

SERVE IN THE OVENPROOF DISHES ON A LARGER PLATE ON A NAPKIN UNDERLINER. SAUCE MAY BE SERVED SEPARATELY.

STUFFED MUSHROOMS

12 large flat mushrooms, stalks removed

juice of ½ lemon

salt, to taste

1 clove garlic, crushed

½ cup white wine

4 ounces chicken livers, trimmed of fat

2 tablespoons butter

1 finely diced shallot

¼ cup cooked spinach leaves (pressed dry)

1 tablespoon chopped chives

⅛ teaspoon ground nutmeg

1 sprig thyme, chopped fine

2 tablespoons heavy cream

¼ cup grated cheddar cheese

½ cup fresh white breadcrumbs

SAUCE

reserved mushroom cooking liquid

¼ cup of heavy cream

1 teaspoon of chopped tarragon

STUFFED MUSHROOMS

1. Preheat oven to 450°F.

2. Cook mushrooms in lemon juice, garlic, and white wine, with a tiny amount of salt, approximately 3 minutes, or until they begin to release their juices. Strain and reserve the cooking liquid from the mushrooms.

3. Sauté chicken livers in a pan with the butter and shallot. Remove from heat when the juices are sealed into the livers, about 30 to 40 seconds. Allow to cool.

4. Blend the cooked, cooled chicken livers in a food processor with the spinach, seasonings and herbs, adding the heavy cream slowly, about 30 seconds.

5. Fill the inverted mushrooms cups with the liver and spinach mixture. Combine the cheese and breadcrumbs, top the mushrooms with the breadcrumbs and cheese mix.

6. Bake mushrooms in 4 ovenproof dishes, 5 minutes, in preheated oven.

SAUCE

1. Reduce mushroom cooking liquid to approx ¼ cup.

2. Add heavy cream.

3. Simmer gently, until the sauce comes to a slightly thick consistency.

4. Finish with chopped tarragon.

Tomato Mousse on a Bed of Black Olives and Balsamic Vinegar

1 cup diced tomatoes, skinned and seeded

4 basil leaves

half rib celery, diced

1 teaspoon tomato paste

1 tablespoon powdered gelatin (or 4 leaves)

salt and freshly ground pepper

3 drops Tabasco sauce

safflower oil, for greasing ramekins

½ cup pitted black olives, sliced finely, for garnish

2 tablespoons balsamic vinegar, for garnish

sprigs of chervil and basil, for garnish

1. In a food processor fitted with a steel blade, blend tomatoes, basil, celery, and tomato paste. Strain mixture through a sieve.

2. Soak gelatin in cold water to soften.

3. Heat the gelatin and ¼ tomato mixture in a bowl over a water bath.

4. Add the cold tomato mixture to the prepared gelatin. Season with salt, pepper, and Tabasco sauce.

5. Pour into lightly oiled ramekins and set in the refrigerator for 3 hours or overnight.

6. Unmold by running a thin knife around edge of mold, dip mold in hot water for a few seconds, invert onto the center of a plate.

SERVES 2

Balsamic vinegar is made from the must of wine grapes.

There are two basic types of gelatin—powdered and leaf. One envelope of powdered gelatin equals one tablespoon of powdered gelatin or four leaves (or sheets) of gelatin.

PRESENTATION

ARRANGE BLACK OLIVES IN CENTER OF PLATES. PLACE THE UNMOLDED TOMATO MOUSSE ON TOP OF THE SLICED OLIVES. DRIZZLE BALSAMIC VINEGAR AROUND THE PLATE. GARNISH WITH CHERVIL AND BASIL.

GUEST CHEF

Bruno Schmidt, Chef, Park Hotel, Kenmare, Co. Kerry

Avocado, King Sitric Style

2 ounces button mushrooms, sliced

¼ red and ¼ green bell pepper, diced

1 teaspoon olive oil

¾ cup heavy cream, divided

2 ripe avocados, peeled, stoned and cut into ¼-inch dice

¼ teaspoon salt

⅛ teaspoon freshly ground pepper

2 egg yolks

1. Preheat broiler. In a small sauté pan over low heat, slowly cook the mushrooms and peppers with the olive oil until softened. Add ½ cup cream. Bring to a boil and simmer, 5 minutes.

2. Add avocado, salt, and pepper.

3. Simmer 90 seconds. Remove the avocados and bell peppers. Place in 2 individual 6-inch ovenproof serving dishes.

4. In a separate saucepan, whisk the egg yolks. Stir in remaining ¼ cup cream. Heat but do not boil.

5. Pour the cream over the diced avocados, mushrooms, and bell peppers. Place under the broiler, and glaze to a golden brown.

SERVES 2

The two most widely marketed avocado varieties are the pebbly textured, almost black, *Haas*, and the green, smooth *Fuerte*. The Haas has a smaller pit and a more buttery texture than the Fuerte.

When purchasing avocados, choose those that yield slightly to gentle palm pressure. They should be heavy for their size and unblemished. Avoid any that have dark, sunken spots. The avocado is the only fruit with a fat content, to which it owes its buttery texture.

PRESENTATION

PLACE THE SERVING DISHES WITH THE GLAZED AVOCADO ON A LARGER PLATE WITH A NAPKIN UNDERLINER.

GUEST CHEF

Aiden McManus, Chef proprietor, King Sitric Restaurant, Howth, Co. Dublin

Cashel Irish Blue Cheese Seafood Bake

SERVES 2

High above Templemore in Co. Tipperary is the Devil's Bit, where legend has it that the mountain was gnashed by the devil in a fit of pique; he threw a morsel down onto the Tipperary plain, where it stands as the Rock of Cashel.

There is a thriving farmhouse-cheese industry in Ireland. Cashel Irish Blue has become well known outside Ireland. It is a soft, mild, blue-veined cheese with an unusually low salt content. It is made in Co. Tipperary from very fresh cows' milk.

PRESENTATION

SERVE IMMEDIATELY ON LARGE PLATE ON A NAPKIN UNDER-LINER.

½ cup mayonnaise

2 tablespoons whipped cream

2 ounces Cashel Irish blue cheese (any blue-veined cheese may be substituted), grated

6 ounces boneless, skinless cod fillets

juice of 1 lemon

½ teaspoon salt

¼ teaspoon freshly ground black pepper

¼ cup fresh white breadcrumbs

1. Preheat oven to 350°F.

2. Combine mayonnaise, cream, and cheese.

3. Cut cod into large cubes, mix with the lemon juice, salt, and pepper.

4. Dry the cod on paper towels, place the seasoned cod into 2 6-inch-diameter individual oven proof serving dishes. Cover with the cheese and mayonnaise mixture, and bake in a preheated oven, 15 minutes.

5. Sprinkle the top with breadcrumbs. Bake further, 2–3 minutes, or until the top crust is golden brown.

Soups

ℳ

SOUP HAS A THOUSAND FACES. IT CAN BE PART OF A MEAL OR THE MEAL ITSELF. SOUPS

can be as simple as the ubiquitous chicken broth, which most of us turn to when we

are ill, as sophisticated as a delicate cream soup, as robust as a potato-and-cabbage

soup, or as sophisticated as a flavorsome lobster bisque. In between are a myriad of

combinations, textures, and consistencies that make Irish soup cookery exciting and

adventurous.

There is a sad and rather curious connection between the famous French chef

Alexis Soyer, soup, and the tragic events of the Great Irish Potato Famine of 1845. At

that time, the ruling British government in Ireland consulted with Soyer, and his charge was to concoct a palatable, low-cost, and nutritious soup that might be served to the starving Irish people.

Soyer composed a series of recipes, all impressively economical. His number one recipe contained one-quarter pound leg of beef to two gallons water, two ounces fat drippings, two onions, and other available vegetables, one-half pound flour, one-half pound barley, three ounces salt, and one-half ounce brown sugar. Recipe number two was even cheaper. For flavor, Soyer recommended mint, bay leaves, thyme, and marjoram. These recipes provoked great criticism from a variety of sources.

The nutritional value of his meatless soup was questioned. Scientists analyzed the soups. The correspondent of *The Times of London* described Soyer's soup as "preposterous," pointing out the debilitating effects of a solely liquid diet. Indeed, the esteemed medical journal *The Lancet* agreed that, while there was nothing wrong with Soyer's soup, it nevertheless could not be considered a "whole food." The story ended sadly, with public resentment at such an hysterical level that the well-meaning Chef Soyer had to leave Ireland secretly to avoid being lynched.

Soup pleases virtually everyone, and has often been referred to as a restorative for those not feeling well or for the weary traveler. It also enjoys the advantage of being inexpensive to prepare. Clever cooks have long known how to use by-products such as bones or vegetable trimmings to create and extract flavors for stocks, which are the basis of appealing and delicious soups.

Traditional Irish soups are simple, filling, and, since the advent of the food processor, easy to make. Food processors have become the biggest time-savers for making soups. With a food processor, the once labor-intensive task of pureeing soup is now a simple chore. In addition, they can chop and slice vegetables in a fraction of the time that it would take most of us to do by hand.

The soups offered in this chapter are innovative and creative. These recipes are as easy to prepare as they are comprehensive, and are traditional Irish favorites.

In order to make great soups, a saying from the computer world is appropriate: "Garbage In = Garbage Out." Similarly, the use of first-class stocks, vegetables, and other quality ingredients provides the basis of great soups.

Mussel and Ham Bisque

3 pounds mussels

1 cup dry white wine

2 cups of water

4 tablespoons olive oil

2 medium onions, diced

4 cloves garlic, chopped fine

2 medium carrots, chopped fine

1 tablespoon whole black peppercorns

2 bay leaves

½ teaspoon string saffron

3 tablespoon all-purpose flour

5 cups fish stock

1 small, meaty ham bone

2 cups heavy cream

salt and freshly ground black pepper

1 teaspoon chopped chives or parsley, for garnish

1. Scrub and debeard mussels. Discard any that are open.

2. Bring white wine and 2 cups water to a boil in a 4-quart saucepan. Add the mussels and cover tightly. Steam mussels until open, 6 minutes. Strain the broth through a fine strainer; set aside. Remove mussels from their shells; set aside.

3. Heat olive oil in a 2-quart heavy bottomed saucepan, add the onions, garlic, and carrots. Simmer, 5 minutes, or until the onions are translucent. Add the peppercorns, bay leaves, saffron, and flour. Continue to cook, stirring constantly, 5 minutes.

continued

If a ham bone is not available, chopped cooked ham can be added five minutes before the completion of the soup.

To debeard mussels pull out the byssus, the prickly beardlike hairs just inside the hinge of the shell. Mussels attach themselves to rocks and each other with these threads. The byssus must be scrubbed from the outer shell and pulled from the inner shell before cooking. Mussels die soon after bearding, so preparation should follow immediately.

PRESENTATION

SERVE IN WARM SOUP PLATES OR BOWLS. SPRINKLE WITH CHOPPED CHIVES OR PARSLEY.

4. Slowly add stock, allowing the soup to thicken before adding more stock. When all the stock has been added in, add ham bone. Simmer slowly, 1 hour, occasionally skimming the foam from the top.

5. Remove the ham bone and any pieces of ham that have fallen off the bone. Dice the ham into ¼-inch pieces. Pour the soup through a medium strainer. Bring the strained soup back to a boil. Skim again. Add cream, and turn heat to a simmer. Add mussels and diced ham. Simmer, 2 minutes. Season to taste with salt (very little will be needed) and pepper.

Jackeen's Cockle-and-Mussel Soup

1 pound cockles, thoroughly washed (littleneck clams may be substituted)

1 pound mussels, thoroughly washed and debearded

²⁄₃ cups white wine

1 bay leaf

1 clove garlic, crushed

3 cups fish stock

1 rib of celery, diced fine

½ white of 1 leek, diced fine

1 potato, peeled and diced fine

²⁄₃ cup milk

1 teaspoon Dijon mustard

salt and freshly ground black pepper to taste

¼ cup cream, lightly whipped, for garnish

1 teaspoon chopped dill, for garnish

1. Heat a 2-quart heavy-bottomed saucepan. Place the cockles and mussels in the saucepan. Add white wine, bay leaf, and garlic. Cover and steam, until all shells are open. Remove and reserve the meat from the shells, strain the liquid, and add to the fish stock.

2. In a separate 2-quart saucepan, sweat vegetables until soft. Add the combined mussel-and-fish liquid, milk, and mustard. Bring to a boil. Simmer, uncovered, 20 minutes.

3. Strain. Place the solids in food processor and pulse, adding the liquid gradually.

4. Season. Add shellfish meat. Return to a boil.

SERVES 4

Irish country people refer to Dublin natives as jackeens. Molly Malone's cockles and mussels were once a common feature of a Dubliner, or *jackeen's*, supper.

PRESENTATION

POUR INTO WARMED SOUP PLATES. ADD LIGHTLY WHIPPED CREAM AND GARNISH WITH DILL.

Dublin Bay Prawn Bisque

SERVES 6–8

Bisque usually denotes a creamy shellfish soup. Classical variations of this soup may be thickened with rice.

In larger shrimp, the intestinal vein contains grit that would interfere with the taste of this dish. Shrimp, both raw and cooked, should feel firm and smell sweet.

Dublin Bay prawns, sometimes known as "Norway Lobster," were often found in the nets of fishing boats looking for other fish. They were sold locally on the Dublin markets. Today, they are scarce and much prized.

PRESENTATION

ARRANGE THE PRAWNS IN SOUP BOWLS AND POUR BISQUE OVER THEM.

GUEST CHEF

Terry McCoy, Chef Proprietor, Red Bank Restaurant, Skerries, Co. Dublin.

4 pounds whole prawns or shrimp

1 pound tomatoes

1 rib celery, diced

2 medium carrots, diced

½ cup chopped mushrooms

1 onion, diced

4 sprigs tarragon

4 sprigs parsley

3 bay leaves

3 cloves garlic, crushed

1 cup dry white wine

4 tablespoons butter

1 tablespoon all-purpose flour

1 tablespoon tomato paste

½ cup brandy

3 egg yolks

1 cup heavy cream

1. Preheat oven to 400°F.

2. Heat the olive oil.

3. Add chopped vegetables, herbs, and wine.

4. Sauté until tender. Add 2 quarts cold water. Bring to a boil.

5. Using a strainer, immerse the prawns in the boiling liquid for 40–50 seconds. Bring liquid back to a boil. Remove the blanched prawns. Allow to cool, shell, and remove the flesh from the prawns. Reserve.

6. Place the prawn shells on a baking sheet.

7. Bake the shells in preheated oven until golden brown, about 20 minutes.

8. In another saucepan, melt butter. Add the flour. Cook gently, 3–5 minutes, stirring continuously. Be careful not to brown flour.

9. Add tomato paste, garlic, tomatoes, baked prawn shells, warm stock, and vegetables. Bring to a boil. Lower heat simmer, 1 hour.

10. Add brandy and simmer, 10 minutes. Strain into another saucepan.

11. In a medium bowl, whisk together egg yolks and cream. Add a little bisque liquid to the egg mixture. When light and fluffy, incorporate into soup. Bring to gentle simmer. Do not allow soup to reboil after the addition of the cream and egg. The bisque should thicken.

Galway Oyster Broth with Dill and Tomato

1 quart fish stock

½ cup heavy cream

8 oysters, shucked, liquor reserved

2 tomatoes, peeled, seeded, and diced

1 tablespoon finely chopped dill

salt and freshly ground black pepper, to taste

1. In a 2-quart saucepan, over high heat, reduce the fish stock by half. When reduced, add the cream and oyster liquor.

2. Add tomato, dill, and oysters. Simmer, 2 minutes.

3. Season with salt and pepper.

SERVES 4

The best oysters in Ireland come from Co. Galway. Clarenbridge, Co. Galway, hosts the world championship oyster-opening competition at its annual festival in September.

PRESENTATION

IRISH CRUSTY BROWN BREAD MAKES AN IDEAL ACCOMPANIMENT FOR THIS SOUP ALONG WITH A GLASS OF GUINNESS.

GUEST CHEF

Richard J. Casburn, Chef, Donnelly's of Barna, Co. Galway.

Connaught Coast Seafood Chowder

Any fish can be used for chowder, and often is, but the very best fish chowder is made with cod or one of its relatives. Salmon or monkfish also make very good chowder. Fish that is delicate or finely textured, such as flounder, mackerel, or sea bass are not good for chowder, as they fall apart too easily. When making chowder, it is best to put the fillets in whole; they will break up by themselves as the fish cooks.

A sabayon is a foamy stirred combination of eggs, cream, and milk or wine.

4 tablespoons butter

1 leek, diced fine

1 onion, diced fine

10 ounces white fish, such as hake, cod, or monkfish

4 ounces fresh salmon, cut into ½-inch dice

2 cloves garlic, crushed

1 sprig fennel, diced fine

zest of ½ lemon, grated

1 teaspoon chopped parsley

4 tomatoes, peeled, seeded, and diced

1 quart fish stock

salt and pepper to taste

2 egg yolks

½ cup heavy cream

4 ounces cooked shrimp, ground into a paste in a food processor

1. Melt butter in a heavy-bottomed 2-quart saucepan. Add leek and onion. Cook until soft, without coloring.

2. Add the fish and continue to simmer gently without coloring.

3. Add garlic, fennel, lemon zest, and parsley.

4. Add chopped tomato and fish stock. Cook gently, approximately 30 minutes. Season to taste.

5. Preheat broiler.

6. Combine egg yolks and cream. Whisk vigorously over hot-water bath until thickened. Add the shrimp paste to the egg and cream mixture. Ladle soup into soup bowls. Spoon the *sabayon* on top of the soup. Glaze under the broiler until golden brown. Serve immediately.

Arklow Fish Stew in a Pastry Crust

2 onions, sliced

2 leeks, diced fine

4 potatoes, peeled and diced

1 clove garlic, crushed

1 bay leaf

1 quart water

1 cup dry white wine

2 cups chopped raw fish, such as cod, halibut, hake, and/or small shrimp

1 egg yolk beaten with 1 tablespoon heavy cream, for egg wash

3 ounces prepared puff pastry

1. Preheat oven to 350°F.

2. In a heavy-bottomed 3-quart saucepan, simmer the vegetables, garlic, and bay leaf in 1 quart water and white wine, 30 minutes.

3. Add fish and simmer, 5 minutes, over low heat. Remove the bay leaf.

4. Place the soup in an ovenproof 6-cup casserole dish. Brush the top edge of the dish with the egg wash to create a seal.

5. Roll out the puff pastry. Place on top of casserole. Brush the top of the pastry with egg wash.

6. Bake in preheated oven, 20 minutes. Serve immediately.

SERVES 6

Bay leaves are aromatic, smooth leaves of the laurel tree and are in sauces, soups, stocks, chowders, stews, fish preparations, and *bouquets garni*. They are best used fresh, but keep their flavor well when dried.

Ulster Cream of Potato Soup with Smoked Salmon and Chives

According to Theodora Fitzgibbon, in *Irish Traditional Food*, Saint John's Day was the traditional time for digging potatoes in Co. Antrim, Ulster. On this day, the fishermen had a salmon dinner with new potatoes.

PRESENTATION

SERVE IN WARM SOUP BOWLS. SPRINKLE WITH DICED SMOKED SALMON AND CHOPPED CHIVES.

4 tablespoons butter

¼ leek, chopped coarse

½ carrot, chopped coarse

½ onion, chopped coarse

1½ pounds potatoes, peeled and diced

1 quart chicken stock

¼ cup heavy cream

4 ounces smoked salmon, diced, for garnish

2 tablespoons chives, chopped fine, for garnish

1. Melt butter over medium heat in a 3-quart heavy-bottomed saucepan. Gently cook vegetables and potatoes.

2. Add the chicken stock and simmer, uncovered, 30 minutes. Strain.

3. In a food processor fitted with a steel blade, puree the solids. Add the liquid in a steady stream. Add cream. Season to taste.

Tipperary Creamy Mushroom Soup

1 tablespoon butter

3 leeks, white part only, thinly sliced

1 pound mushrooms, thinly sliced

½ cup all-purpose flour

1 cup nonfat milk

½ cup dry white wine

10 cups chicken stock

4 potatoes, peeled and diced

1 bulb garlic, roasted (see below)

1 cup light evaporated milk

2 teaspoons mixed fresh herbs, such as parsley, thyme, sage, and basil

2 tablespoons sherry

salt and freshly ground black pepper, to taste

fresh chives, chopped, for garnish

1. Melt butter in a 3-quart saucepan. Sauté leeks and mushrooms until soft.

2. Stir in flour and cook until all white from flour has disappeared.

3. Stir in nonfat milk and cook, stirring, until smooth.

4. Add wine and stock, stirring until smooth.

5. Add potatoes, cover, and simmer, 45 minutes.

6. When garlic is roasted, squeeze into a food processor, and puree with evaporated milk, herbs and sherry.

7. Whisk into soup. Do not allow soup boil after adding evaporated-milk mixture.

8. Simmer soup, 5 minutes, over low heat. Season to taste.

Agaricus bisporus is the common supermarket button mushroom. Mild in flavor, it is cultivated in hothouses, and is always available. Store in the refrigerator, loosely wrapped in paper towels, and use as soon as possible.

Sage is a member of the mint family, and is one of the more pungent herbs. Sage leaves are long, narrow, grayish-green ovals with a coarse texture. They are aggressive in aroma and flavor, slightly musty, especially when heated.

PRESENTATION

SERVE IN WARM SOUP PLATES OR BOWLS. SPRINKLE CHOPPED CHIVES.

Celeriac Soup with Smoked Bacon and Potato Bread

SOUP

1 tablespoon unsalted butter

2 medium onions, diced

1 head celeriac, peeled and diced

2 ounces low-salt smoked bacon, chopped

1 bay leaf

1 quart chicken or vegetable stock

salt and ground white pepper

whipped cream, for garnish

chervil, for garnish

POTATO BREAD

1½ pounds boiling potatoes, peeled and diced

¼ cup all-purpose flour

⅛ teaspoon salt

1 tablespoon unsalted butter, melted

⅛ teaspoon mixed herbs, such as parsley, sage, or thyme

2 tablespoons clarified butter

SOUP

1. Melt butter in a 2-quart, heavy-bottomed saucepan. Sauté the onions and bacon, 3–5 minutes.

2. Add diced celeriac, bay leaf, and stock. Bring to a boil.

3. Simmer, gently, uncovered 20 minutes.

4. Skim excess fat. Remove bay leaf.

5. Puree soup in a food processor until smooth. Adjust seasoning.

POTATO BREAD

1. Preheat a heavy-bottomed frying pan.

continued

SERVES 6

Potato bread is also known in some regions of Ireland as boxty. In the United States, celeriac is better known as celery root. It is not the root of ordinary celery and does not develop large stalks above the ground.

PRESENTATION

POUR SOUP INTO WARMED BOWLS OR PLATES. GARNISH WITH A SWIRL OF LIGHTLY WHIPPED CREAM AND A SPRIG OF CHERVIL. SERVE THE POTATO BREAD ON THE SIDE.

GUEST CHEF

Tina Walsh, Co. Kilkenny

2. Boil the potatoes and mash to a puree. While the potatoes are still hot, mix with flour, herbs, and salt.

3. Add the melted butter, knead briefly. On a lightly floured surface, roll out the potato mixture to ½-inch thickness.

4. Using a 2-inch round biscuit cutter, cut out individual circles. Add a little clarified butter to the hot pan and cook circles until both sides are golden brown. Repeat until all potato mixture is used.

Potato and Cabbage Soup

2 onions, peeled and diced

1 leek, washed and diced

2 large boiling potatoes, peeled and sliced

4 tablespoons butter

½ head green cabbage, shredded

salt and freshly ground white pepper

¼ teaspoon nutmeg

1 bay leaf

1 cup milk

3 cups chicken stock

2 tablespoons lightly whipped heavy cream, for garnish

1 teaspoon chopped parsley, for garnish

1. In a 1-quart heavy bottomed saucepan, sauté onions, leeks, potatoes in butter until soft.

2. Add cabbage, season with salt and white pepper, bay leaf, and nutmeg.

3. Simmer, 3–4 minutes.

4. Add milk and stock. Bring to a boil, reduce heat, and simmer slowly, approximately 30 minutes.

5. Remove bay leaf and transfer soup to a food processor. Puree until smooth. Adjust seasoning.

Originally this soup was traditionally served on Monday in Ireland. It was usually based on the leftovers from the traditional Sunday dinner of boiled bacon, cabbage and mashed potatoes.

PRESENTATION

GARNISH WITH LIGHTLY WHIPPED CREAM AND CHOPPED PARSLEY.

Lentil and Coriander Soup

SERVES 8

Sweat, in a culinary sense, means to cook foods slowly without allowing them to color, so as to bring out the flavors of the individual food.

Coriander is much esteemed as a seasoning. Its finely ground seeds are a major ingredient of curry powder. In Ireland, coriander leaves are used for soups, and the seeds are often used to flavor cakes.

PRESENTATION

FINISH SOUP BY WHISKING IN THE CREAM AND BUTTER. POUR INTO WARMED SERVING PLATES.

GUEST CHEF

Michel Flamme, Chef de Cuisine, The Kildare Hotel & Country Club, Straffan, Co. Kildare.

½ cup shallots, diced fine

1 rib celery, diced

4 cloves garlic, crushed

1 cup onion, diced

1½ tablespoons tomato paste

1 tablespoon finely chopped fresh coriander

10 cardamom seeds

1 teaspoon sugar

3 tomatoes, peeled, seeded, and diced

1 cup lentils (soaked in cold water 2 hours, drained)

1 quart chicken stock

½ cup white wine

2 tablespoons heavy cream

4 tablespoons butter

1. Sweat shallots, celery, garlic, and onions over low heat in a 2-quart saucepan, 2 minutes

2. Add coriander, cardamom, sugar, tomato, and lentils

3. Add stock and wine and simmer, over low heat uncovered 1 hour. Skim regularly.

4. Strain the solids into a food processor, add the remaining liquid to the solids and puree until smooth, about 30 seconds.

Cream of Watercress Soup with Warm Herbal Drop Scones

SOUP

1 large onion, diced

½ cup diced leek

½ cup diced celery

2 tablespoons butter

2 medium potatoes, peeled and diced

1 quart chicken or vegetable stock

½ cup heavy cream

6 ounces watercress, well washed

½ cup of whipped heavy cream for garnish

8 sprigs of watercress for garnish

DROP SCONES

³/₄ cup all-purpose flour

1 teaspoon salt

1 teaspoon baking powder

2 tablespoons milk

2 eggs

¼ cup melted butter

1 tablespoon chopped mixed fresh herbs, such as parsley, basil, and rosemary

4 tablespoons safflower oil

SOUP

1. In a 2-quart heavy-bottomed saucepan, over medium-high heat, sweat the onion, leek, and celery in butter, until soft.

2. Add potato and chicken or vegetable stock. Simmer gently, uncovered, 25 minutes.

SERVES 8

Watercress has grown and been eaten in Ireland since prehistoric times. Its mild peppery flavor makes it a popular salad green and garnish.

PRESENTATION

POUR SOUP INTO WARMED PLATES, GARNISH WITH A SWIRL OF WHIPPED CREAM, AND TOP WITH A TINY SPRIG OF WATERCRESS. SERVE WARM DROP SCONES SEPARATELY.

GUEST CHEF
Tina Walsh, Co. Kilkenny

continued

3. Add cream and watercress and simmer, 2 minutes. In a food processor fitted with a steel blade, puree until smooth.

4. Season to taste.

SCONES

1. Sift together the flour, salt, and baking powder.

2. Blend in milk, eggs, butter, and herbs.

3. Pass this batter through a fine-mesh strainer into a small bowl. Refrigerate, covered with plastic wrap, 10 minutes.

4. Heat the safflower oil in a heavy-bottomed pan. Pour a tablespoon of batter onto the pan. Cook on both sides, about 30–40 seconds per side or until golden brown.

Lettuce and Nutmeg Soup

SERVES 6

Nutmeg comes from the inner kernel of the fruit of the nutmeg tree, and is native to the West Indies. The spice is highly aromatic but slightly bitter.

PRESENTATION

POUR INTO WARMED SOUP PLATES AND SERVE WITH THE CROUTONS.

GUEST CHEF

Eugene McGovern, Catering Manager, Trinity College, Dublin

2 cups Boston (Bibb) lettuce leaves

½ cup finely diced leeks

½ cup finely diced onion

½ cup finely diced celery

1 pound potatoes, peeled and diced

1 quart chicken stock

⅛ teaspoon nutmeg

½ cup heavy cream

1 cup ¼-inch cubes fresh bread

2 tablespoons oil or clarified butter, (See note below)

2 cloves garlic, crushed

1. Blanch lettuce leaves in boiling salted water, drain, and plunge into ice-cold water.

2. Simmer vegetables and potato in the chicken stock, 50 minutes.

3. Strain the the solids. Blend in a food processor. Add the liquid to the solids and process until smooth.

4. Combine the drained lettuce leaves with some of the pureed soup. Puree in the food processor.

5. Return to saucepan and add nutmeg. Bring to a boil. Add cream. Correct seasoning and consistency. Add stock to achieve smooth consistency and check for salt and pepper.

6. Fry bread in garlic-flavored clarified butter or oil until golden brown. Place on kitchen paper towels to dry.

Chilled Armagh Apple and Apricot Soup

SERVES 4

In flavor and texture the apricot is often compared to the peach. Unlike the peach, however, an apricot's flavor improves upon cooking and preserving.

Some of Ireland's finest apple orchards are in Co. Armagh, in Ulster.

PRESENTATION

SERVE CHILLED WITH MINT SPRIGS.

1 (approximately 2-ounce) apricot, peeled and stoned

2 Granny Smith apples, peeled, cored, and sliced

²/₃ cup medium-sweet white wine

2 cups vegetable stock

¼ teaspoon grated fresh ginger

2 teaspoons sugar

salt and freshly grund pepper, to taste

6 tablespoons heavy cream

6 sprigs fresh mint, for garnish

1. Place apricot, apple, white wine, stock, ginger, and sugar in a 2-quart heavy-bottomed saucepan. Bring to a boil.

2. Simmer, 15–20 minutes, or until the fruit becomes soft.

3. In a food processor, blend until smooth. Chill. Add cream.

GUEST CHEF

Dermot McEvilly, Chef, Cashel House Hotel, Connmeara, Co. Galway

Potato and Sorrel Soup

1 onion, diced fine

2 tablespoons butter

1 pound potatoes, peeled and diced

1 small bunch sorrel, or 1 cup sorrel leaves

4½ cups chicken stock

¼ cup heavy cream

salt and freshly ground black pepper, to taste

3–4 shredded sorrell leaves, for garnish

2 tablespoons lightly whipped cream, for garnish

1. In a heavy-bottomed 3-quart saucepan over medium heat, cook onion in butter until soft.

2. Add the potatoes, sorrel, and stock.

3. Simmer until potatoes are tender.

4. Add cream. Strain solids, and place in a food processor fitted with a steel blade. Process solids until smooth. While adding the liquid, blend until smooth.

5. Return to heat. Season with salt and pepper.

SERVES 4–6

For vegetarians, use stock or water and omit the dairy products. This soup can also be served chilled. Wild sorrel grows in great abundance in the marshy meadows of Ireland.

PRESENTATION

SERVE IN WARMED SOUP PLATES WITH THREADS OF RAW SORREL AND A TEASPOON OF LIGHTLY WHIPPED CREAM.

Leek and Irish Cashel Blue Cheese Soup

3 leeks, sliced fine (white only)

1 onion, diced fine

1 rib celery, diced fine

2 medium potatoes, diced small

3 tablespoons unsalted butter

4½ cups chicken stock

½ cup heavy cream

3 tablespoons Irish Cashel Blue cheese or other blue-veined cheese

1. In a heavy-bottomed 3-quart pot over medium-high heat, gently cook or sweat the leeks, onion, celery, and potato in butter, without coloring until onions are soft.

2. Add chicken stock. Cook, 30 minutes, until all vegetables are tender.

3. Strain. In a food processor fitted with a steel blade blend the soup to a smooth puree.

4. Return to saucepan. Bring to a boil and skim. Add cream.

5. Season to taste.

SERVES 6

Inoculating cheese with mold spores will, over time, produce a blue-veined interior. Blue-veined cheeses are generally pungent; they can range in taste from the mild Irish variety to the moist creaminess of Gorgonzola to the firm, slightly crumbly, Stilton.

PRESENTATION

GRATE THE CHEESE INTO SOUP. SERVE IN WARMED SOUP BOWLS.

GUEST CHEF

Bruno Schmidt, Chef, Park Hotel, Kenmare, Co. Kerry

Fish &
Seafood Dishes

IRISH FISH AND SEAFOOD ARE OUTSTANDING, NOT ONLY IN THE VARIETY OF SPECIES

caught, but also in freshness. No place in Ireland is more than sixty miles from the

sea. In addition, her unspoiled lakes and rivers yield an abundance of freshwater fish.

The warm currents of the Gulf Stream bring many kinds of fish to Irish coastal

waters; while the colder waters to the north bring an equal variety. Cod, haddock, whit-

ing, pollack, hake, ling, monkfish, and plaice are the most plentiful. Black sole, turbot,

bass, and brill are available in lesser quantities. Salmon, of course, has always been the

most popular of Irish fish. Irish smoked salmon is considered by many to be the finest

in the world.

Salmon was the most highly regarded fish in ancient Ireland, where it was roasted and served with honey. In today's Irish kitchens, it is cooked in many different ways.

The life cycle of the salmon is interesting. Eggs are laid in November or December in the gravel of upstream river beds. After about two years, the young salmon changes color from brown to silver and heads for the sea where it spends about eighteen months. In the sea, it feeds on small fish and builds up its food stock, since it will not eat on its return to the river. Only one percent of young salmon survive this long journey.

Salmon fishing in Ireland is strictly regulated. The freshwater season opens on New Year's Day, and great efforts are made by anglers to catch the first salmon of the season, which usually fetches a high price from a local restaurant.

Trout have a similar life pattern to salmon. Brown trout are much prized. More than thirty other species of freshwater fish are found in Irish waters.

Shellfish have always been plentiful in Ireland, with Galway Bay oysters and Dublin Bay prawns being the most famous. Over a hundred years ago, when Dublin was a very busy port, fishing boats from all over Europe would anchor off Lambay Island in Dublin Bay for shelter and rest before continuing their journeys. These fishermen had their womenfolk on board, and the women cooked their freshly caught shellfish on board, and sold them on the streets of Dublin as Dublin Bay prawns.

Mussels have long been cultivated in Ireland's waters, especially around Wexford. Scallops and crab are also special, but lobster is the aristocrat of the Irish shellfish family. The preparation of fish and shellfish is a strength of many Irish chefs; there are many restaurants specializing in seafood cookery.

ROUND FISH OR FLATFISH

All fish can be classified as either round or flat. Round fish can be cooked whole or cut off the bone into fillets. Large round fish, like salmon, can be cut crosswise into steaks. The fillets of some round fish are thick enough to cut crosswise. Flatfish, such as flounder, cannot be satisfactorily cut into steaks or slices. They are either cooked whole or cut from the bone into fillets.

The fat content of fish ranges from 0.1 percent for haddock to 20 percent for eel. Fat content has a great effect on what cooking method should be chosen. Lean fish are those that are low in fat. Among this group are flounder, sole, cod, bass, and halibut. The fat fish group includes salmon, trout, tuna, and mackerel. Lean fish can easily become dry if overcooked. Fat fish can tolerate more heat without becoming dry.

1. Lean fish are especially well suited to sautéing, since the cooking method supplies fat that the fish lack. Fat fish may also be sauteed, as long as you take care not to use too much fat, which would make the fish greasy.

2. Fish is usually given a coating of flour, breading, or other starchy product before it is sauteed. This forms a crust that browns attractively, enhances the flavor, and helps hold the fish together and reducing sticking.

3. Fish may be soaked in milk briefly before dredging in the flour. This helps the flour form a better crust.

4. Clarified butter or oil are the preferred fats for sautéing and pan frying. Whole butter is likely to burn, unless the fish pieces are very small.

5. Use a minimum of fat, about $\frac{1}{8}$ inch, or just enough to cover the bottom of the pan.

6. Small items, such as shrimp or scallops, can be sautéed over high heat. Large items, such as whole fish, require lower heat to cook evenly.

7. Very large fish may be browned in fat, then finished in the oven, uncovered.

8. Brown the most attractive side—the presentation side—first. For fillets, this is the flesh side against the bone, not the skin side.

9. Handle fish carefully during and after cooking to avoid breaking the fish or the crisp crust.

10. Sauté or fry fish, at the last moment, just prior to serving.

GENERAL GUIDELINES FOR COOKING FISH

Pan Frying and Sauteing

Baking

1. Season fish with salt, pepper, and lemon juice before cooking.

2. Place fish on oiled or buttered baking sheets and brush tops well with oil or butter.

An alternative method is to dip the fish in oil or melted butter to coat both sides and place on ungreased baking sheet.

3. Apply toppings, if desired, such as seasoned bread crumbs, lemon slices, mushrooms or other vegetable garnish, or sauce.

4. Bake the fish at 350°F until done. If the fish is lean and doesn't have a moist topping, baste with oil or butter during baking.

Poaching

1. Use a cold poaching liquid for fish and shellfish, and heat just below boiling until the surface of the poaching liquid barely moves. This prevents the outside of the fish from cooking before the inside and helps prevent fish from falling apart. Also, if a whole fish is placed directly into hot liquid the skin will split.

2. When poaching a whole fish, first wrap it in cheesecloth. The cheesecloth preserves the shape of the fish and facilitates removal from liquid. Remove fish pieces with a slotted spatula. Handle all poached fish as delicately as possible.

3. Almost all types of fish are suitable for poaching; the exception is fish with very soft, fatty flesh, as these tend to fall apart in the poaching liquid.

Testing for doneness

1. The fish should just separate into flakes; that is, it is beginning to flake but does not fall apart easily.

2. If bone is present, the flesh separates from the bone, and the bone is no longer pink.

3. The flesh has turned from translucent to opaque (usually white, depending on the type of fish).

Nuggets of Salmon with Mushrooms, Connemara Style

2 pounds salmon fillet, pin bones removed

½ teaspoon salt

¼ teaspoon freshly ground black pepper

1 tablespoon lemon juice

4 tablespoons butter

1 tablespoon safflower oil

1 shallot, diced finely

8 ounces mushrooms, sliced

¼ cup white wine

½ cup heavy cream

1 teaspoon finely chopped fennel

4 fennel leaves, for garnish

1. Cut salmon into 2-ounce pieces.

2. Season salmon with salt, pepper, and lemon juice.

3. Melt butter in a skillet. Add safflower oil. Add salmon, and sauté over high heat, 6 minutes, turning at least twice.

4. Remove salmon from pan, dry on paper towels, and keep warm.

5. Discard butter, oil, and liquid. Add shallot and mushrooms to skillet. Add white wine and cook, 4 more minutes, over high heat until the liquid reduces by ⅓.

6. Add heavy cream and cook over moderate heat until cream becomes thick, about 2 minutes.

7. Add chopped fennel.

SERVES 4

The small pin bones on salmon fillets may be removed with a tweezer, or small long-nosed pliers.

Fennel grows wild, but it is the cultivated plant that is valued for its leaves and seeds, the flavor of which resembles anise. The fennel stalks often reach five or six feet, supporting delicate feathery leaves and blossoms. The stalks and leaves are traditional seasoning for fish dishes; the seeds are often used in cookies, pastries, and sweet pickles.

PRESENTATION

PLACE MUSHROOM SAUCE ON WARM PLATE. ARRANGE THE SALMON NUGGETS ON TOP OF THE SAUCE. GARNISH WITH WHOLE FENNEL LEAVES.

Baked Liffey Salmon Filled with an Herbed Lobster and Cream Stuffing, *Grainne Ni Mhaille*

The fiery queen *Grainne Ni Mhaille* (Grace O' Malley) was a warrior legend. During one of her campaigns, she arrived at Howth Castle in Dublin, where she was not welcomed. She kidnaped the lord's son, enticing him onto her ship. The conditions for his return were that an extra table setting should always be laid for dinner at the castle, and that the gates should always be left open, a tradition which continues to this day.

PRESENTATION

CUT THE SALMON IN HALF AND SERVE ON LARGE WARM PLATE. SERVE IMMEDIATELY. ASPARAGUS TIPS AND HOL-LANDAISE SAUCE MAKE AN IDEAL ACCOMPANIMENT TO THIS DISH.

4 ounces cooked lobster tail

1 teaspoon chopped parsley

1 teaspoon chopped chives

2 tablespoons heavy cream

juice of 1 lemon

Worcestershire sauce

2 tablespoons butter, melted

4 3-ounce salmon pieces cut from the fillet, preferably from the tail

6 ounces spinach leaves, cleaned and stemmed

8 ounces prepared puff pastry

salt and freshly ground black pepper, to taste

3/4 teaspoon nutmeg

1 egg mixed with 1/4 cup milk, for egg wash

1. Preheat oven to 400°F.

2. Chop lobster into 1/4 inch dice. In a medium bowl, combine lobster with herbs, cream, lemon juice, Worcestershire sauce, and melted butter.

3. Make a pocket in salmon fillets (slit fillet with a thin bladed sharp knife in a lateral slice without cutting all the way across). Fill the pocket with the lobster mixture.

4. Blanch spinach by plunging it into boiling water for 5 seconds. Shock the spinach in ice-cold water immediately after it is removed from the boiling water.

5. Remove spinach from the water, shake off excess, and lay out on a flat

surface. Season with salt, pepper, and nutmeg. Wrap the salmon fillets in the spinach leaves.

6. On a lightly floured surface, roll out puff pastry to ¼-inch thickness. Wrap the salmon and spinach in the puff pastry to form a parcel approximately 6 inches long x 2 inches wide. Brush liberally with egg wash, place on sheet pan, seam side down, and bake in the preheated oven, 17 minutes.

Roasted Peppered Salmon with Tomato-and-Basil Relish

SALMON

1 pound salmon fillet, trimmed, with all pin bones removed

1 tablespoon cracked black peppercorns

1 teaspoon chopped dill, divided

1 whole lime

oil, for greasing

SAUCE

2 shallots, diced fine

1 tablespoon finely shredded basil leaves

2 teaspoons olive oil

1 cup dry white wine

2 cloves of crushed garlic

6 large plum tomatoes, skinned, seeded, and chopped roughly into large chunks

PEPPERED SALMON

1. Preheat oven to 350°F.

2. Cut salmon into 4 equal parts.

3. Coat salmon with cracked peppercorns and ½ teaspoon dill. Grate a little lime zest over salmon.

4. Place on a lightly oiled sheet pan. Bake in preheated oven, 6–8 minutes.

TOMATO-AND-BASIL RELISH

1. In a medium saucepan, place 1 teaspoon olive oil, garlic, and diced shallots. Sauté over medium heat, 1 minute, without coloring.

2. Add white wine and juice of the lime. Reduce by half.

3. Add tomato chunks and basil leaves. Mix and gently heat, 1 minute.

SERVES 4

This dish works particularly well with farm-raised salmon.

Pepper was the first Oriental spice introduced to the west, and was a mainstay of trade with Rome. Of the more than 2,000 described species of pepper, the most prolific and commercially important, *Piper nigam*, is the source of most peppercorns—both black and white.

PRESENTATION

PLACE THE TOMATO-AND-BASIL RELISH IN THE CENTER OF A WARMED DEEP-DISH PLATE. ARRANGE THE SALMON ON TOP. FRESH FLOWERING HERB SPRIGS MAY BE USED TO DECORATE.

GUEST CHEF

John Coughlan, "MasterChefs," Dublin.

Pan-Fried Salmon with Sorrel, Apple, and Scallion Relish

4 4–6 ounce salmon fillets, boneless and skinless

salt and freshly ground black pepper, to taste

juice of 1 whole lemon

1 tablespoon of vegetable oil

4 tablespoons butter, divided

2 Granny Smith apples, diced small

1 bunch scallions, chopped

1 small bunch sorrel, shredded (about 8 leaves)

1 teaspoon chopped parsley

1 lemon, sliced, for garnish

1. Dry salmon on paper towels and season with salt, pepper, and lemon juice.

2. Add 1 tablespoon vegetable oil and 12 tablespoons butter to a large skillet and heat over medium/high heat. Place the salmon fillets (presentation side down) on the hot skillet. Fry until golden brown, turning at least twice.

3. In a separate saucepan, gently cook over medium heat in the remaining butter the diced apples, scallions (spring onions), about 2 minutes. Divide among 4 plates.

4. Place the cooked salmon fillets on top.

SERVES 4

Many people regard sorrel only as a herb, but the leaves can be used for salads, soups, and sauces, as well as in egg and fish dishes. Sorrel's high acidity causes it to discolor when it is cooked in iron pots, or when it is chopped with a non–stainless-steel knife.

PRESENTATION

SPRINKLE SHREDDED SORREL AND CHOPPED PARSLEY OVER THE SALMON. GARNISH WITH SLICED OR QUARTERED LEMON WEDGES.

GUEST CHEF

Colin O'Daly, Chef, Roly's Bistro, Dublin

Pan-Seared Fillet of Salmon with Roasted Peppers and Pineapple Compote

SERVES 4

Asparagus comes in two varieties: white and green. The green is said to have a much stronger flavor, and the white one more tender and delicate. The difference between them is one of cultivation. White asparagus is planted eight to ten inches below the ground, and gathered as soon as the tip breaks the surface. Green asparagus has the benefit of the sun's rays during its growth.

PRESENTATION

MOLD THE RELISH (PINEAPPLE AND PEPPER MIXTURE) IN THE CENTER OF A PLATE. SET SALMON ON TOP AND PLACE POACHED ASPARAGUS SPEARS AROUND THE EDGE OF THE PLATE. DRIZZLE ANY REMAINING JUICE FROM THE RELISH AROUND THE SALMON.

GUEST CHEF

Terry Doran, Chef, Ballymac Restaurant, Co. Antrim

4 8-ounce salmon fillet steaks

1 tablespoon olive oil

1 teaspoon dill

salt and white pepper, to taste

1 each roasted green, yellow, and red pepper, peeled, seeded, and dice fine
To prepare, place the peppers on aluminum foil, lightly brush with oil, and set roast in a 350°F preheated oven 20 minutes. Remove from oven and seal in a plastic bag, allow to cool, peel seed, and dice.)

2 tablespoons white-wine vinegar

¼ cup diced fresh pineapple

1 teaspoon brown sugar

20 green asparagus spears, washed and trimmed

2 tablespoons butter

SALMON

1. In a large skillet, over high heat, sear salmon fillets on both sides in the olive oil.

2. Season with chopped dill, salt, and milled peppercorns. Remove from skillet and keep warm.

3. In a separate saucepan, over medium heat, cook gently the mixed peppers without coloring.

4. Add wine vinegar to the peppers and cook slowly for 6–8 minutes.

5. Add the diced pineapple and finish with brown sugar.

ASPARAGUS

1. With string, tie asparagus into 3 upright bundles.

continued

2. Fill 2-quart saucepan (tall enough to hold the asparagus upright) ¾ full with water, add ½ teaspoon salt, and bring to a boil.

3. Place the asparagus spears with the tips pointed upwards into the water (tips protruding above the water), simmer, 1 minute. Remove from saucepan and shock in ice-cold water.

4. Remove string from asparagus. Heat asparagus gently, about 10 seconds, in a saucepan with warmed butter. Gently lift the asparagus with a slotted spoon onto warmed serving dish.

Gratin of Cod with Tomatoes, Bacon, and Dill

oil, for greasing

1 teaspoon olive oil

3 ounces lean bacon, diced

2 onions, diced fine

2 pounds cod boneless and skinless fillets

4 large tomatoes, skinned, seeded, and chopped (to peel tomatoes, immerse in boiling water for 30 seconds, cool in cold water and remove skin, split in half, and with a teaspoon scoop out the seeds).

2 tablespoons fresh chopped dill

1 cup fresh white breadcrumbs (to prepare fresh breadcrumbs, remove crust from any white bread and pulse in a food processor)

½ cup grated cheddar cheese

1. Preheat oven to 375°F.

2. Lightly oil six individual ovenproof gratin dishes.

3. Heat 1 teaspoon olive oil in a skillet. Add the chopped bacon. Fry until bacon is crisp and fat rendered. Pour off excess fat.

4. Add onion to the skillet and sauté until soft, without coloring.

5. Slice cod fillet into six equal portions.

6. Place a layer of onion mixture on bottom of each dish. Place cod on top.

7. In a medium bowl, combine tomatoes, bacon, dill, breadcrumbs, and cheese. Liberally coat each portion of cod.

8. Place cod in prepared gratin dishes. Bake at 375°F, 20 minutes.

SERVES 6

Au gratin, refers to a mixture of crumbs and grated cheese with enough butter or oil to hold it together. The mixture is spread on food, and baked or broiled until golden brown and crisp.

PRESENTATION

SERVE EACH OVENPROOF INDIVIDUAL DISH ON LARGE PLATE WITH A NAPKIN UNDERLINER.

Grilled Halibut Steak with Parsley Butter

SERVES 4

Halibut is the largest of the flat-fish. It is usually cut into steaks or fillets, then broiled or grilled. Halibut is also popular smoked.

Parsley butter, is also known as maître d' hotel butter, is called as a compound butter, or hard sauce. Parsley has been cultivated for thousands of years in Ireland. In imperial Rome, parsley was fashioned into crowns for banquet guests. This it was hoped would prevent drunkenness at the table.

Of all natural fats, butter is by far the best tasting and most easily digested. While overconsumption of butter is frowned upon by nutritionists, butter in small quantities still remains a perfect enrichment for delicate foods. It was Jonathan Swift, the celebrated Dean of Saint Patrick's Cathedral in Dublin and author of *Gulliver's Travels*, who coined the phrase; "She looks as if butter wouldn't melt in her mouth."

HALIBUT

4 six-ounce boneless halibut steaks, skinned

½ cup white wine

juice of 1 lemon

1 teaspoon freshly ground black pepper

4 lemon wedges

1 tablespoon chopped chives

2 tablespoons olive oil

¼ pound butter, melted

PARSLEY BUTTER

3 tablespoons finely chopped parsley

½ pound butter, softened

1 tablespoon lemon juice

⅛ teaspoon each salt and pepper

HALIBUT

1. Preheat broiler or grill.

2. Place the halibut steaks in a dish large enough to lay them flat. Mix white wine, and lemon juice to make a marination. Cover the steaks with the marination. Cover dish with plastic wrap and marinate in refrigerator, 2 hours.

3. Remove halibut from the marination and pat dry with paper towels. Sprinkle with pepper.

4. Brush lightly with olive oil and butter, place on hot grill. Grill both sides until cooked, about 2 minutes on each side depending on the thickness of the halibut. If using a broiler, place halibut onto a flat grilling tray. Alternatively, mark halibut on the grill to make a lattice pattern on one side

of the fish, remove, place on a sheet pan and finish cooking in a 375°F oven, approximately 3 minutes.

PARSLEY BUTTER

1. Add lemon juice and parsley to butter and blend in a food processor.

2. Season with salt and pepper.

3. Shape butter into 1-inch thick tube; roll in parchment paper, twisting each end. Place in freezer, 1½ hours.

4. Allow to thaw, approximately 1 minute, unwrap, and slice into medallions. Place in ice water while the halibut is being grilled.

PRESENTATION

PLACE HALIBUT STEAKS ON WARMED PLATE. SERVE WITH PARSLEY-BUTTER MEDALLIONS, CHOPPED CHIVES, AND LEMON WEDGES.

Deirdre's Seafood and Saffron Shell

1 large potato, peeled and diced into ¼" cubes

1 pound prime cuts of fish, including salmon, sea trout, mussels, monkfish, and/or shrimp

1 tablespoon butter

1 small onion, finely diced

½ cup white wine

1 teaspoon saffron powder or fresh saffron threads

½ cup fish stock or water

½ cup heavy cream

2 tablespoons grated cheddar cheese

salt and ground pepper

1. Preheat oven to 425°F.

2. Boil potato in unsalted water until soft, about 20 minutes.

3. Cut fish into even-sized pieces approximately 1-inch square.

4. Over medium-high heat, melt butter in a medium saucepan. Add diced fish, onions, wine, saffron, stock, and seasoning.

5. Bring to a boil. Simmer gently, 5 minutes.

6. Remove fish with a slotted spoon and keep warm.

7. Return liquid to boil. Add cream and reduce until it reaches a thick, creamy consistency.

8. Return fish to sauce.

9. Reheat and place into coquille (scallop) shells or ovenproof dishes.

10. Place potatoes on top and sprinkle with cheddar.

11. Glaze quickly under broiler or bake at 425°F in a preheated oven for 5 minutes.

SERVES 4

Saffron is the world's most expensive spice. Some 75,000 stigmas of crocus are required to produce one pound of saffron. It is used primarily for coloring and flavoring rice, cakes and bread, soups, and fish dishes.

PRESENTATION

PLACE SHELL OR OVENPROOF DISH ON A PLATE WITH NAPKIN UNDERLINER. THIS DISH IS IDEALLY ACCOMPANIED BY IRISH BROWN BREAD.

GUEST CHEF

Matt Dowling, CERT, Dublin

Roast Fillet of Hake with Potato and Black-Olive Sauce

SERVES 4

Hake is a member of the cod family—its meat is white, soft, flaky, and tender. It is a very common type of fish in Ireland.

PRESENTATION

PLACE A HEAPING TABLESPOON OF THE POTATO IN THE CENTER OF A WARMED PLATE. SPOON SAUCE AROUND THE POTATO. PLACE FISH ON TOP OF POTATO. SERVE IMMEDIATELY.

GUEST CHEF

John Howard, Le Coq Hardi Restaurant, Ballsbridge, Dublin

HAKE

1 pound new potatoes, peeled

4 tablespoons virgin olive oil

salt and freshly ground black pepper, to taste

2 cloves garlic, crushed

1 teaspoon chopped dill

1 teaspoon chopped chervil

2½ pounds hake fillet, boneless, skin on

SAUCE

¼ cup virgin olive oil

¼ cup black olives, pitted and chopped

salt and freshly mulled black pepper, to taste

juice of 1 lemon

2 teaspoons chopped dill

4 large tomatoes, skinned, seeded, and diced

HAKE AND POTATOES

1. Preheat oven to 400°F.

2. Cook potatoes in boiling salted water until soft, about 20 minutes. Warm olive oil.

3. While still warm, mash the potatoes with a fork. Add olive oil, salt, pepper, garlic, and chopped herbs. Keep warm.

4. Heat olive oil in a skillet until it becomes quite hot. Place the hake in an ovenproof skillet and turn quickly, ensuring that the skin side becomes very crispy. Roast in preheated oven, 2–3 minutes.

SAUCE

1. Warm the olive oil. Add the sliced olives.

2. Add salt, pepper, lemon juice, dill, and diced tomato. Warm gently.

Steamed Fillet of Hake, Kenure House

SERVES 4

Kenure House was a paladin mansion made famous during the filming of *Ten Little Indians*. On the grounds of the now-demolished house was a garden; among the many plants gone wild was horseradish root. Horseradish has a rough, thin, light-brown skin and white flesh that, when sliced or grated, releases an acrid oil. Because the pungent character of horseradish is highly volatile, the root is rarely cooked.

Hake is a very fine fish, grossly underrated in Ireland. Spanish fishermen take great risks in Irish coastal waters to catch hake. It is considered the champagne of fish in Spanish markets.

PRESENTATION

DRY HAKE ON PAPER TOWELS. PLACE ONTO WARM OVEN-PROOF PLATES, AND COAT WITH SAUCE. PLACE UNDER VERY HOT BROILER AND GLAZE TO A GOLDEN BROWN. GARNISH WITH LEMON AND WATERCRESS.

GUEST CHEF

Terry McCoy, Chef/Proprietor, The Red Bank Restaurant, Skerries, Co. Dublin

HAKE
1½ pounds hake, boneless and skinless fillet

¼ cup prepared horseradish sauce

½ cup heavy cream, whipped

SAUCE
4 tablespoons cold butter, cut into 6 equal parts

3 cups fish stock

4 lemon wedges, for garnish

watercress, for garnish

HAKE

1. Remove pin bones from hake. Cut into 4 equal portions.

2. Fold whipped cream into horseradish sauce.

3. Spread the cream-and-horseradish mixture onto the fish and fold the fillets in half.

4. Bring 3 cups fish stock to a boil in a steamer pot.

5. Place the fish on a bamboo steamer, cover, and steam over stock, 5 minutes.

6. Remove fish from the steamer and keep warm. Reserve stock.

SAUCE

1. Reduce reserved fish stock by ⅔.

2. Remove from heat.

3. Add butter to stock, piece by piece, and shake saucepan until butter has been totally absorbed into the stock.

4. Serve immediately.

Fillet of Sea Bass and Shrimp with Wild Mushrooms and Nettle Butter

BASS

4 sea bass fillets, skin on (6–8 ounce)

½ teaspoon sea salt

1 teaspoon freshly ground black pepper

8 tablespoons butter

1 tablespoon olive oil

24 small shrimp, shelled

2 cups shiitake mushrooms, quartered

dill, for garnish

NETTLE BUTTER

12 tablespoons of unsalted butter

¼ cup chopped nettles (if nettles are unavailable, sorrel can be substituted)

¼ teaspoon salt

1 teaspoon of lemon juice

BASS

1. Dry bass fillets on paper towels. Season with salt and pepper.

2. In a large skillet, over medium high heat, melt butter with olive oil. When very hot, sauté bass on both sides until golden brown (bass skin should be cooked until crisp). Remove from skillet and keep warm. Add the shrimp to the skillet and cook, 2 minutes.

3. In a separate skillet, over medium heat in 1 tablespoon of olive oil, sauté the mushrooms slowly. Keep warm.

SERVES 4

Sea bass are caught in small quantities around Ireland. They are usually broiled, or pan seared, with the descaled skin left on. The name bass is given to several kinds of fish with spiny dorsal fins. Sea bass is much prized by chefs in Ireland because of its firm, white flesh. The French refer to this fish as *loup de mer* or *sea wolf*, because of its voracious eating habits. Striped bass, from the same family is also caught around Ireland's coastline. It is stronger in taste and resembles salmon.

PRESENTATION

PLACE MUSHROOMS ON WARMED SERVING PLATE. PLACE FISH ON TOP OF THE MUSHROOMS. ARRANGE THE SHRIMP AROUND THE SEA BASS. PLACE A ROUND OF NETTLE BUTTER ON TOP OF EACH BUNDLE OF FISH. GARNISH WITH DILL.

GUEST CHEF

Colin O' Daly, Chef, Roly's Bistro, Dublin

continued

NETTLE BUTTER

1. Soften butter and blend with chopped nettles.

2. Add salt and lemon juice.

3. Roll finished butter in parchment paper and form into a cylinder.

4. Tighten paper roll at each end and refrigerate until needed.

Turbot Fillets with Savory Herb-and-Tomato Crumble

SERVES 4

Turbot is a large flatfish, caught on the Atlantic coast of Ireland. It is found in limited quantities in American waters. Called the "pheasant of the sea," turbot has white flesh, and is so delicate and delicious that the simplest cooking methods suffice.

PRESENTATION

SPOON TOMATO AND MUSTARD SAUCE ONTO A WARMED PLATE. PLACE THE TURBOT ON TOP (ALLOW THE EXCESS JUICE TO DRAIN FROM THE TURBOT BEFORE PLACING ON TOP OF SAUCE).

4 6-ounce boneless and skinless turbot fillets (sole may be substituted)

2 tablespoons butter

1 teaspoon olive oil

2 tablespoons Dijon mustard

¼ cup dry white wine

2 shallots, diced fine

2 tablespoons chopped mixed herbs (equal amounts parsley, tarragon, and chervil)

1 cup fresh white breadcrumbs

½ cup heavy cream

1 cup plum tomatoes, peeled and seeded

1. Preheat oven to 325°F.

2. Over high heat, in a large heavy-bottomed skillet, sear the turbot fillets in butter and olive oil.

3. Remove fillets from the pan. Gently pat dry paper towels

4. Lightly brush fillets with 1 tablespoon mustard.

5. In a medium saucepan heat the white wine with the shallots. In a medium bowl, combine the breadcrumbs and chopped herbs. Add the white wine mixture. Consistency should be loose.

6. Spread breadcrumb mixture evenly over each fillet.

7. Place the turbot on a lightly oiled sheet pan. Bake in preheated oven, 6–7 minutes, or until fish is cooked and topping is golden brown.

8. Whisk mustard and cream together in a small saucepan. Reduce until the sauce thickens. Add tomatoes and gently heat.

Baked Fillets of Flounder with Cabbage, Smoked Bacon, Roasted Potatoes, and a Grain Mustard Sauce

FLOUNDER

3 strips smoked bacon, diced fine

½ head savoy cabbage, shredded fine

4 boneless, skinless fillets (about 12 ounces total)

salt and freshly ground black pepper

vegetable-oil spray

SAUCE

⅔ cup strong fish stock

¼ cup heavy cream

1 teaspoon grain mustard

1 tablespoon lemon juice

ROASTED POTATOES

2 large potatoes, peeled

1 teaspoon olive oil

½ teaspoon chopped parsley

¼ teasoon freshly ground black pepper

salt, to taste

FLOUNDER

1. Preheat oven to 425°F.

2. In a skillet, fry bacon until crispy. Drain, reserving 1 tablespoon bacon fat.

3. In a heavy-bottomed saucepan over medium heat, bring ⅔ cup water to a boil. Add finely shredded cabbage. Cover with tightly fitting lid. Cook, about 30 seconds.

4. Combine the cabbage and the bacon fat (cabbage should be cooked yet crisp).

continued

SERVES 2

Cabbage is one of the most popular vegetables in Ireland, and is available all year 'round. Savoy cabbage has smooth, tightly packed leaves.

PRESENTATION

PLACE CABBAGE ON WARMED PLATES CAREFULLY LIFT THE FLOUNDER FROM THE BAKING PAN AND PLACE ON TOP OF THE CABBAGE. GARNISH WITH THE ROASTED POTATOES. POUR THE SAUCE AROUND THE FISH.

GUEST CHEF
Derek Dunne, Dublin

5. Dry fillets with a paper towel. Season with salt, pepper, and lemon juice.

6. Lightly oil or spray a small baking pan. Carefully fold each end of the flounder fillets, place on the pan, and bake in preheated oven, about 3 minutes.

SAUCE

1. Reduce fish stock by half and add cream. Reduce again by ⅓. Add grain mustard.

ROASTED POTATOES

1. Preheat oven to 375°F.

2. Using a sharp knife, shape each potato into long, narrow, barrel-shaped pieces about 2 inches long and ½ inch in diameter.

3. Place potatoes in cold salted water, bring to a boil, cook for 15 minutes. Cool.

4. Dry potatoes with paper towels. Heat olive oil in a heavy-bottomed ovenproof skillet. Add potatoes.

5. Place into a preheated oven. Roast, 5 minutes.

6. Remove potatoes from the skillet, and sprinkle with chopped parsley.

Poached Sole Fillets in a Clonmel Cider Sauce

Cider is a mildly fermented apple juice, it is produced in large quantities in Clonmel Co. Tipperary.

PRESENTATION

GENTLY PAT FILLETS DRY WITH PAPER TOWELS. PLACE THEM ON SERVING PLATES. POUR THE REDUCED SAUCE OVER THE FISH FILLETS AND GLAZE UNDER BROILER UNTIL GOLDEN BROWN. GARNISH WITH THE APPLE SLICES. SERVE WITH KING SITRIC BROWN BREAD (RECIPE, PAGE 235).

GUEST CHEF

Aiden Mc Manus, Chef / Proprietor, King Sitric Restaurant, Howth, Co. Dublin

4 4-ounce fillets lemon or grey Atlantic sole, boneless and skinless

2 tablespoons fish stock

¼ cup cider

1 apple, cut into 6 wedges

4 tablespoons salted butter, cut into 6 pieces

2 tablespoons unsalted butter, plus additional for greasing

¼ cup heavy cream

1. Fold the fillets in half, and place in a lightly buttered shallow poaching dish.

2. In a separate saucepan bring fish stock and cider to a boil.

3. Pour the liquid over fillets, cover with a parchment paper, lid and gently poach, 2 minutes.

4. Meanwhile, in a skillet over low heat, gently sauté apple wedges in the salted butter until soft.

5. Remove fillets from the dish.

6. Reduce fish cooking liquid to two tablespoons. Remove from heat and whisk in unsalted butter one piece at a time. Combine with heavy cream.

Poached Fillets of Sole and Oysters with Spinach and Gratine Riesling Sauce

4 sole fillets (black sole is ideal, but grey Atlantic sole may be used)

4 oysters, shucked

1 cup fish stock, divided

2 tablespoons butter, divided

½ cup Riesling wine

6 ounces spinach leaves, stemmed and shredded

¼ teaspoon salt

¼ teaspoon freshly milled black pepper

¼ teaspoon ground nutmeg

1 ounce walnuts

1 egg yolk

¼ cup heavy cream whipped

flowering herbs for garnish

2 cooked crayfish, for garnish

1. Fold the fillets. Poach sole and oysters in ½ cup fish stock with 2 tablespoons butter, 1–2 minutes.

2. Remove from stock and set aside.

3. Combine wine and remaining fish stock with the poaching stock. Reduce to 5 tablespoons, or until syrupy.

4. In a separate saucepan, cook spinach with 2 tablespoons of butter, salt, pepper, and nutmeg. Cover, and cook over medium heat, 10 seconds.

5. Add walnuts. Cook, 20 seconds.

6. In a bowl, fold the egg yolk into the whipped cream. Whisk the mixture into the fish stock syrup. Remove from the heat.

SERVES 2

Black sole or Dover sole (as it is known outside of Ireland) is highly esteemed by Irish chefs for its firm white flesh and its delicate flavor. It derives its name from the Latin word for sandal, *Solea*, supposedly from its resemblance to the sole of a shoe.

PRESENTATION

PLACE THE WELL-DRAINED SPINACH ON THE CENTER OF A WARMED PLATE. ARRANGE THE SOLE AND OYSTERS OVER THE SPINACH. SPOON THE SAUCE OVER THE FISH AND GLAZE UNDER A VERY HOT BROILER. GARNISH WITH FLOWERING HERBS AND COOKED CRAYFISH.

GUEST CHEF

Bruno Schmidt,
Chef, Park Hotel, Kenmare,
Co. Kerry

Roast Pike with Lovage, Bacon, and Chicken Sauce

SERVES 4

Lovage is an aromatic herb used extensively in Irish cooking since ancient times. A celerylike plant, it is a member of the parsley family. Its leaves are frequently added to salads, and its seeds are used in candy making.

Pike is a most maligned fish in Ireland, and so undervalued that it rarely appears on menus. Preparation is similar to other round fish. The flesh, typical of freshwater fish, abounds in small bones which need to be extracted with tweezers. Care should be exercised when handling whole fresh pike. They have sharp teeth. Due to the heaviness of the head and many bones, the proportion of usable flesh is no more than one-quarter of the whole fish.

PRESENTATION

POUR THE SAUCE ONTO THE CENTER OF A WARMED PLATE, PLACE THE PIKE ON TOP.

GUEST CHEF

Gerry Galvin, Drimcong House, Moycullen, Co. Galway

4 strips bacon, chopped fine

4 x 6 ounces pike, boned and skinned

salt and freshly milled black pepper, to taste

2 tablespoons all-purpose flour

¼ cup clarified butter

1 tablespoon lemon juice

1 clove garlic, crushed

1¼ cups chicken stock

1 tablespoon finely chopped lovage

1 teaspoon balsamic vinegar

1. Cook bacon in a dry skillet over high heat until crisp. Drain on a paper towel.

2. Season pike with salt and pepper and dust lightly with flour.

3. Sear pike in clarified butter in a very hot separate ovenproof skillet.

4. Drench with lemon juice, sprinkle with chopped bacon and garlic and roast in a 400°F oven for 8 minutes.

5. Bring the chicken stock to a boil in a medium saucepan. Add lovage and balsamic vinegar. Reduce by ⅓.

Bay Scallops in White Wine and Butter Sauce

16 large scallops, shelled

1 teaspoon lemon juice

²⁄₃ cup white wine

¼ cup finely diced onion

8 tablespoons butter, cut into 4 pieces

1 tablespoon finely chopped, chives for garnish

salt and freshly ground black pepper

1. Halve scallops and lay on a absorbent paper towels to dry.

2. Heat lemon juice and white wine in a pan. Add scallops and poach (cook over very low heat without boiling), 1 minute.

3. Remove scallops and keep warm.

4. Add onion to the scallop stock. Reduce stock by half.

5. Allow to cool slightly and add the butter one piece at a time, shaking the pan while adding.

6. Season the sauce, strain onto warmed plates.

SERVES 4

Scallops are commonly found in the coastal waters of Ireland. Queen scallops, with their delicate roe are considered the best. Although scallops can be broiled or deep fried in breadcrumbs, the preferred cooking method in Ireland is to gently poach them and serve with a light sauce.

PRESENTATION

ARRANGE THE SCALLOPS ON WARM PLATES. COAT WITH THE REMAINING SAUCE AND GARNISH WITH CHOPPED CHIVES.

Portrush Scallops with Baby Leeks in a Citrus Vinaigrette

SCALLOPS

18 large scallops, in shell

1 carrot, julienned, cut into 2-inch strips

2 baby leeks, julienned, white portions cut into 2-inch strips

½ teaspoon olive oil

2 tablespoons chopped scallions

1 tablespoon butter

VINAIGRETTE

2 medium oranges, peeled, seeded, and segmented

1 lemon, peeled, seeded, and segmented

½ cup extra-virgin olive oil

SCALLOPS

1. Open and separate scallops.

2. Slice scallops horizontally, with the roe attached; and pan fry in a heavy-bottomed skillet heated to high heat with olive oil, 10 seconds.

3. Remove scallops from the pan, keep warm. Discard oil add the scallions, and cook, 30 seconds.

4. Return scallops to the pan and toss with scallions, 15 seconds.

5. Blanch carrots and leeks in boiling salted water for 30 seconds. Strain and shock in ice-cold water.

VINAIGRETTE

1. Place orange and lemon segments in a food processor fitted with a steel blade. Pulse pureed.

2. Gradually add the oil while the machine is running.

3. Pass through a fine mesh strainer and set aside.

SERVES 4

In Ireland, scallops tend to be larger than those in the United States; diners prefer the coral, which is the roe, attached.

While the straight-sided sauté pan is the more familiar name for a skillet in Ireland, the flare-sided skillet, also called a frying pan, has American roots. They evolved as slightly different approaches to the same process—rapid stove-top cooking in fat. Cast iron is the traditional material used for skillets; it is heavy, and is an excellent conductor of heat. With continuous use it develops a seasoning, which enables it to function like a non-stick finish.

PRESENTATION

WARM THE VINAIGRETTE AND POUR ONTO WARMED DEEP-DISH PLATES. ARRANGE THE SCALLOPS, WITH ROE ON TOP OF THE VINAIGRETTE. GENTLY TOSS THE WELL DRAINED VEGETABLES IN 1 TABLESPOON BUTTER AND DIVIDE EQUALLY AMONG FOUR PLATES.

GUEST CHEF

Sandra Griffin, Chef / Owner, Magherabouy House Hotel, Co. Antrim

Baked Stuffed Lobster, *Uisce Beahta*

Live lobsters should be cooked the day they are purchased. To keep lobster tails from curling during the cooking process, insert a metal or bamboo skewer completely through the middle. Remove the skewer when the lobster is cooked.

Uisce Beatha is Gaelic for Irish whiskey; it means "the water of life."

PRESENTATION

PLACE LOBSTER SHELLS ON A WARMED PLATTER. SERVE WITH LEMON.

4 1½-pound lobsters, cooked, and split lengthwise

8 tablespoons clarified butter

1 rib of celery, diced fine

3 cloves of garlic, crushed

¼ cup onion, diced fine

12 large shrimp, deveined and cut into large pieces

2 tablespoons Irish whiskey

1¼ cups fresh white breadcrumbs, divided

1 tablespoon paprika

juice of ½ lemon

2 teaspoons parsley, chopped fine

2 teaspoons tarragon, chopped fine

salt and pepper

1 lemon, quartered, for serving

1. Preheat oven to 350°F.

2. Bring 3 quarts water to a boil.

3. Drop the live lobsters into the boiling water. Simmer, 3 minutes.

4. Remove lobsters and place under cold running water to prevent further cooking.

5. Remove claws from cooked lobster. Crack the claws and remove meat.

6. Butterfly each lobster (cut lengthwise through the underside without cutting all the way through).

7. Remove tail meat, and discard sac. Slice the tails into medallions.

8. Heat the butter in a large skillet and, over medium heat, sauté celery, garlic and onion, 1 minute. Add shrimp and cook, 2 minutes. Pour Irish

whiskey on to a dry portion of the skillet and ignite (pour the whiskey, always pour away from the open flame, and then return to the flame to ignite. Never hold the bottle close to an open flame during this process). Remove from heat, and place the mixture in a bowl.

9. Add sliced cooked lobster tail, 1 cup breadcrumbs, paprika, lemon juice, herbs, salt, and pepper to the shrimp and vegetable mixture. Mix gently to a paste, continue mixing until a moist consistency is achieved.

10. Place whole lobster claws onto the butterflied lobster shells.

11. Cover lobster claws with the shrimp mixture. Spread evenly over each lobster. Sprinkle with reserved breadcrumbs.

12. Place on a sheet pan and bake in preheated oven, 5–8 minutes, or until golden brown.

Ballyferriter Lobster Gaby

1 1½-pound lobster

¼ cup dry white wine

freshly ground black pepper, to taste

1 shallot, diced fine

4 tablespoons butter, divided

1 teaspoon tomato paste

⅛ teaspoon paprika

¼ cup fish stock

1 tablespoon brandy

1 teaspoon arrowroot

¼ cup cream

1 teaspoon lemon juice

1. Cook live lobster in boiling water, 10 minutes. Remove and cool under cold water to prevent any further cooking.

2. Split lobster in half lengthwise. Remove all meat from shells and claws and cut into 1-inch squares. Discard remaining lobster. Wash the 2 half shells. Allow shell to drain and dry. Reserve for final presentation.

3. In a small sauce pan, over medium heat, place white wine, lemon juice, pepper, shallots, 2 tablespoons butter, tomato paste, paprika, and all but 1 teaspoon fish stock. Reduce by ⅓.

4. Reduce the heat, and add the diced lobster meat, brandy, and cream.

5. Simmer, 2 minutes. Dissolve arrowroot in remaining teaspoon fish stock. Add to sauce. Stir until sauce thickens.

6. Stir in remaining butter.

This lobster dish was first prepared by Chef Maes' mother, and is named in her honor. Chef Maes wraps lemon halves in cheesecloth for serving with this dish. The cheesecloth prevents lemon pits from dropping on the lobster.

Arrowroot is a fine white powder derived from a tuber found mainly on St. Vincent, an island in the West Indies.

PRESENTATION

PLACE LOBSTER IN THE DRY AND WARMED RESERVED SHELLS. GLAZE UNDER A VERY HOT BROILER UNTIL THE TOP TURNS GOLDEN. SERVE WITH LEMON.

GUEST CHEF

Geert Maes, Gaby's Restaurant, Killarney, Co. Kerry

Mullaghmore Lobster Soufflé, *Classiebawn*

SERVES 8

A classic soufflé dish is best, because the straight sides force the expanding soufflé upward. Always position the oven rack in the middle of the oven for baked soufflés.

This lobster dish was first prepared by the author at Classeibawn Castle in Co. Sligo. It was served to the Mountbatten family.

PRESENTATION

SERVE IMMEDIATELY.

3/4 cup unsalted butter, plus additional for greasing

3/4 cup all-purpose flour

2 cups boiling milk

8 eggs, separated

1/4 teaspoon salt

1/8 teaspoon nutmeg

1 2/3 pounds cooked lobster flesh

1. Preheat oven to 325°F.

2. Lightly butter 2 large soufflé molds (7-inch diameter) or 8 individual ramekins.

3. Over medium heat, melt butter in a medium saucepan. Stir in flour.

4. When flour and butter become a smooth paste, gradually whisk in boiling milk. Cool slightly.

5. One at a time, beat the egg yolks, into the milk mixture. Season with salt and nutmeg.

6. Cut lobster into 1/2-inch cubes. Add to egg mixture.

7. In a clean copper or stainless steel bowl, whisk the egg whites until stiff. Fold gently, in thirds, into the egg mixture.

8. Pour the soufflé mixture into soufflé molds. Place into a water bath (water for the bath should be boiling to ensure immediate heat transfer to the soufflés). Bake in preheated oven, 85 minutes for the larger soufflé molds; 45 minutes for individual ramekins.

Salads, Dressings & Cold Sauces

***

ALTHOUGH RELATIVELY NEW TO THE IRISH MENU, SALADS HAVE NOW BECOME A VERY

popular feature in many Irish restaurants and homes. In the past, salads featured on

Irish menus were confined mostly to first courses, or as accompaniments to cold

poached salmon or cold cooked meats. Indeed, the only two major salad items general-

ly featured on menus were the ubiquitous tossed green salad or mixed salad.

Compound or complex mixed salads were confined mainly to vegetable and potato

salads. Cucumber, lettuce, tomato, and hard-boiled eggs usually accompanied these

dishes. Featured salad courses within menus were the exception.

There has, however, been a complete turnaround in this area. Now, a vast array of salads and adventurous combinations are offered, with all types of dressings and cold sauces. Warm salads are particularly popular. Varieties of greens, such as lollo rosso, mache, and arugula were all unknown in Ireland until recent times.

Herba salata, the Latin equivalent of salted greens, is the origin of the word *salad*. This suggests that the earliest salads were mixtures of salted, pickled greens. This culinary variation had evolved, by the time of Imperial Rome, into mixtures of greens served with a fresh herb garnish and an oil-and-vinegar dressing. It was in the early twentieth century that the famous French chef, Escoffier created a salad of celery, partridge breast, and truffles, with a dressing of virgin olive oil from Provence, and mustard from Dijon. From this creation, we have progressed to the variety of salads served today.

The possibility of salad combinations is limited only by the imagination of the chef. They may include leaf greens, raw and cooked vegetables, fruit, meat, game, fish, poultry, legumes, rice, and pasta. These are often served *Tiede* (warm).

Vinaigrettes

BASIC VINAIGRETTE

1 part wine vinegar

Salt and freshly ground black pepper, to taste

3 parts olive oil

1. Place vinegar bowl.

2. Add salt and pepper.

3. Whisk in oil gradually, until it forms an emulsion, or simply blend in a food processor, 20 seconds.

4. Shake before use.

LEMON DRESSING

Use lemon juice instead of vinegar.

MUSTARD DRESSING

Add ½ teaspoon mustard per cup dressing.

FINE HERBES DRESSING

Add 1 tablespoon finely chopped herbs, such as parsley, chives, tarragon, or chervil per cup dressing.

MARSEILLAISE DRESSING

Add ½ clove crushed garlic per cup dressing.

PAPRIKA DRESSING

Add ¼ cup finely chopped onions, and paprika to taste.

ANCHOVY DRESSING

Add 1 teaspoon anchovy paste per cup dressing.

SPICY DRESSING

Add English mustard, chili sauce, and chutney to taste.

ROQUEFORT DRESSING

Add ¼ cup Roquefort cheese, rubbed through a sieve, to 1 cup dressing.

Proportions of oil and vinegar may be adjusted according to personal taste. Keep in mind that the strength of vinegars varies from one brand to another.

Balsamic vinegar is made from the juice of white grapes. It is aged in wood barrels for several years. The vinegar is dark brown, with a mellow, sweet-and-sour character. The finest balsamic vinegar is carefully aged for decades, and is extremely expensive.

Balsamic Vinaigrette

½ cup plus 2 tablespoons olive oil

⅓ cup balsamic vinegar

1 tablespoon diced shallot

1 teaspoon chopped marjoram

Combine all ingredients in a food processor. Process 20 seconds.

Sherry Vinaigrette

½ cup sherry vinegar

⅓ cup light olive oil

⅓ cup walnut oil

1 teaspoon diced shallot

Combine all ingredients in a food processor. Process 20 seconds.

Orange Vinaigrette

½ cup olive oil

¼ cup white-wine vinegar

3 tablespoons fresh orange juice

2 teaspoons grated orange zest

Combine all ingredients in a food processor. Process 20 seconds.

Limantour Vinaigrette

⅔ cup olive oil

2 tablespoons Dijon mustard

⅓ cup white wine vinegar

1 teaspoon fresh lemon juice

¼ teaspoon chopped fresh thyme

freshly ground black pepper

Combine all ingredients in a food processor. Process 20 seconds.

Hazelnut Vinaigrette

⅓ *cup plus 2 tablespoons white wine vinegar*

½ *cup hazelnut oil*

⅛ *teaspoon salt*

freshly ground black pepper

Combine all ingredients in a food processor. Process 20 seconds.

Tarragon Citrus Dressing

¼ *cup orange juice*

¼ *cup lemon juice*

¼ *cup lime juice*

¼ *cup rice-wine vinegar or champagne vinegar*

½ *cup pure virgin olive oil*

1 *teaspoon chopped garlic*

1 *teaspoon finely diced shallots*

salt and freshly ground black pepper, to taste

½ *teaspoon chopped fresh tarragon*

Combine all ingredients and mix vigorously.

½ cup low-fat yogurt may also be added to this dressing.

Homemade Mayonnaise

MAKES 3 CUPS

Mayonnaise will keep, if refrigerated, at least 5 days. Allow it to return to room temperature, then stir to combine.

Flavor mayonnaise with chopped tarragon, tarragon vinegar, or chopped chives. Try adding slightly whipped fresh cream.

2 egg yolks

1 whole egg

1 tablespoon Dijon mustard

⅛ teaspoon salt

freshly ground black pepper, to taste

¼ cup lemon juice

2 cups olive oil

1. Combine egg yolks, whole egg, mustard, salt, and pepper, and half the lemon juice in the bowl of a food processor. Process 1 minute.

2. With the motor running, pour in the olive oil in a slow, steady stream. When all the oil is in, shut motor off, and scrape down sides of bowl with a spatula.

3. Taste mayonnaise. Correct seasoning, if necessary. Scrape mayonnaise into a storage container, cover, and refrigerate until ready to use.

Aioli

MAKES 4 SERVINGS

Mustards are prepared from a combination of ground white, black, or brown mustard seeds. One of the most famous of mustards is Dijon mustard, named after the region from which it comes in France. It contains the husks of black seeds, salt spices and white wine.

4–6 garlic cloves, crushed, to taste

1 egg

1 teaspoon fresh lemon juice

1 teaspoon Dijon mustard

½ teaspoon freshly ground white pepper

¾ cup oil (half peanut, half olive oil)

1. Place garlic in food processor.

2. Add egg, lemon juice, mustard, and seasoning.

3. With the machine running, slowly add oils, until mixture reaches consistency of mayonnaise.

Cashel Blue Cheese Dressing

2 cups mayonnaise

1 cup sour cream

2 tablespoons grated Parmesan cheese

2 cloves garlic, crushed

1 teaspoon Worcestershire sauce

½ cup buttermilk

¼ teaspoon salt

2 tablespoons finely diced onion

3 ounces Cashel blue cheese, crumbled (other blue cheese may be substituted)

1. In a medium bowl, combine all ingredients, except blue cheese.

2. Whisk ingredients until smooth (about 3 minutes). Fold in blue cheese.

SERVES 8

Blue cheese is a piquant, full-flavored cheese, named for the blue mold that produces its flavor. Cashel Blue is produced in Ireland; it is rich and crumbly.

For a lighter dressing, use light mayonnaise and/or light sour cream. This dressing will keep up to three weeks when refrigerated.

Honey Mustard Dressing

1 cup mayonnaise

1 tablespoon honey

1 tablespoon prepared mustard

2 teaspoons lemon juice

1 tablespoon sugar

salt and white pepper

Tabasco sauce, if desired

1. Combine all ingredients in a small stainless steel mixing bowl. Whisk until well blended (about 5 minutes).

2. Refrigerate until ready to use.

MAKES 1 CUP

Depending upon the flower from which it is derived, honey can be quite strong and dark, like buckwheat honey, or pale and delicate, like clover honey.

Morrin's Summer Salad

SALAD

2 tablespoons chopped hazelnuts

¼ cup sliced celery

1 red apple

2 scallions

1 onion, diced

1 chicken breast, grilled, cooled, and sliced

salt and freshly ground black pepper, to taste

¼ cup sliced strawberries

¼ cup sliced peaches

1 cup mixed salad greens

HAZELNUT VINAIGRETTE

¼ cup white-wine vinegar

½ cup hazelnut oil

⅛ teaspoon salt

freshly milled black pepper

DRESSING

Whisk oil into vinegar. Season to taste.

SALAD

Toss all the salad ingredients with the dressing in a large bowl.

SERVES 4

This recipe was developed at the Imperial Hotel in Cork by Executive Chef John Morrin. It was first served at a banquet for the late Speaker of the House, Tip O' Neill.

PRESENTATION

SERVE THIS SALAD WITH THE MIXED GREENS.

GUEST CHEF

John Morrin, Chef, Imperial Hotel, Cork

Warm Smoked Chicken Salad with Creamed Lentils and Roasted Garlic

ROASTED GARLIC

1 head of garlic

½ cup garlic oil or light olive oil

LENTILS

1 cup green lentils, soaked 2 hours in cold water

2 tablespoons each diced carrot, leek, and onion

1 teaspoon chopped parsley

½ teaspoon chopped fresh tarragon

½ cup heavy cream

CHICKEN

oak wood shavings, for smoking

2 6-ounce boneless chicken breasts (or prepared smoked and cooked chicken breasts)

1 tablespoon melted butter

Salt and freshly ground milled black pepper, to taste

VINAIGRETTE

6 tablespoons olive oil

2 tablespoons tarragon vinegar

salt and freshly milled pepper, to taste

2 cups mixed salad greens

2 tablespoon black olives

ROASTED GARLIC

1. Preheat oven to 350°F.

2. Using a sharp knife, cut about ½ inch from the top of the garlic bulb, partially exposing the cloves.

3. Arrange in a shallow baking dish. Drizzle with ½ teaspoon oil.

continued

SERVES 4

Lentils have been cultivated since the Bronze age. These pulses are 25 percent protein, more than any other legume, and are rich in vitamin B, iron, and phosphorus.

As it roasts in the oven, garlic becomes sweet and develops a buttery texture.

PRESENTATION

COAT THE BASE OF THE PLATES WITH THE LENTILS. PLACE SALAD GREENS AND OLIVES IN THE CENTER OF THE PLATE AND ARRANGE CHICKEN BREAST ON TOP. SERVE WHILE THE CHICKEN IS WARM.

GUEST CHEF

**John Coughlan,
MasterChefs, Corporate & Event
Catering, Dublin**

4. Roast garlic, 45–60 minutes, until soft, brushing often with oil.

5. Let cool. Separate cloves and peel.

LENTILS

1. Bring 6 cups salted water to a boil in a 2 quart saucepan. Add lentils.

2. Reduce heat and simmer, 5 minutes. Skim, add diced vegetables, tarragon, and parsley. Cook, 8 minutes.

3. Drain lentils. Let stand, so that the excess liquid may drain off. Mix the lentils with garlic cloves. Add cream.

CHICKEN

1. Place oak shavings in aluminum-foil container in a heavy-bottomed saucepan. Place over stove or grill until shavings begin to smoke.

2. Brush chicken breasts with melted butter and sprinkle with milled peppercorns arrange chicken breasts on rack above wood shavings. Cover the container. Smoke, 8–10 minutes.

3. Remove chicken from smoking rack. Allow to cool slightly. Slice each cooked chicken breast into 3 slices.

VINAIGRETTE

1. Mix vinegar in a bowl or food processor with salt and pepper.

2. Beat in the oil gradually until it forms an emulsion, or blend in food processor for 30 seconds.

3. Toss the mixed salad greens and olives in vinaigrette.

Lobster and Vegetable Salad

Old recipes indicated that lobster be cooked for 15 minutes to the pound. The modern approach is to cook lobster for 2–5 minutes with a carry over cooking time in the stock for 15 minutes.

PRESENTATION

SERVE CHILLED. PLACE LOB-STER SALAD IN LETTUCE BOWL AND GARNISH WITH JULIENNE VEGETABLES, LEMON AND AIOLI DRESSING.

2 pounds cooked lobster meat

4 green peppercorns

2 teaspoons Dijon mustard

pinch fresh, chopped thyme

pinch fresh, chopped basil

pinch fresh, chopped chives

salt and pepper, to taste

1 head iceberg lettuce

½ cup julienned yellow squash

½ cup julienned zucchini

¼ cup julienned red bell pepper

¼ cup julienned yellow bell pepper

1 lemon

aioli dressing (recipe page 116)

1. Cut lobster meat into ¾ inch cubes. Mix with peppercorns, mustard, herbs, and salt and pepper. Mix gently and refrigerate, 6–8 hours.

2. Prepare lettuce bowl by cutting head of lettuce in half. Gently pull out the center of the head. Remove all but 3 to 4 layers of lettuce leaves, creating a bowl.

Warm Salad of Emyvale Duck with Orange and Balsamic Dressing

DUCK

2 duck breasts, cut in half and trimmed of excess fat

salt and freshly milled black pepper, to taste

1/4 cup vegetable oil

DRESSING

1/4 cup dry sherry

1 tablespoons finely diced shallots

1 small carrot, diced fine

1 clove garlic, crushed

1/2 cup chicken stock (recipe, page 274)

2 tablespoons freshly squeezed orange juice

2 tablespoons balsamic vinegar

2 whole cloves

1 teaspoon chopped fresh thyme

1/4 cup extra-virgin olive oil

1/4 teaspoon of ground nutmeg

SALAD

2 cups arugula, rinsed, coarse stems removed

1 Belgian endive, cut into thin strips

1 small head radicchio, cut into thin strips

SERVES 4

Emyvale, in Co. Monaghan, is the home of Silverhill duck farms. Many consider the ducks raised there some of the finest in Europe.

PRESENTATION

CUT DUCK INTO 1/2-INCH-LONG SLIVERS. ARRANGE ARUGULA, ENDIVE, AND RADICCHIO ON SERVING PLATES. TOP WITH DUCK. POUR DRESSING OVER, AND SERVE WARM.

1. Rub duck breasts with salt and pepper. Heat vegetable oil in large skillet over moderately high heat.

2. Add duck, skin side down, reduce heat, and cook until skin is crisp and golden brown. Turn and cook, about 5 minutes. Remove and set aside.

3. Drain off all excess fat from skillet. Deglaze skillet with sherry, scraping up browned particles from bottom of pan. Add shallots, garlic, and carrot. Sauté, 2 minutes.

4. Add chicken stock, orange juice and vinegar. Bring to a boil. Add cloves, thyme, and ground nutmeg. Reduce heat and simmer until liquid is reduced to about 1 cup.

5. Strain the sauce into a bowl. Discard vegetables and seasonings. Pour the liquid into a food processor, add olive oil in a steady stream, and blend for 30 seconds.

Warm Rabbit Salad with Thyme Vinaigrette

SALAD

4 ounce prepared, trimmed rabbit loin

salt and freshly milled black pepper, to taste

3 tablespoons clarified butter

8 cherry tomatoes

1/4 cup toasted pine nuts

2 slices lean bacon, diced and cooked

2 slices bread

1 clove garlic, crushed

4 leaves mâche lettuce

4 leaves radicchio

4–5 iceberg lettuce leaves

VINAIGRETTE

3–6 tablespoons olive oil, to taste

1 teaspoon mustard

1 tablespoon malt vinegar

salt and pepper, to taste

1/8 teaspoon sugar

1 sprig thyme, chopped

SALAD

1. Cut loin of rabbit into thin slices, and season with salt and pepper. Sauté in clarified butter in a heavy-bottomed skillet over high heat.

2. Sauté the cherry tomatoes, pine nuts, and bacon in the pan with the cooked rabbit, 10 seconds. Just prior to serving, remove from pan and place in bowl.

continued

SERVES 1

Rabbit is the most common Irish mammal. It eats all sorts of young vegetation, including crops. Rabbit, however is not native to Ireland—it was introduced in medieval times by the Normans.

Thyme is a popular herb in Ireland. It is a pungent, and should be used sparingly in warm salads

PRESENTATION

COMBINE WARM RABBIT, CHERRY TOMATOES, PINE NUTS, AND BACON PIECES, WITH THE MÂCHE AND RADICCHIO LETTUCE. ADD THE VINAIGRETTE, AND TOSS. SERVE THE WARM RABBIT SALAD IN CUPPED ICEBERG LETTUCE LEAVES.

GUEST CHEF

Richard J. Casburn, Chef, Donnelly's of Barna, Co. Galway

3. Cut bread into even cubes. Fry bread in hot garlic. Combine 2 cloves of crushed garlic with clarified butter. When cooked to a golden brown, place on kitchen paper towels to dry. Season with salt and pepper.

VINAIGRETTE

1. Combine all ingredients in a food processor. Process, 30 seconds.

Corned Beef and Cabbage Salad

CORNED BEEF AND CABBAGE

1 pound small new potatoes

2 cups finely shredded savoy cabbage

1 tablespoon finely diced onion

⅓ cup grated carrot

2 tablespoons mayonnaise

12 thin slices of cooked corned beef

DRESSING

1 cup olive oil

3 tablespoons vinegar

1 tablespoon mustard powder

1 bunch watercress, for garnish

1 teaspoon chopped chives, for garnish

1 head radicchio

CORNED BEEF AND CABBAGE

1. Cook new potatoes, skin on, in boiling salted water, about 25 minutes, or until tender.

2. Strain and allow to cool. When cold, peel and slice into coin shapes. Place in a bowl.

3. Mix the cabbage with the potatoes. Add onion, carrot, and mayonnaise.

DRESSING

1. Combine all ingredients together in a food processor and blend for 20 seconds.

SERVES 4

Traditionally two cuts of beef are used for pickling in Ireland: the brisket and the silversides tail end of beef.

Corned beef and cabbage is probably the one dish that is most clearly thought of as typically Irish in the United States.

PRESENTATION

ARRANGE RADICCHIO LEAVES ON CHILLED PLATES. SPOON THE CABBAGE AND POTATO SALAD ONTO THE LEAVES. ARRANGE THE CORNED BEEF SLICES IN ALTERNATE LAYERS ON TOP OF THE CABBAGE AND POTATOES. DECORATE EACH WITH ¼ BUNCH OF WATERCRESS. DRIZZLE WITH DRESSING.

Noel's Mushroom Salad

SERVES 5

Mushrooms have been an Irish favorite for many centuries, and still hold a popular place in Irish kitchens. There are many wild varieties, but this recipe calls for the cultivated variety.

PRESENTATION

SERVE THE MUSHROOM SALAD ON CHILLED PLATES WITH MIXED SALAD GREENS. SPRINKLE WITH CHOPPED SCALLIONS.

MUSHROOMS

12 ounces cultivated mushrooms

2 tablespoons lemon juice

DRESSING

1 tablespoon mild mustard

4 tablespoons extra-virgin oil

2 tablespoons lemon juice

1 teaspoon chopped parsley

2 cloves garlic, crushed

SALAD

2 cups mixed salad greens

2 tablespoons roughly chopped scallions

1. Wash mushrooms in cold water with lemon juice added. Drain and dry. Slice mushrooms thin and place in bowl.

2. Mix all other ingredients for dressing in a bowl, or blend in a food processor, 20 seconds.

3. Pour the dressing over the mushrooms and mix.

Traditional Cold Irish Potato Salad

1–6 peeled, cooked potatoes (about 6 ounces, total), chilled

1 tablespoon finely diced chives

½ cup mayonnaise

¼ teaspoon salt

1 tablespoon finely diced onion

¼ teaspoon freshly milled black pepper

1 teaspoon chopped parsley

1 cup mixed salad greens

1. Cut potatoes into ½ inch dice.

2. Mix potatoes with chives, mayonnaise, onions, salt, and pepper.

3. Correct the seasoning with salt and pepper. Sprinkle with chopped parsley. Refrigerate before serving.

SERVES 2

Some of the most popular varieties of potatoes used in Ireland include Kerr's Pinks, King Edwards, Golden Wonders, and Records. Legend has it that Sir Walter Raleigh introduced the potato to Ireland at his estate in Youghal, Co. Cork, in 1623. What he probably planted was the sweet potato—the Virginian potato did not arrive in Ireland until much later.

PRESENTATION

PLACE THE POTATO SALAD ON A CHILLED PLATE SURROUNDED BY MIXED SALAD GREENS.

Beef, Lamb & Pork Dishes

DURING THE MIDDLE AGES, THE FARE OF THE COMMON MAN WAS SALT PORK AND MUTTON;

beef was the privilege of the wealthy. By the eighteenth century, England had a reputation as a nation of beef eaters. Beef has only been popular in Ireland for about a century. Prior to the nineteenth century the Irish had eaten beef only on special occasions.

In Ireland, beef was consumed mostly by the landed gentry, most natives lived on a bare subsistence of oatmeal, milk, and potatoes, as well as game or fish, when available.

Corned beef was eaten with boiled cabbage on feast days, such as New Year's Eve or Saint Patrick's Day. Spiced beef is an Irish specialty: It is corned beef with a mixture of spices, cloves, ground nutmeg, and cinnamon rubbed into it. Grilled steaks, roasted ribs, and tenderloins are cut into tournedos. Medallions of tenderloin are widely consumed with different sauces and garnishes, along with stewed beef braised with stout.

It has been said that what beef is to England, lamb is to Ireland. Lamb or mutton is the essential ingredient of Irish stew (modern tastes prefer lamb).

Lamb is the meat from a sheep under a year old; above that age the animal is called a *hoggett*, and its meat is called *mutton*. The best Irish lamb is marketed when it is five to seven months old, and is known as *Spring, Summer,* or *early lamb*. The demand for lamb in preference to mutton is partly due to the fact that the lamb carcass provides smaller cuts of more tender meat. Mutton tends to be well-ripened by long hanging before cooking. As it is usually fatty, it needs a good deal of trimming.

Mutton pies were common in Kerry and are still served every year at Puck Fair in Killorglin. Fairend of lamb (known as commercial rack in the United States) is very popular either roasted with garlic and rosemary, or sliced into cutlets or chops. Lamb shanks, braised with root vegetables has also become popular again in Irish restaurants. Lamb's liver is also much prized in Ireland.

Pigs are the only farm animals native to Ireland. Pork makes up a sizeable part of the Irish diet, and almost every part of the animal is put to good use. Roast pork, ham, bacon, gammon, sausages, and blood puddings have been popular from the earliest times. Although unknown in the United States, shoulder of bacon is much loved by the Irish people.

The pig also provides the major part of the hearty Irish breakfast, including rashers (slices of bacon), sausages, and black-and-white pudding. Regional varieties of by-products range from *crubeens* (pigs feet) to Dublin Coddle to cured pork dishes.

Pork should be pale pink with firm, white fat. Nearly all cuts of pork are considered prime; that is, they can broiled or roasted. The majority of cook books, even the most recent, recommend that pork be well done to the point of dryness, thus minimizing the danger of the parasite *trichina*. However, scientists now recommend a safe internal core temperature for pork of 170°F, so that the pork remains moist and tender.

Layered Slices of Top Round of Beef Braised in Smithwicks Ale

1½ pounds top round of beef

6 tablespoons all-purpose flour

¼ teaspoon salt

½ teaspoon freshly milled black peppercorns

4 tablespoons butter

1 tablespoon olive oil

1½ cups sliced onions

¾ cup Smithwicks ale (any ale may be substituted)

1½ cups homemade or purchased brown sauce or classic demi-glace *(recipes pages 278, 279)*

1 teaspoon chopped parsley

1. Preheat oven to 325°F.

2. Slice beef into 8 equal slices.

3. Dust the beef in flour with salt and pepper added.

4. Heat butter and oil in a heavy-bottomed pan. Sear beef slices. Remove and keep warm.

5. Add onions to the pan in which beef was seared. Sauté, 2 minutes.

6. Add ¼ cup ale to the onions to deglaze the pan.

7. In an ovenproof casserole, layer first the onions, then the beef, alternating the onions and meat.

8. Combine *demi-glace* and remaining ale in the pan. Simmer, 1 minute. Pour over meat.

9. Place lid on casserole and cook in preheated oven, until fork tender, approximately 50 minutes. Correct seasoning. Sprinkle with chopped parsley and serve.

SERVES 4

Braising is used primarily for less tender cuts of meat; it requires that food be covered by the braising liquid, then covered and baked in a relatively low oven.

Medallions of Beef with Madeira Sauce and Traditional Ulster Champ

Champ is a beloved dish in Ulster. The flavorings in champ vary from region to region. In other parts of Ireland, nettles, chives, and parsley are used with or instead of scallions.

Tenderloin of beef is known as *fillet of beef* in Ireland.

PRESENTATION

PLACE CHAMP INTO THE CENTER OF A WARMED PLATE. MAKE A WELL IN THE CENTER. SPOON SOME SAUCE INTO THE WELL AND AROUND THE EDGE OF THE PLATE. PLACE THE TENDERLOIN BESIDE THE CHAMP, AND PLACE A BUNCH OF WATERCRESS ON TOP OF THE BEEF.

GUEST CHEF

Noel McMeel, Co. Derry, Northern Ireland

BEEF
¼ cup Madeira

½ cup beef stock

1 cup heavy cream

salt and freshly ground black pepper

8 2-ounce pieces beef tenderloin, trimmed

6 bunches watercress

ULSTER CHAMP
1½ pounds all-purpose potatoes

8 scallions

1½ cups milk

4 tablespoons butter

salt and pepper, to taste

BEEF

1. Bring Madeira to a boil. Simmer to reduce by ½. Add beef stock, and reduce by ⅓. Add cream, and reduce further until the sauce becomes thick. Season with salt and pepper.

2. Grill tenderloins until they reach the required doneness.

ULSTER CHAMP

1. Peel and roughly cut potatoes. Place in a saucepan and cover with salted cold water.

2. Simmer about 20–25 minutes, or until tender.

3. Drain. Place over low heat for a few minutes to dry out.

4. Wash scallions and chop fine.

5. Combine the milk and butter in a small saucepan. Bring to a boil.

6. Place scallions in boiling liquid. Remove from heat. Let sit for a few minutes so the scallions can infuse the milk with flavor.

7. Mash potatoes. Stir in milk mixture until potatoes are smooth. Season with salt and pepper.

Maggie Kerrigan's Beef Stew

SERVES 6

Maggie Kerrigan lived on Moore Street, in Dublin, home to the famous open-air produce market. She cooked this hearty stew for the street vendors of Moore Street.

PRESENTATION

SERVE IN DEEP DISH. THIS HEARTY DISH MAKES FILLING MEAL AND IS USUALLY SERVED WITH HOT CRUSTY BREAD.

2½ pounds boneless beef (rump or chuck)

¼ cup all-purpose flour

4 tablespoons olive oil

2 cloves garlic, crushed

3 cups brown beef stock

1 bay leaf

½ teaspoon salt

¼ teaspoon ground black pepper

3 slices lean bacon

2 small onions, sliced

18 button mushrooms

4 tablespoons tomato paste

12 small potatoes

4 tablespoons of butter

2 teaspoons chopped parsley

1. Preheat oven to 325°F.

2. Cut beef into large cubes and roll them in flour. In a large skillet over high heat, fry meat cubes in olive oil until browned on all sides.

3. Add the garlic and cook with beef, 1 minute. Remove beef from the skillet. Place beef in a 3-quart ovenproof casserole.

4. Bring stock to a boil. Add meat to cover, along with the bay leaf, salt, and pepper. Stir well, cover with lid, and cook in the oven, approximately 1 hour.

5. Slice the bacon into 1-inch segments and fry in a skillet over medium heat with onions and mushrooms, about 2 minutes. Pour off and discard fat. Stir in the tomato paste. Add to stew. Continue cooking until the meat is tender, about 1 hour. Skim fat.

6. Peel potatoes and, in a separate saucepan, boil, 10–12 minutes, or until tender. Drain, toss in butter with parsley. Arrange over top of casserole when fully cooked.

Mullingar Beef Tenderloin Steaks on a Bed of Spinach with a Red-Wine Sauce

TENDERLOINS
4 6-ounce beef tenderloins

salt and freshly ground black pepper

1 teaspoon olive oil

2 tablespoons butter

SPINACH
1½ cups spinach leaves

1 tablespoon butter, melted

⅛ teaspoon nutmeg

Salt and freshly ground black pepper, to taste

RED-WINE SAUCE
1 cup red wine

1 shallot, diced fine

1 bay leaf

1 cup simple brown sauce or demi-glace *(recipes pages 278, 279)*

2 tablespooons unsalted butter

1 bunch chives, chopped fine

4 sprigs chervil

TENDERLOINS

1. Season beef with salt and pepper.

2. In a large skillet over high heat, sear the tenderloins in olive oil and 2 tablspoons butter to desired doneness.

SPINACH

1. Remove and discard spinach stems. Put the leaves in a sink or large bowl full of cold water.

2. Swish leaves around. Allow spinach to stand for a few minutes, allowing any dirt or grit to sink to the bottom.

continued

SERVES 4

The tenderloin is the most tender cut of beef. Classically, the tenderloin provides the *chateaubriand*, a two-person portion cut from the head of the tenderloin, also known as the *double fillet*.

Like onion and garlic, the shallot is a bulbous member of the lily family. Its taste is similar to—but milder than—that of the onion. Shallots are used mainly as a flavoring agent in sauces, stews, and soups.

PRESENTATION

PLACE ¼ OF THE SPINACH ON EACH OF 4 WARMED PLATES. ARRANGE THE TENDERLOINS ON TOP. POUR THE SAUCE AROUND THE BASE OF THE PLATES. GARNISH WITH CHIVES AND CHERVIL.

GUEST CHEF

John Moloney, Chef, Tinakilly Country House and Restaurant, Co. Wicklow

3. Lift the leaves from the water. If very gritty, repeat rinsing process.

4. Blanch the spinach in boiling salted water for 10 seconds, shock in ice-cold water. Drain; squeeze out any excess water.

5. Toss with melted butter, salt, pepper, and nutmeg.

RED-WINE SAUCE

1. Place wine in a medium saucepan with shallots and bay leaf. Over medium heat, simmer until only 1 tablespoon liquid remains

2. Add brown sauce, or *demi-glace*. Return to a boil. Reduce heat.

3. Whisk in 2 tablespoons butter. Correct seasoning.

Roasted Sirloin of Beef Crusted with Peppercorns and Fresh Herbs

SIRLOIN OF BEEF

2 pounds trimmed sirloin of beef

1 teaspoon vegetable oil

½ teaspoon chopped parsley

½ teaspoon chopped chervil

½ teaspoon rosemary

½ teaspoon chopped thyme

1 clove garlic, crushed

2 tablespoons butter

1 tablespoon assorted crushed peppercorns; black, white, and pink

salt to taste

TARRAGON BUTTER SAUCE

3 tablespoons malt vinegar

1 teaspoon finely diced shallots

1 bay leaf

½ teaspoon crushed black peppercorns

3 tablespoons water

3 egg yolks

8 ounces butter, clarified, hot

juice of half lemon

¹⁄₁₆ teaspoon cayenne pepper

½ teaspoon chopped tarragon

ROASTED SIRLOIN OF BEEF

1. Sear sirloin of beef in a very hot ovenproof skillet with a 1 teaspoon of vegetable oil, set to roast in a preheated 375°F oven until cooked to desired degree of done-

SERVES 4

It's best to allow roasts to sit from 15 to 30 minutes, depending upon size, before carving. This allows the juices to recirculate, and the internal temperature to equalize. As a rule, carve only what is needed. Slice into the meat with a steady sawing motion, keeping the knife as level as possible. Use a carving knife with a long narrow blade, about 8 to 10 inches long and 1 inch wide, made of a material that can be sharpened and will hold an edge, such as high-carbon steel. Also useful is a two-pronged long carving fork to hold the meat in place and to lift meat onto the serving platter.

PRESENTATION

LET BEEF REST BEFORE IT IS CARVED. SERVE THICKLY SLICED WITH THE BUTTER SAUCE.

GUEST CHEF

Michael Clifford, Cork

ness. (Desired doneness can be checked using an instant read thermometer: medium rare gives a core temperature reading of 120°F, medium 140°F, and well done 160°F.)

2. Combine herbs, garlic, butter, pepper, and salt and place on top of cooked sirloin.

3. Return to the oven for 2 more minutes until butter has melted and peppercorns and fresh herbs have crusted.

TARRAGON BUTTER SAUCE

1. Reduce vinegar with shallots, bay leaf, and peppercorns to approximately 1 tablespoon liquid.

2. Add water and strain, reserving liquid.

3. In a food processor, combine the warm reduction and egg yolks.

4. Switch on food processor and slowly pour in the hot clarified butter in a thin stream. Butter must be hot (120°F) to cook the egg yolks. Or, vigorously whisk the egg yolks over a water bath by hand, and slowly trickle in the butter.

5. Add lemon juice, cayenne, and chopped tarragon.

Pinwheel of Beef and Colcannon, *Niamh Chinn Oir*

BEEF PINWHEEL

6 8-ounce bottom round steaks, pounded thin about ½-inch thick

4 tablespoons Dijon mustard

1 tablespoon freshly ground black pepper

6 slices Canadian bacon

6 portabello mushrooms, about 2 inches in diameter, trimmed

4 tablespoons butter

1 teaspoon olive oil

¾ cup onions, diced

1 carrot, diced fine

1 rib celery, diced fine

1 leek, diced fine

¼ teaspoon chopped fresh thyme

1 bay leaf

4 tablespoons tomato paste

½ cup all-purpose flour

1 cup red wine

1 bunch chives, for garnish

1 quart beef stock

COLCANNON

6–8 medium all-purpose potatoes

1 small head savoy cabbage

1¼ cup milk

1 onion, diced fine

2 tablespoons butter

salt and pepper, to taste

continued

SERVES 6

Niamh Chinn Oir is Gaelic for *Niamh* (pronounced *Niav*) of the golden tresses. She was the beautiful maiden in Irish mythology who enticed *Oisin* (pronounced *Osheen*) to *Tir Na N-Og*—the land of eternal youth.

PRESENTATION

PLACE A MOUND OF COLCANNON IN THE CENTER OF A WARMED PLATE. POUR SAUCE AROUND THE COLCANNON. SLICE EACH OF THE PINWHEELS AT AN ANGLE INTO SIX SLICES. ARRANGE SLICES, OVERLAPPING, ON TOP OF THE COLCANNON. GARNISH WITH CHIVES.

BEEF PINWHEEL

1. Preheat oven to 350°F.

2. Season steaks with mustard and pepper.

3. Lay bacon on top of steaks. Place portabello mushrooms on top.

4. Roll steaks into spirals and secure with wooden skewers.

5. Heat butter and olive oil in a heavy-bottomed ovenproof skillet (or casserole) and, over high heat, sear the beef. Remove and keep warm.

6. Place the onions, vegetables, thyme, and bay leaf in the casserole and sauté, 1 minute, over low heat.

7. Mix in tomato paste and flour. Cook over low heat, 1 minute.

8. Add red wine and beef stock and whisk until smooth and slightly thick.

9. Return beef to sauce. Cover casserole and bake in preheated oven, 1 hour 30 minutes.

10. Check for doneness, remove from oven and allow to cool slightly.

11. Take beef out of sauce and remove wooden toothpicks or butcher string.

12. Strain the sauce through a fine-mesh strainer. Season to taste.

COLCANNON

1. In a pot large enough to hold them, cover potatoes with cold salted water. Bring to a boil. Boil 20 minutes, or until tender. Remove potatoes. Let dry, then mash.

2. Chop cabbage finely. Boil separately in salted water about 3 minutes.

3. In a saucepan, heat milk with onion.

4. Drain cabbage and add to mashed potatoes. Stir in butter; season with salt and pepper.

5. Pour warm milk and onions over potatoes and beat together until creamy.

Grilled Guinness-Marinated Sirloin Steaks with Chived Potato and Tomatoes

MARINATION

1½ cups Guinness stout

1½ cups chicken stock

2 sprigs thyme

1 teaspoon Worcestershire sauce

½ teaspoon milled peppercorns

1 bay leaf

¼ pound unsalted butter, cut in 4 pieces

STEAKS

4 10-ounce trimmed sirloin steaks

ground black pepper to taste

CHIVED POTATO AND TOMATO

2 large cooked potatoes, peeled and sliced lengthwise

1 clove garlic, crushed

1 teaspoon olive oil

1 tablespoon chopped chives

4 plum tomatoes, peeled, seeded, and cut in chunks

1 teaspoon pepper

SERVES 4

Guinness is synonymous with great stout. Stout is a strong, dark, malty-tasting beer and is Ireland's most popular drink and a national treasure. The Guinness family began brewing its stout in 1759, along the banks of Dublin's River Liffey at St. James Brewery, where it has been produced ever since.

PRESENTATION

PLACE GRILLED CHIVED POTATO AND TOMATO ONTO THE CENTER OF A WARMED PLATE. LAY THE SIRLOIN STEAKS TO ONE SIDE. POUR SAUCE AROUND THE STEAK.

MARINATION

1. Combine all the ingredients except butter in a deep dish. Mix thoroughly. Totally immerse the trimmed steaks in marination and refrigerate, 8 hours.

2. Pour the marination into a saucepan and bring to a boil, skimming off foam that rises to the surface. Reduce marinade by half.

3. Remove from heat. Strain through fine mesh strainer.

continued

4. When slightly cooled, whisk in butter, one piece at a time, until it is totally incorporated into sauce.

GRILLED SIRLOIN

1. Grill steaks to desired doneness.

CHIVED POTATO AND TOMATO

1. Rub potatoes with garlic, oil, salt, and freshly milled black peppercorns.

2. Lay flat on a sheet pan and grill on both sides until golden brown.

3. Overlap the potatoes into a circle. Place tomato chunks on top of potatoes and sprinkle with chopped chives.

Ballymaloe Steak-and-Oyster Pie

1½ pounds top round beef

12 shucked oysters (retain juices from oysters)

2 tablespoons butter

1 teaspoon vegetable oil

1 onion, chopped fine

1 tablespoon all-purpose flour

2½ cups beef stock

2 cups sliced mushrooms

1 4-ounce sheet prepared puff pastry

1 egg lightly beaten with 1 tablespoon milk

salt and freshly ground black pepper, to taste

1. Preheat oven to 350°F.

2. Trim beef of any excess fat or sinew. Cut into 1-inch cubes.

3. Heat butter with oil in an ovenproof deep skillet or casserole. Sear beef cubes in oil.

4. Add the onions, cook, about 1 minute. Remove beef and onions from the skillet.

5. Add flour to the skillet and stir to a smooth paste. Cook, 2 minutes, over low heat.

6. Slowly whisk in the stock to achieve a smooth consistency. Add mushrooms and oyster liquor. Return the beef and onions to the skillet and stir. Add salt and pepper. Simmer for 1½ hours over low heat, stirring occasionally. Adjust consistency with additional stock, as needed.

7. Remove from skillet, check seasoning, place into ovenproof serving pie dish.

continued

SERVES 4–6

Shucked oysters should be plump, uniform in size, have a good clear color, and smell of the sea; their liquor (liquid) should be also be clear. Store live oysters in the refrigerator (larger shell down), covered with a damp towel, for up to three days. The sooner they are eaten, the better. If any shells open during storage, tap them—if they don't close, throw them out.

PRESENTATION

LET THE PIE REST FOR 10 MINUTES AFTER REMOVING FROM THE OVEN. USE A SHARP SERRATED KNIFE TO SLICE THE PIE. IDEALLY, THIS PIE DISH SHOULD BE IS ACCOMPANIED BY SEASONAL GREEN VEGETABLES.

GUEST CHEF

**Myrtle Allen,
Chef Proprietor, Ballymaloe
House, Shanagarry, Co. Cork.**

8. On a lightly floured flat surface, roll out the puff pastry to ¼-inch thickness. Cover pie dish with pastry, pressing the edges down firmly around the edges of the pie dish. Brush with egg wash and place in preheated oven. Bake, 20 minutes, or until the pastry crisps and turns a golden brown color. Lift the lid of the cooked pastry and slip in the oysters. No further cooking is necessary.

Traditional Irish Lamb Stew

INGREDIENTS

3 pounds deboned, lean lamb shoulder

1½ cups sliced onions

1 cup sliced leeks

1 cup sliced celery

2 tablespoons chopped parsley

3 sprigs thyme

salt and pepper, to taste

16 small potatoes, peeled

1½ cups carrots, cut into 2-inch-long batons

2½ quarts chicken stock

1. Trim lamb of excess fat and bone. Cut into 2-inch chunks.

2. In a pot large enough to hold lamb, cover chunks with cold water. Bring to a boil. Boil, 10 minutes. Drain and cool under cold water.

3. In a 4-quart pot, layer the meat, onions, leeks, celery, and herbs. Cover with stock. Simmer, 1 hour.

4. Add potatoes and carrots after 30 minutes time.

5. When cooked, sprinkle with chopped parsley.

SERVES 8

The stew should be skimmed periodically to remove fat. When fully cooked, the finished stew should be white in color, with a slightly peppery flavor.

Traditional Killorglin Lamb Pie with Thyme and Roasted Parsnips

SERVES 4

Lamb is closely associated with Ireland and is, essentially, a sheep less than one year old.

PRESENTATION

SERVE THE BAKED PIE ON A PLATE WITH A NAPKIN UNDERNEATH

1 small shoulder of lean lamb, deboned, bones reserved

3 tablespoons tomato paste

¼ pound butter

2 cloves garlic, crushed

1 cup button mushrooms, trimmed

3 onions, diced

4 carrots, diced

4 tablespoons all-purpose flour

1 whole parsnip, peeled, and split in half lengthwise

salt and freshly ground black pepper, to taste

4 small sprigs thyme

BOUQUET GARNI

1 large sprig thyme

1 small bunch parsley

4 bay leaves

1 rib celery, cut into 3-inch lengths, tied with string around parsley, thyme, and bay leaves

STOCK

1. Preheat oven to 400°F.

2. Roast the lamb bones in with the parings of carrots and onions.

3. When bones are browned, discard any excess fat and place in a 4-quart stock pot with tomato paste. Cover with 3 quarts water. Bring to a boil. Simmer, 40 minutes, and strain.

LAMB PIE

1. Cut lamb into one inch cubes. Saute over low heat in butter with crushed garlic until lightly browned.

2. Add mushrooms, onions, and carrots. Sauté, 2 minutes.

GUEST CHEF

**Colin O'Daly,
Chef, Roly's Bistro, Dublin**

3. Add the flour and incorporate with the vegetables, mushrooms, and lamb. Stir well and cook, 1 minute.

4. Slowly add the strained stock (approximately 4 cups) stirring constantly. Add the bouquet garni and simmer over low heat, 1 hour. Skim.

PARSNIPS

1. Preheat oven to 350°F.

2. Place parsnip on a small roasting pan, season with salt and pepper, and roast 20–25 minutes. Allow the roasted parsnips to cool slightly, cut ½-inch dice, and add to the cooked lamb stew.

BAKING THE PIE

1. Preheat oven to 350°F.

2. Divide the combined lamb and parsnips into 4 individual dishes. Place a sprig of thyme on each.

3. On a lightly floured surface, roll out puff pastry to ¼-inch thickness. Cover each pie with pastry. Brush with egg wash. Bake, 10–15 minutes, or until the pastry is golden brown and crisp.

Peppered Leg of Lamb with a Ginger, Red-currant, and Vinegar Glaze

SERVES 6

Because of its delicate yet distinctive flavor, lamb is usually cooked as simply as possible. Lamb flesh spoils much faster than beef and should be eaten as soon as possible after purchase. Lamb cooked until medium-rare will be tender and succulent; overcooking lamb makes it dry and tough.

Ginger is a rhizome, which is the part of the plant used in cooking. Resembling a thick knobby root, fresh ginger has thin, pale-brown skin and moist, pale gold flesh. It has a pungent, slightly hot flavor and a lively, fresh aroma.

PRESENTATION

POUR THE SAUCE ONTO A WARM PLATE, SLICE THE MEAT FROM THE LEG OF LAMB, AND SERVE OVER THE SAUCE. THIS DISH MAY BE ACCOMPANIED WITH A PUREE OF LEEKS AND NEW POTATOES WITH MINT.

GUEST CHEF

John Morrin, Executive Chef, Imperial Hotel, Cork

2 tablespoons each of red, green, and black peppercorns, crushed

4 cloves garlic—2 crushed, 2 slivered

salt

1 tablespoon oil

1 5–6 pound leg of lamb

1 sprig rosemary

1½ pounds roughly chopped vegetables—onions, celery, carrots, and leeks

2 tablespoons all-purpose flour

¼ cup raspberry vinegar

1 tablespoon peeled and chopped ginger

¼ cup red-currant or cranberry jelly

1½ cups chicken stock (see recipe page 274)

1. Preheat oven to 375°F.

2. Crush mixed peppercorns with crushed cloves of garlic, salt, and a little oil.

3. Remove outer layer of skin from lamb.

4. Make six incisions in the surface of the lamb, and insert the peeled cloves of garlic and pieces of rosemary.

5. Rub peppercorn mixture into the lamb.

6. Roast the leg of lamb on the top of chopped vegetables, until medium rare, about 1 hour.

7. Remove the leg of lamb from the roast pan and keep warm.

8. Pour off excess fat.

9. Add flour to the roasting pan to make a roux. Stir constantly until flour is fully cooked.

10. Add raspberry vinegar, ginger, and jelly. Incorporate with the roux and cook, two minutes.

11. Add chicken stock and whisk to a smooth consistency. Bring to a boil. Strain through a fine-mesh strainer.

12. If required, correct the consistency of the sauce with additional chicken stock. It should be slightly thickened.

Braised Lamb Shanks with Roasted-Garlic Mashed Potatoes

This old recipe is now a popular comfort food.

PRESENTATION

SERVE THE LAMB SHANKS ON WARMED PLATES WITH MOUNDS OF ROASTED-GARLIC MASHED POTATOES.

LAMB SHANKS

¼ cup vegetable oil

4 tablespoons butter

4 lamb shanks

1 bay leaf

2 celery ribs, diced

2 small carrots, sliced

2 medium onions, sliced

salt and ground pepper, to taste

2 cloves garlic, crushed

1 teaspoon chopped rosemary

1 teaspoon chopped thyme

1 cup red wine

1 tablespoon tomato paste

6 cups brown stock

⅓ cup all-purpose flour

ROASTED-GARLIC MASHED POTATOES

3 pounds all-purpose potatoes, peeled and quartered

salt and freshly ground black pepper

4 heads roasted garlic, peeled and mashed

2 ounces butter

1 cup milk

1 tablespoon chopped parsley

LAMB SHANKS

1. Preheat oven to 400°F.

2. Heat oil and butter in a heavy-bottomed skillet. Sear the lamb shanks on all sides. Remove shanks, and reserve the oil and butter.

3. Place shanks in a roasting pan with the bay leaf, celery, carrots, and onion. Bake, in a preheated oven, 20 minutes.

4. Reduce oven temperature to 350°F. Season lamb shanks with salt, pepper, garlic, rosemary, and thyme.

5. Add red wine, tomato paste, and stock to the lamb shanks. Return to oven, cover with a tightly fitting lid or aluminum foil. Braise until tender, approximately 1 hour.

6. Remove from oven. Lift the lamb shanks out of sauce and keep warm.

7. Skim any fat from the stock, strain through a fine-mesh strainer.

8. In a separate pot, mix the reserved oil and butter and flour. Add the strained braising stock, slowly whisking until a smooth consistency is achieved.

9. Return lamb shanks to sauce and simmer, 15 minutes. Correct seasoning.

ROASTED-GARLIC MASHED POTATOES

1. In a medium pot, cover potatoes with salted water. Bring to a boil, reduce to a simmer, and cook until tender, about 20 minutes.

2. Drain and mash potatoes.

3. In a small saucepan, combine garlic, butter, and milk, bring to a boil.

4. Turn heat under potatoes to low. Mash in garlic-and-milk mixture, stirring until a smooth paste is formed. Season with salt and pepper and serve with chopped parsley.

Roasted Rack of Wicklow Lamb with an Herb Crust and Mint-Butter Sauce

SERVES 2

The minted-butter sauce can be made without a food processor by whisking the reduction and egg yolks over a water bath until the egg yolks thicken. Then add the clarified butter in a steady trickle.

PRESENTATION

CARVE THE LAMB CAREFULLY BETWEEN EACH BONE. POUR THE ROAST PAN GRAVY ONTO THE CENTER OF A WARMED PLATE, ARRANGE 3 LAMB CUTLETS ON TOP AND SPOON A LITTLE MINTED SAUCE OVER EACH CUTLET.

1 2-pound rack of lamb, trimmed and Frenched

1 clove garlic, crushed

1 sprig rosemary, chopped

¼ teaspoon salt

¼ teaspoon freshly ground black pepper

1 tablespoon olive oil

4 tablespoons butter

1 teaspoon chopped parsley

½ teaspoon chopped tarragon

½ chopped teaspoon basil

2 tablespoons tomatoes, seeded, skinned, and roughly chopped

1 cup fresh breadcrumbs

1½ cups chicken stock

1 teaspoon arrowroot

SAUCE

2 tablespoons tarragon vinegar

1 tablespoon lemon juice

1 bay leaf

¼ cup water

2 egg yolks

½ cup clarified butter

6 mint leaves, finely chopped

LAMB

1. Preheat oven to 350°F.

2. Trim excess skin and fat from lamb rack, rub the crushed garlic on the outside of the lamb and sprinkle with chopped rosemary, salt, and pepper.

3. Cover the exposed, Frenched bones with aluminum foil to prevent burning. Place on a roasting pan with the olive oil and roast in preheated oven, 20 minutes, or until the lamb reaches a core temperature of 140°F.

4. Melt butter in a small saucepan. Mix in herbs and tomatoes. Add breadcrumbs, and mix until moist.

5. Spread the herbed bread mixture over the lamb. Return it to the oven and roast, 5 minutes. Remove from oven, let rest in a warm place.

6. To make gravy, pour off excess fat from the roasting pan and deglaze with chicken stock. Mix arrowroot with 1 teaspoon of stock. Add the arrowroot and thicken the pan juices. Strain and set aside.

MINT-BUTTER SAUCE

1. Place vinegar, lemon juice, bay leaf, and water in a small saucepan. Reduce to 2 tablespoons.

2. Remove bay leaf. Place warm reduction in a food processor with the egg yolks. Blend at high speed until the egg yolks thicken, about 30 seconds.

3. Heat the clarified butter to 120°F and pour slowly into the food processor set on high speed, about 2 minutes.

4. Add the chopped mint leaves and process.

Traditional Dublin Coddle

Dubliners' traditionally enjoyed this *tightener* (a filling supper) accompanied by Irish soda bread on Saturday evenings, particularly after several pints of Guinness. It is said to have been much liked by Dean Swift.

PRESENTATION

SERVE IN DEEP-DISH PLATES. SPRINKLE WITH CHOPPED PARSLEY.

1½ pounds lean ham or slab bacon, cut into 8 1-inch chunks

8 lean pork sausages

2 pounds potatoes, peeled and sliced

1 sprig thyme

2 large onions, sliced thin

1 tablespoon chopped parsley

salt and ground pepper, to taste

1 quart vegetable or chicken stock

1. Blanch ham or bacon, with sausages, in boiling water, 5 minutes.

2. Drain and cool. Place the sausage and ham/bacon into a 4-quart casserole with potatoes, thyme, onions, and parsley.

3. Season. Cover with stock.

4. Cover, and gently simmer, 1 hour or until fork tender. Do not allow to become mushy.

Lamb Cutlets (Chops) with a Basil Crêpe and Braised Vegetables

CRÊPE BATTER

½ cup all-purpose flour

2 eggs

1 cup milk

¼ cup water

2 tablespoons chopped basil

salt and pepper, to taste

1 tablespoon olive oil

LAMB

12 lamb cutlets, trimmed and Frenched

salt and pepper

1 tablespoon olive oil

¼ cup Madeira

1 cup chicken stock

1 tablespooon arrowroot

6 mint leaves, chopped fine

4 sprigs rosemary

BRAISED VEGETABLES

1 small eggplant

1 zucchini

1 small onion

2 tomatoes, skinned and seeded

1 tablespoon olive oil

2 cloves garlic, crushed

½ cup thinly sliced mushrooms

1 teaspoon chopped parsley

½ teaspoon chopped thyme

¼ teaspoon ground pepper

¼ teaspoon salt

continued

The Skellig Hotel stands on the site of an 1891 coast-guard station. The restaurant provides a spectacular view of beautiful Dingle Bay. From the restaurant, diners can watch Fungie, a bottlenosed dolphin, perform his acrobatics in the bay. No one knows why this dolphin has made his home in Dingle but, since his arrival, he has become a great friend and tourist attraction.

PRESENTATION

ON EACH OF FOUR WARMED PLATES, PLACE A SPOONFUL OF VEGETABLES TO ONE SIDE. FOR EFFECT, THE CRÊPES MAY BE SHAPED INTO ROUNDS BY USING A LARGE CUTTER. PLACE A PANCAKE ON TOP, ADD A SECOND LAYER OF VEGETABLES AND A SECOND PANCAKE. PLACE THE LAMB CUTLETS BESIDE THE CREPES AND VEGETABLES. POUR THE GRAVY AROUND THE PLATE. DECORATE WITH A SPRIG OF ROSEMARY.

GUEST CHEF

Patrick Clement, Skellig Hotel, Dingle Co. Kerry

CRÊPES

1. Using a standing mixer, mix flour, eggs, milk, water, basil, and seasoning (or whisk vigorously by hand).

2. Coat a 6–8" diameter nonstick crêpe pan with a little oil. Heat.

3. Pour a thin layer of the pancake batter onto the pan. Swirl around the base.

4. Lightly brown the pancakes on both sides.

5. Turn out onto parchment paper and hold until ready to use.

BRAISED VEGETABLES

1. Preheat oven to 350°F.

2. Split the eggplant into quarters lengthwise. Slice eggplant, zucchini, onions, and tomatoes thin.

3. In a casserole, heat a tablespoon of olive oil.

4. Add all vegetables, mushrooms, garlic, thyme, and parsley. Sauté on top of the stove, about 2 minutes. Add salt and pepper.

5. Cook, covered, in the preheated oven, 2 –3 minutes.

LAMB

1. Season cutlets with salt and pepper. Sear over high heat in olive oil, turning each cutlet at least twice, about 6 minutes.

2. Remove the cutlets. Set aside and keep warm.

3. Pour off fat from the skillet and deglaze over high heat with the chicken stock and Madeira. Reduce until 2 tablespoons liquid remain.

4. Thicken gravy with arrowroot dissolved in a little cold chicken stock, strain. Add the finely mint leaves. Simmer, 1 minute

Traditional Cork Crubeens

Hind feet are usually preferred for crubeens, because they have more meat on them. The forefeet are called *trotters*. Crubeens were a common food in Ireland, often eaten with soda bread. They can be eaten hot or cold, and are nawed like corn on the cob.

PRESENTATION

SERVE SIMPLY, ON A WARMED PLATE WITH A TOSSED MIXED SALAD OF SEASONAL GREENS.

GUEST CHEF

**Declan Ryan,
Chef Proprietor, Arbutus Lodge,
Cork**

BRINE

1 gallon water

1 cup honey

1 cup brown sugar

1 cinnamon stick

4 bay leaves

1 cup kosher or other coarse salt

CRUBEENS

4 pigs' feet

2 carrots, chopped

1 rib celery, chopped

1 onion, diced

1 cup white-wine vinegar

8 tablespoons butter, melted

3 cups dried breadcrumbs

¼ teaspoon allspice

1. Mix all brine ingredients.

2. Place pigs' feet in brine mixture, 2 days.

3. Tie the pigs' feet, 2 at a time, onto wooden dowels, so they keep their shape while cooking.

4. Place in a 4-quart stock pot with the vegetables. Cover with water and add vinegar.

5. Simmer over low heat for 6–7 hours. Remove from heat and let cool.

6. When cooled, split each crubeen in half, roll in melted butter and dried breadcrumbs mixed with a pinch of allspice.

7. Preheat broiler. Warm the crubeens slowly under the broiler or in an oven until they are warm on the inside and crisp on the outside.

Pan-Seared Loin of Pork with Derry Apple Relish

1 2-pound boneless loin of pork trimmed of excess fat and sinew

3 tablespoons unsalted butter

1 onion, diced

¼ cup all-purpose flour, seasoned with salt and pepper

1 tablespoon safflower oil

2 Granny Smith apples, cored and sliced

1 rib celery, diced fine

1 teaspoon finely chopped sage

½ teaspoon chopped rosemary

¼ teaspoon ground cinnamon

2 teaspoons orange zest

1½ cups apple cider

salt and freshly round black pepper

fresh basil leaves, for garnish

1. Slice pork into 8 equal pieces.

2. In a heavy-bottomed skillet, over medium heat, melt butter. Add onion and celery, sweat, without coloring, 2 minutes. Transfer to 2-quart casserole.

3. Dust pork pieces with seasoned flour.

4. In a skillet, over high heat, sear pork pieces in the oil. Remove.

5. Arrange apples on top of onion in the casserole. Add the pork, mixed with the remaining ingredients.

6. Bring to a boil. Cover, lower heat, and simmer, 1 hour.

SERVES 4

The French word *ragout* has come to mean a simple well-seasoned stew.

Celery has been cultivated since the seventeenth century. Legend has it that the wearing a wreath of its leaves on one's head prevented hangovers.

PRESENTATION

TRANSFER THE PORK, APPLE, AND ONIONS TO A SERVING PLATTER. REDUCE THE COOKING LIQUID BY HALF. STRAIN AND POUR OVER THE PORK. GARNISH WITH FRESH BASIL LEAVES.

GUEST CHEF

**Noel McMeel,
Co. Derry.**

Cured Boneless Pork Cutlets with Barley-Stuffed Cabbage Parcels

1 loin of pork (4 rib bones, about 2 pounds)

2 ounces pearl barley

1 bouquet garni (peppercorns, bay leaf, thyme, parsley stalks, wrapped in cheesecloth)

4 large cabbage leaves

¼ cup finely diced carrot

2 tablespoons each finely diced onions, celery, and leek

1 tablespoon butter

8 tablespoons fresh breadcrumbs

1 teaspoon ground pepper

2 tablespoons chopped parsley

2 tablespoons melted butter

PORK CURE

1 gallon water

1 cup honey

1 cup brown sugar

1 cinnamon stick

4 bay leaves

1 cup kosher or other coarse salt

1. In a refrigerator, soak pork overnight in cure.

2. In a separate bowl soak overnight barley in cold water.

3. Remove pork from cure and place in a 4-quart stock pot with a bouquet garni. Cover with fresh water, bring to a boil, and simmer, 2 hours. Remove loin and keep warm. Reserve cooking water.

4. Preheat oven to 450°F.

continued

SERVES 4

The pig is the only farm animal native to Ireland—all other species were introduced. Cabbage is by far the most common vegetable in Ireland; it was first introduced in the seventeenth century, and the present variety was imported from the Orient in the nineteenth century.

PRESENTATION

REMOVE PARCELS FROM COOKING LIQUID. PLACE INTO THE CENTER OF WARMED ENTREE PLATES. CARVE THE PORK LOIN INTO 4 EQUAL PORTIONS. PLACE A PORTION OF THE SLICED PORK OVER THE CABBAGE PARCEL, AND POUR A LITTLE OF THE COOKING LIQUID ON TO THE PLATE. BOILED POTATOES ARE TRADITIONALLY SERVED WITH THIS DISH.

GUEST CHEF

Patrick McLarnon, Chef, Ardtara House Hotel, Upperlands, Co. Derry

5. Drain barley and place in a medium saucepan. Cover with $1\frac{1}{2}$ cups cold water. Bring to a boil and simmer, 30–35 minutes. Drain and cool

6. Remove the hard center vein from each cabbage leaf. Blanch in boiling salted water until tender, about 1 minute. Plunge into ice water to stop the cooking process and retain bright green color. Pat dry.

7. In a skillet, over medium heat, sauté carrot, onion, leek, and celery in 1 tablespoon butter and 2 tablespoons cold water. Cover with a tight-fitting lid and simmer, approximately 1 minute, or until the vegetables are soft. Remove from heat and cool.

8. Combine vegetables with breadcrumbs, barley, pepper, and parsley.

9. Lay the blanched cabbage leaves on a clean, flat surface. Divide the barley mixture into 4 equal parts. Place 1 portion on the center of each cabbage leaf.

10. Fold in the outer edges of the cabbage. Shape to form a parcel.

11. Place the cabbage parcels, folded side down, onto the base of an ovenproof flat casserole dish. Brush with melted butter, and cover with $1\frac{1}{2}$ cups of the cooking liquid from the pork. Cover with a tight fitting lid and cook, 25–30 minutes in preheated oven.

Boyne Valley Honey-Braised Pork Tenderloin with Snowpeas and Grapes

2 10-12 ounces pork tenderloins, trimmed of excess fat and sinew

2 large potatoes, peeled

4 threads saffron or ½ teaspoon turmeric

1 tablespoon finely diced shallots

1 clove garlic, crushed

4 tablespoons butter, divided

1 teaspoon chopped parsley

2 tablespoons honey

1 teaspoon mild mustard

1 tablespoon sherry vinegar

½ cup chicken stock

2 tablespoons sliced black olives

3 cups trimmed snow peas, julienned

1 tablespoon olive oil

1 whole red bell pepper, julienned

½ teaspoon chopped thyme

½ teaspoon chopped sage

½ cup halved seedless grapes

¼ teaspoon salt

½ teaspoon ground pepper

string or small wooden skewers

1. Preheat oven to 400°F.

2. Butterfly pork tenderloins. Pound until ¼-inch thick.

3. Peel and boil potatoes in water to cover with saffron or turmeric,

Like its relative, ginger, turmeric is a rhizomeùan underground stem. It resembles ginger externally, but its color and flavor are very different. Turmeric is bright yellow-orange, and has a pungent, slightly acrid flavor.

PRESENTATION

POUR THE SNOWPEA, OLIVE, AND GRAPE SAUCE ONTO A PLATE. REMOVE THE STRING FROM THE PORK AND SLICE. PLACE THE SNOW PEAS ON THE PLATE ALONG WITH THE PORK SLICES.

GUEST CHEF

Peter Brady, Dublin

about 25 minutes. Drain. Dry potatoes over medium heat, 1 minute. Cool, puree with hand masher.

4. In a skillet shallots and garlic in 2 tablespoons butter. Combine with potatoes and chopped parsley. Cool.

5. Place potato mixture in center of butterflied pork tenderloin, folding to enclose. Tie with string or use toothsticks to hold the overlap.

6. In a small saucepan, warm honey. Coat pork. Melt 1 ounce of butter in a skillet. Place the pork tenderloins in the skillet and toss to coat the pork in the butter. Place in a 400°F preheated oven and roast for 10 minutes.

7. Remove the pork from the skillet, discard the excess fat, add the mustard and sherry vinegar, chicken stock, and olives to the *roasting skillet*.

8. Blanch snow peas in boiling water, 30 seconds. Strain and plunge into ice water.

9. In a skillet, heat olive oil. Add the peppers, snow peas, herbs, and grapes. Season with salt and pepper. Toss over high heat, 30–50 seconds

Boiled Limerick Ham Shanks with Mustard-Grain Cream and Crisp Cabbage

SERVES 4

The pig was probably the first animal to be raised as domesticated livestock in Ireland. Indeed, to this day, it is not uncommon to find butcher shops in Ireland divided into pork and others. Pig is most versatile, with almost every part of the animal being put to some gastronomic use. Irish ham and bacon has been renowned for centuries.

In Ireland, only the leg of the pig is called ham, all else is bacon. Limerick is celebrated for its great bacon and ham.

PRESENTATION

POUR THE SAUCE ONTO THE CENTER OF A WARMED PLATE. SPOON THE SLICED CABBAGE OVER THE SAUCE. PLACE THE TRIMMED HAM SHANK ON TOP, AND GARNISH WITH FLAT LEAF PARSLEY. CHAMP MAKES AN IDEAL ACCOMPANIMENT TO THIS TRADITIONAL IRISH DISH.

GUEST CHEF

Terry Doran, Chef, Ballymac Restaurant, Co. Antrim

4 1½-pound ham shanks

¼ pound butter, divided

½ small head savoy cabbage, finely shredded

salt and ground pepper, to taste

⅔ cup heavy cream

2 teaspoons coarse-grain mustard

flat-leaf parsley, for garnish

1. Trim ham shanks, and clean ends of the bones.

2. Soak overnight in cold water to remove excess salt.

3. Rinse the shanks and place in a 4-quart stock pot.

4. Cover with fresh cold water and bring to a boil. Simmer, 1 hour. Remove shanks. Reserve liquid.

5. In a heavy-bottomed skillet, over medium heat, melt 2 tablespoons butter. Add ½ cup ham stock, then savoy cabbage, stirring to coat.

6. Season with salt and pepper. Cover, reduce heat. Stir occasionally, until tender, about 3 minutes.

7. Reduce 1 cup ham stock to half its volume.

8. Add cream and coarse-grained mustard. Simmer until the sauce thickens slightly.

9. Whisk in remaining butter, in pieces.

Veal, Poultry & Game Dishes

THERE IS NO PRECISE DEFINITION OF VEAL. THE WORD IS MOST OFTEN USED TO DESCRIBE A

young calf (one–three months old). However, in Ireland, animals up to nine months

are considered veal. Milk-fed veal is considered premium. Its delicate flesh is firm and

creamy white with a pale gray tinge. Other calves are fed on grain or grass, which

results in a slightly coarser texture and stronger flavor. Unlike beef, veal requires very

little aging. However, because veal comes from young animals, it lacks the extensive

intramuscular fat, known as *marbling*, typical of good beef. The best indication of quali-

ty in veal is its pale color, and fine texture.

Veal is delicate, so it must be cooked very gently. Breading seals in the flavor of thinner cuts of veal. Overcooking veal will toughen and ruin it. High-quality veal produced in Ireland is exported throughout the world.

The choicest cuts of veal come from the loin and tenderloin, the rib section, (from which veal chops are cut), and the top, bottom, and eye rounds. The remaining usable flesh is tougher, and better suited for slow-cooking methods, such as roasting or braising, or for use ground for pâtés, sausages, meatballs, or mousses. Veal bones are high in natural gelatin and are preferred by many Irish chefs for making stock. It provides a rich body and mild flavor.

The most popular poultry in Ireland are chicken, turkey, and duck. Pigeon and guinea fowl are also frequently featured on menus.

Chicken is a common menu item everywhere because of its versatility; chicken can be roasted, boiled, grilled, braised, fried, poached, steamed, broiled, pan-fried, deep-fried, stir-fried, or sautéed.

POINTS TO REMEMBER

In order to prevent bacterial growth, do not stuff poultry until just before roasting. Only stuff the bird ¾ full to allow for expansion during cooking.

Do not salt poultry until after cooking. Salt draws out the natural juices from the meat and will make it dry.

Poultry is done when the juices run clear and the meat near the bone at the thickest part is no longer pink. Drumsticks should move easily in their sockets. Large birds can be tested with an instant-read thermometer, which should register at least 170°F when inserted into the thigh's thickest part.

Bacteria on raw poultry can contaminate other food it comes in contact with, so it is vital that hot soapy water is used to thoroughly wash hands, cutting boards, and any utensils used in its preparation. A further recommendation is to rub the cutting board with a paste of salt and vinegar, then rinse in hot soapy water.

Fresh poultry is very perishable. When purchased, it should not have an off odor or color, and should be quite dry. If poultry is packaged, there should not be any accumulated liquid on the tray or in the bag. Fresh poultry should be used within one or two days of purchase, or frozen immediately. Refrigerating fresh poultry does not kill off organisms that cause food spoilage; it only slows their growth. Spoiled meat will have a definite off odor and a slimy surface. Discard any meat that is of questionable freshness.

Game furnishes some of the most tasty and wholesome of all meat—it is rich in flavor, high in protein and minerals, and low in fat. Game in Ireland includes game birds, venison, and wild rabbit. The pheasant has been held in high esteem for centuries in Ireland since it was first introduced from China. To this day, it is the most popular of all the feathered game on Irish menus.

Venison is a most healthful meat, and is also very flavorsome and moist when properly aged or marinated. As in the United States, venison is commercially produced in Ireland. However, Irish chefs favor the unique flavor and taste of the wild variety. Venison should be deep red, with very little outside fat or marbling. Because of its leanness, aging, marinating, and the introduction of fat during the roasting process is vital.

In general, the variety of game available depends on the shooting seasons; however, domesticated species, particularly rabbit, are becoming very popular in Ireland.

Game is distinguished by its texture and taste, which differs significantly from that of poultry and farmyard animals. It is generally darker, stronger tasting, and, often, tougher, according to the age and type of animal. Game meat responds by far the best to roasting. Older game can be casseroled or braised, or made into pies, pâtés, or terrines. Marinating in a mixture of oil, vinegar, wine, or beer, with herbs and spices, helps to make tough meat tender, and enhances the taste.

Baked Spinach-and-Cheese-Stuffed Veal Cutlets with Oven Roasted Potatoes

To *turn* foods, slice them carefully into equal-sized ovals.

PRESENTATION

POUR SAUCE IN THE CENTER OF A WARMED PLATE. SLICE THE VEAL AT AN ANGLE, ABOUT ¼ INCH THICK, AND ARRANGE NEATLY ON TOP OF SAUCE. PLACE THREE POTATOES ON EACH PLATE AND SPRINKLE WITH CHOPPED CHIVES.

VEAL

1 cup fresh spinach leaves, washed and stemmed

2 tablespoons Dijon mustard

1 clove garlic, crushed

4 tablespoons grated Parmesan cheese

salt and ground pepper to taste

1 tablespoon all-purpose flour

4 4-ounce veal cutlets

3 tablespoons olive oil

wooden toothpicks

SAUCE

1 finely diced shallot

2 tablespoons butter

½ cup port wine

2½ cups beef stock

salt and freshly ground pepper

1 tablespoon chopped chives

POTATOES

12 small peeled and "turned" potatoes

4 tablespoons butter

1 tablespoon olive oil

1 tablespoon lemon juice

salt and freshly ground black pepper, to taste

chopped chives, for garnish

VEAL

1. Preheat oven to 350°F.

2. Place the spinach leaves in a sink or large bowl full of cold water.

Swish the leaves, then allow to stand for a few minutes to allow any dirt or grit to sink to the bottom. Lift the spinach leaves out of the water. Repeat if the spinach is very gritty.

3. Blanch spinach leaves in boiling salted water, about 10 seconds. Rinse in ice cold water, drain, and squeeze out all excess moisture.

4. Chop spinach and combine in a bowl with the lightly beaten egg along with the mustard, garlic, cheese, salt, and pepper.

5. Flatten cutlets between plastic sheets, and pound until about ¼-inch thick. Spread spinach mixture about ¼-inch thick over one side of the veal.

6. Carefully roll veal. Use wooden toothpicks or butcher's string to secure.

7. Lightly dust with flour, and season with salt and pepper.

8. Sear over high heat in a skillet with olive oil, making sure to seal the seam.

9. Place veal on a small roasting pan, place in a preheated oven, and roast, 6–8 minutes.

10. Allow to relax, 2 minutes, in a warm place. Remove the toothpicks.

SAUCE

1. In a medium saucepan, over low heat, sauté the shallots in butter.

2. Add port. Reduce by half.

3. Add beef stock, and reduce to a smooth consistency.

4. Season to taste and strain.

POTATOES

1. Preheat oven to 350°F.

2. Parboil potatoes for 8 minutes. Drain and pat dry.

3. Melt the butter with the olive oil in a heavy bottomed ovenproof skillet. Place the "dried" potatoes on the skillet, and toss until they are fully coated.

4. Sprinkle lemon juice over the potatoes.

5. Place in preheated oven and roast, 40 minutes, or until tender.

6. Season with salt and pepper.

Veal Escalopes with Orange Butter and Roasted Vegetable Salad

ROASTED VEGETABLE SALAD

½ cup thickly sliced carrots

½ cup thickly sliced parsnips

½ cup thickly sliced Jerusalem artichokes

1 cup ½-inch chunks rutabaga, peeled and diced

½ cup diced onion

3 cloves garlic, crushed

2 tablespoons olive oil

¼ teaspoon salt

½ teaspoon freshly ground black pepper

1 cup basic vinaigrette dressing (recipe page 113)

1 cup mixed salad greens

VEAL

4 2-ounce veal cutlets (pounded flat)

salt and ground pepper

2 whole eggs

1 teaspoon chopped basil

1 teaspoon chopped thyme

2 tablespoons grated cheddar cheese

2 cloves garlic, crushed

6 tablespoons all-purpose flour

1 cup safflower oil

1½ cups fresh white breadcrumbs

4 tablespoons butter

juice of 1 orange

2 oranges, peeled, pith removed, and segmented

1 grapefruit, peeled, pith removed, and segmented

continued

Veal cutlets are more commonly known as escalopes (thin slices) in Ireland. Veal cutlets are the United States version of chops (with the bone attached).

Veal must be cooked very gently. Moist cooking methods are the most appropriate. Breading the cutlets helps seal in the veal's precious moisture. The delicate flavor of veal can easily be overpowered by strongly flavored sauces.

PRESENTATION

PLACE THE VEAL CUTLET ON A WARMED PLATE, COAT WITH THE ORANGE BUTTER, AND GARNISH WITH ORANGE AND GRAPEFRUIT SEGMENTS. ADD THE VEGETABLE SALAD AND WATERCRESS.

SALAD

1. Preheat oven to 400°F.

2. Place the prepared vegetables and garlic, with the olive oil and seasonings, in an ovenproof heavy-bottomed skillet. Over high heat, shake and toss the vegetables to make sure that all of the vegetables are well coated with the oil.

3. Place in preheated oven. Roast the vegetables, about 15 minutes, or until they are caramelized, and soft but firm. Remove from oven and cool.

4. When vegetables are cool, toss them gently with the dressing. Refrigerate. Serve the salad with mixed greens.

VEAL

1. Season cutlets with salt and pepper.

2. In a bowl, beat the eggs. Add herbs, cheese and garlic.

3. Dredge cutlets in flour, then dip in the herbed egg and cheese mixture. Coat with breadcrumbs.

4. Gently pat the breaded veal with a heavy knife, cover, and refrigerate, 30 minutes.

5. Heat oil in a large heavy-bottomed skillet. Place the cutlets in the oil and fry over moderate heat until golden brown on both sides.

6. Remove the veal cutlets from the pan and set on paper towels to drain excess oil. Keep warm.

7. In a separate medium saucepan, simmer the butter and orange juice until lightly browned.

Lady Linda's Veal Pinwheel with Garlic-Butter-Crumb Tomatoes

GARLIC BUTTER CRUMB TOMATOES

4 medium skinned and seeded tomatoes

1 cup fresh white breadcrumbs

2 cloves garlic, crushed

½ teaspoon finely chopped basil

¼ teaspoon salt

¼ teaspoon ground black pepper

½ teaspoon finely chopped parsley, divided

4 tablespoons melted butter

VEAL

4 4-ounce veal (cutlets)

4 slices prosciutto

4 leaves fresh sage

¼ cup shredded mozzarella cheese

salt and freshly ground pepper

2 tablespoon olive oil

2 tablespoons diced onion

30 capers

2 tablespoons Irish whiskey

1 cup brown sauce or demi-glace

½ cup heavy cream

4 small bunches watercress, for garnish

TOMATOES

1. Preheat broiler.

2. Cut tomatoes in half.

continued

SERVES 4

Flaming the whiskey is a dramatic part of this dish. The real purpose of flaming foods is to impart flavor and character to the dish. This occurs only after the impurities have been burned off. When flaming this dish, tilt the pan away and pour the whiskey onto a dry part of the pan. For safety, keep the alcohol some distance away from the naked flames, and never add alcohol to a flaming pan. Remove the pan from the flame before adding it.

PRESENTATION

REMOVE THE VEAL FROM THE SAUCE. REMOVE THE WOODEN SKEWERS. SLICE THE VEAL AT A 45-DEGREE ANGLE INTO FOUR PIECES. POUR THE SAUCE ONTO THE CENTER OF A WARMED PLATE, AND PLACE 2 TOMATO HALVES THE SAUCE. SHINGLE THE VEAL SLICES AROUND THE TOMATOES. PLACE A SMALL BUNCH OF WATERCRESS ON TOP OF EACH SERVING OF VEAL.

3. Combine breadcrumbs, garlic, basil, and ½ teaspoon parsley with warmed, melted butter.

4. Place crumb mixture into the tomato halves. Broil tomatoes, 10 inches from heat source, until browned and heated through.

5. Sprinkle with remaining parsley. Serve immediately.

VEAL PINWHEEL

1. Pound the veal slices until very thin, about 5–6 inches in diameter. Place 1 slice prosciutto, sage leaf, and 1 tablespoon mozzarella on top of each veal slice. Fold the edges inward, and square the slices of veal. Roll the slices of veal into a pinwheel and secure with wooden toothpicks.

2. Season the veal with salt and pepper. In a heavy-bottomed skillet, sear the veal on all sides, 2–3 minutes, in olive oil. Remove from skillet and keep warm.

3. Pour off fat. Add the onion and capers to the skillet. Over medium heat, cook the onions and capers until they soften.

4. Add the whiskey to the skillet. Away from the naked flame, ignite and allow to burn off. Return to medium heat and add the brown sauce. Add cream.

5. Return the veal to the skillet and allow to simmer, 3 minutes. Correct seasoning.

Kiwi-and-Gin Sauced Tenderloin of Veal with Asparagus Soufflé

4 6-ounce veal tenderloins slices

MARINADE

4 tablespoons olive oil

2 cloves garlic, crushed

1 sprig rosemary

1 sprig thyme

3 tablespoons white wine

6 crushed peppercorns

SAUCE

3 tablespoon Cork Dry Gin, or other

3 kiwis, peeled and diced

12 green peppercorns (in brine)

1 cup veal stock

salt and freshly ground black pepper, to taste

4 tablespoons butter, cut into pieces

ASPARAGUS SOUFFLÉ

3 tablespoons whole-wheat flour

1 cup skim milk, divided

3 eggs, separated

1 cup cooked asparagus, diced

½ teaspoon chopped tarragon

½ teaspoon marjoram

2 tablespoons grated Parmesan

salt and ground pepper, to taste

VEAL

1. Combine marinade ingredients.

continued

Most American asparagus is green, with slender to medium-thick stalks. In Ireland, one sees purple-streaked thickish stalks, and the prized soft white asparagus. Asparagus should be cooked only until they are tender-crisp and bright green, about eight minutes in boiling seasoned water.

Marjoram (also known as sweet marjoram) is a perennial herb from the mint family; it is often confused with oregano. It has a similar flavor and leaf shape, but is slightly milder and sweeter.

Pork tenderloin may be substituted for veal in this recipe.

PRESENTATION

POUR THE SAUCE ONTO THE CENTER OF A WARMED PLATE. PLACE THE TENDERLOIN ON TOP. SERVE THE ASPARAGUS SOUFFLÉ ON A SEPARATE PLATE.

GUEST CHEF
Michael Cllifford, Cork

2. Marinate veal, approximately 1 hour, refrigerated.

3. In a skillet, over medium/high heat, sear veal on both sides in oil, approximately 3 minutes per side.

4. Remove from the pan and set aside. Pour off oil.

5. Add gin, kiwis, and peppercorns to the skillet. Bring to a boil.

6. Add veal stock and simmer, 1–2 minutes.

7. Strain through a fine-mesh sieve.

8. Season to taste. Whisk in the butter pieces.

ASPARAGUS SOUFFLÉ

1. Preheat oven to 350°F. Lightly oil four ramekin molds.

2. In a heavy-bottomed saucepan, whisk together the flour and half the milk until well blended. Add remaining milk and stir.

3. Bring to a boil, reduce to a simmer, and cook, until thickened.

4. Over low heat, whisk in the egg yolks, one at a time, stirring constantly. Add asparagus, tarragon, marjoram, one tablespoon grated cheese, salt, and pepper. Remove from heat.

5. Beat egg whites in a clean bowl until stiff. Fold into the cooled egg-yolk-and-asparagus mixture, one-third at a time.

6. Pour mixture into the ramekins. Sprinkle with remaining cheese.

7. Bake soufflés in bain marie on the lowest rack of the oven, 30–40 minutes. Do not open oven while cooking.

Honey-Glazed Breast of Duck with Peppercorn Dressing on a Bed of Spiced Celeriac

4 small skinless 2–3 oz. duck breasts

1 teaspoon ground black pepper

3 tablespoons honey

1 tablespoon soy sauce

1 cup chicken stock

1 medium head celeriac

4 tablespoons butter

1 teaspoon chopped ginger

salt, to taste

4 mint leaves, for garnish

DUCK BREAST

1. Preheat oven to 400°F.

2. Rub duck breasts with pepper. In a heavy-bottomed ovenproof skillet, over high heat, sear the duck breasts on each side, about 2 minutes, depending on the size of the duck breasts. Remove from the skillet and coat with honey.

3. Return duck to the skillet.

4. Place skillet in preheated oven, 4 minutes (the center of the duck should be pink).

5. Remove duck from the skillet and pour off the fat. Add soy sauce and chicken stock, and simmer, reducing slightly to concentrate the flavor. Strain through a fine-mesh sieve.

SPICED CELERIAC

1. Peel celeriac and slice into 2-inch long strips.

2. In a medium saucepan, over low heat, melt the butter. Sauté the celeriac with ginger until tender, about 4 minutes.

SERVES 4

Until recently in Ireland, the primary cooking method for duck was roasting, usually until well done.

However, in recent years, many chefs and diners discovered that duck breast is more flavorful when cooked medium rare. In this recipe, the honey caramelizes on the duck breast and gives it a dark, crisp crust.

PRESENTATION

USING A 3-INCH OPEN RING MOLD, SHAPE THE CELERIAC ON THE CENTER OF A WARMED PLATE. SLICE DUCK BREAST ON THE BIAS, AND OVERLAY AROUND CELERIAC. POUR THE COMBINATION OF PAN JUICES, CHICKEN STOCK, AND SOY SAUCE AROUND THE DUCK. GARNISH WITH MINT LEAVES.

Roast Templenoe Duck with Rhubarb-and-Honey Sauce

Racks serve to raise items being roasted from the bottom of the roasting pan. Strongly flavored vegetables such as carrots, leeks, celery, and onions may be chopped roughly and used for this purpose; this is something known as a *bed of roots*. The advantage of a vegetable rack is that it greatly enhances the flavor of the roasting pan juices, which serve as a basis for accompanying sauce.

PRESENTATION

CARVE THE DUCK. POUR THE STRAINED SAUCE ONTO THE CENTER OF 4 WARMED PLATES. ARRANGE THE CARVED DUCK ON TOP.

1 4-pound duck

4 tablespoons unsalted butter

2 tablespoons honey

¼ cup Irish Mist liqueur

1 bunch watercress, washed and stemmed

1 pound rhubarb, washed and chopped

2 cups of chicken stock

1. Preheat oven to 350°F.

2. Rub the outside of the duck with the butter. Place on a rack set in a roasting pan. Roast in a preheated oven, 1¼ hours.

3. Place the honey, Irish Mist, watercress, mustard, and rhubarb in a medium saucepan. Cover with 1 cup chicken stock and simmer over medium heat until the rhubarb has softened, about 2 minutes.

4. After roasting, remove duck from roast pan. Set aside. Pour off fat from the pan, deglaze with the remaining chicken stock, reducing slightly.

5. Pour the rhubarb sauce into the roasting pan and simmer, 3 minutes. Strain and serve.

Roasted Chicken with Walnuts and Tarragon

1 4-pound roasting chicken, cavity rinsed, patted dry

½ lemon

6 tarragon sprigs

1 tablespoon olive oil

salt and freshly ground black pepper, to taste

½ cup roughly chopped walnuts

½ cup white wine

1 cup plain yogurt

1 tablespoon lemon juice

2 tablespoons whole-grain mustard

1 teaspoon honey

1. Preheat oven to 375°F. Place lemon half in the chicken cavity with tarragon sprigs. Truss securely. (See side note.)

2. Brush the chicken all over with olive oil. Season with salt and pepper.

3. Place chicken on its side on a rack in a shallow baking pan. Roast in the preheated oven, 20 minutes. Turn chicken onto its other side, brush with oil and roast, 20 minutes. Turn breast-side up, and baste with the pan juices. Roast, 20 to 25 minutes, until golden brown.

4. Transfer chicken to a warm platter.

5. Pour off all but 2 tablespoons of fat from the roasting pan. Add walnuts to the pan and sauté over moderately high heat until brown.

6. Add the wine. Scrape the pan well with a wooden spoon. Increase the heat, and reduce liquid by half while continuing to stir and scrape. Add the yogurt, lemon juice, mustard, and honey. Bring to a boil, simmer, 2 minutes, then strain through a fine-mesh sieve.

SERVES 4

Trussing means to secure the legs and wings of the chicken close to its body. Trussing holds the bird together during the roasting process, so that when it is finished, it has an attractive appearance and even shape. The simplest method is to lay string across and under neck opening, then draw string up and over wings and under drumsticks. Pull ends toward you between drumstick and breast on each side, and cross over.

Native walnuts have virtually disappeared from Ireland. In the nineteenth century, walnut trees were decimated as their wood was used to make gun stocks.

Braised Young Chicken with Cabbage, Bacon, and Rosemary

1 1–1½ pound chicken, cut into serving pieces, portions skin on.

salt and ground pepper, to taste

½ cup chicken stock

3 tablespoons butter, divided

½ cup thinly shredded savoy cabbage

1 slice Canadian bacon, julienned

4 cloves

½ cup brown sauce or demi-glace

1 sprig rosemary

2 sprigs lavender, optional, for garnish

1.   Preheat oven to 350°F.

2.   Season the chicken with salt and pepper. Sear the chicken pieces, skin side down first, in a heavy-bottomed skillet. Remove chicken. Pour off fat.

3.   Return chicken to the skillet, and add the chicken stock. Simmer, covered, in oven, approximately 15 minutes, or until the chicken is cooked.

4.   In a medium saucepan, place 2 tablespoons butter. Over low heat, sauté savoy cabbage with bacon and cloves, about 3 minutes. The cabbage should remain crisp. Season with salt and pepper.

5.   In a separate small saucepan, bring *demi-glace* to a boil and add rosemary. Allow to reduce slightly and strain. Remove the chicken from the skillet with a slotted spoon. Strain the pan juices into the *demi-glace*, whisking to combine. Finally, whisk 1 tablespoon butter into the sauce just prior to serving.

SERVES 2

Cloves are powerfully scented, hard, dried flower buds. They are useful as a spice for baking, pickling, and in beverages.

PRESENTATION

PLACE THE CABBAGE INTO A WARMED DEEP-DISH PLATE. ARRANGE THE BABY CHICKEN NEATLY ON TOP OF THE CABBAGE. POUR SAUCE AROUND THE CHICKEN. GARNISH WITH SPRIGS OF FRESH LAVENDER.

GUEST CHEF

Bruno Schmidt,
Head Chef, Park Hotel,
Kenmare, Co. Kerry

Crab-Stuffed Chicken Breast with
Broccoli–Cream-Cheese Mousse

SERVES 4

Darragh is an Irish name dating from ancient clan times. Its literal translation is The Tall Dark One.

To *braise* generally means to cook food in a small amount of liquid in an airtight pot. This creates a moist, steamy cooking environment that gently breaks down hard-to-chew connective tissue and releases the food's own juices. Any casserole with a tight-fitting lid is suitable for braising. Stewing is similar to braising, but uses smaller pieces of meat and more liquid.

PRESENTATION

RUN THE TIP AROUND THE EDGE OF THE BROCCOLI MOUSSE MOLD. INVERT ONTO THE CENTER OF A WARMED PLATE. ON MOLD, ARRANGE THE SLICED CHICKEN ON TOP, AND SURROUND WITH THE SAUCE.

CHICKEN

4 boneless, skinless, chicken breasts

3 ounces ground chicken

1 clove garlic, crushed

1/2 teaspoon freshly ground black pepper

1/8 teaspoon ground nutmeg

4 ounces crabmeat

1/4 cup heavy cream

2 cups chicken stock

BROCCOLI MOUSSE

4 ounces cooked broccoli

1/4 teaspoon salt

1/8 teaspoon pepper

2 ounces cream cheese

1 clove garlic, crushed

1 egg white

1 tablespoon heavy cream

SAUCE

2/3 cup chicken stock

2/3 cup heavy cream

2 tablespoons Dijon mustard

1/2 teaspoon garlic, crushed

1/2 teaspoon salt

1/2 teaspoon white pepper

1/4 teaspoon chopped chives

CHICKEN

1. Preheat oven to 375°F.

2. Make a horizontal pocket in the chicken breasts with a sharp knife. Do not cut all the way across.

3. In a bowl, mix the ground chicken, garlic, pepper, nutmeg, crabmeat, and cream.

4. Spoon the stuffing in the chicken pocket. Seal the edges with toothpicks or wrap the breasts in foil.

5. Place the chicken in a shallow ovenproof dish and cover with the chicken stock. Place in a preheated 375°F oven, cover with a lid, and braise (see note on braising) for 20 minutes. Remove chicken from dish and on a rack let cool for 2 minutes before slicing.

BROCCOLI MOUSSE

1. Preheat oven to 350°F.

2. Season broccoli with salt and pepper.

3. Place cheese, broccoli, garlic, and egg white in the bowl of a food processor. Using the pulse function, add the cream slowly.

4. Lightly grease 4 1-cup molds or ramekins. Gently spoon the broccoli mousse into the molds, place in oblong baking pan, and fill pan with hot, but not boiling, water to reach the middle of the molds. Bake in a preheated oven, 20 minutes, or until firm in the center.

SAUCE

1. In a heavy skillet, over medium heat, simmer chicken stock, 10 minutes.

2. Reduce liquid by one-third. Add heavy cream. Simmer, 1 minute, over low heat.

3. Add mustard, garlic, salt, pepper, and chives and simmer, 2 to 3 minutes.

Arbutus Lodge Chicken Hibernia with Leek Pilaf

SERVES 4

Bulgur is a type of cracked wheat. Made of partly debranned, par-boiled wheat, it is generally used whole or cracked. It is a popular product in health-food stores.

Hibernia is the Latin name for Ireland.

PRESENTATION

POUR SAUCE IN THE CENTER OF A WARMED PLATE. PACK A RAMEKIN MOLD WITH THE LEEK PILAF; UNMOLD THE PILAF ONTO THE SAUCE. SLICE THE GRILLED CHICKEN BREASTS AND FAN OVER THE LEEK PILAF. SPRINKLE WITH CHOPPED CHIVES.

GUEST CHEF

**Declan Ryan,
Chef Proprietor,
Arbutus Lodge, Cork**

CHICKEN

4 boneless chicken breasts, skin on

salt and ground pepper, to taste

½ cup sliced shiitake mushrooms, stems removed

2 cups chicken stock

1 tablespoon Irish whiskey

¼ cup heavy cream

1 ounce arrowroot, dissolved in a small amount of cold liquid, optional

chopped chives, for garnish

LEEK RELISH

3 whole leeks, white part only

2 tablespoons butter

3 cloves garlic, crushed

1 cup cracked bulgur

2 cups vegetable stock

½ cup finely diced carrot

½ cup finely diced celery

½ cup finely diced red bell pepper

2 scallions, diced fine

1 teaspoon marjoram

1 tablespoon chopped parsley

CHICKEN

1. Preheat broiler.

2. Season the chicken breasts with salt and pepper. Broil about 3 minutes on each side. Make sure the skin is crispy.

3. In a skillet, over medium heat, cook sliced mushrooms in chicken stock with the whiskey, about 2 minutes.

4. With a slotted spoon, remove mushrooms to a small bowl. Keep warm. Reduce mushroom stock by half.

5. Add cream to mushroom reduction. Further reduce by $\frac{1}{3}$.

6. If necessary, the sauce may thickened with arrowroot. Correct seasoning with salt and pepper. Stir in mushrooms. Remove from heat and keep warm.

LEEK PILAF

1. Wash the leeks carefully. Split in half lengthwise, slice into half rounds.

2. Heat butter in a large saucepan. Add the garlic and leeks and sauté, 3 minutes. Add the bulgur. Mix well.

3. Stir in the stock, diced carrot, celery, red bell pepper, scallions, and marjoram.

4. Cover saucepan tightly and simmer, 40 minutes, or until bulgur is tender and liquid has been absorbed. Fluff with a fork. Mix in parsley.

Venison Sausage with Rutabaga Puree, Red Cabbage, and Apple

SERVES 4

This is an ideal filling and flavor-some meal that most definitely falls into the comfort-food category.

Rutabagas are known as swedes in Ireland. The Rutabagais is a member of the cabbage (brassica) family and is, in fact, a cross between a turnip and a wild cabbage.

PRESENTATION

SPOON THE PUREED RUTABA-GA INTO A PASTRY BAG. PIPE A BORDER AROUND THE INNER EDGE OF A WARMED PLATE. PLACE RED CABBAGE IN THE CENTER. SLICE THE VENISON SAUSAGE LENGTHWISE ON THE BIAS. PLACE ON TOP OF THE RED CABBAGE.

RUTABAGA

1 pound rutabagas, peeled and quartered

4 tablespoons butter, divided

2 cloves garlic, crushed

salt and freshly ground pepper, to taste

RED CABBAGE

1 small head red cabbage

1 small onion, chopped fine

2 teaspoons vegetable oil

$\frac{1}{2}$ teaspoon freshly ground black pepper

$\frac{1}{2}$ cup red wine

2 small baking apples, peeled, cored, and sliced into thin rounds

3 tablespoons honey

$\frac{1}{2}$ teaspoon lemon juice

VENISON SAUSAGE

1 pound ground venison (shoulder or leg)

1 teaspoon each chopped parsley, sage, and chives

1 clove garlic, crushed

$\frac{1}{4}$ cup fresh white breadcrumbs

1 egg, well beaten

1 tablespoon olive oil

salt and ground pepper, to taste

$\frac{1}{2}$ teaspoon of salt

RUTABAGA

1. Peel the rutabaga, chop into large dice. Parboil, 7 minutes, in salted water. Drain thoroughly. Place in a medium saucepan. Sauté rutabaga and garlic gently in 2 tablespoons butter until soft.

2. Puree in a food processor or by hand. Add the remaining butter. *Season to taste.*

RED CABBAGE

1. Quarter the red cabbage. Discard the core and finely shred leaves.

2. In a large saucepan, sauté the onion in vegetable oil until soft. Add cabbage, pepper, and red wine. Simmer, covered, 5 minutes.

3. Place apples into red cabbage. Stir in vinegar, honey, and lemon juice. Continue to cook, covered, 8 minutes, or until apples are tender and liquid is absorbed.

VENISON

1. Mix ground venison, herbs, garlic, and breadcrumbs.

2. Add egg to the venison mixture. Process in a food processor fitted with a steel blade, 10 seconds. Season with salt and pepper.

3. Divide into quarters and roll into sausage lengths.

4. On a skillet, over high heat, fry in olive oil until golden brown.

5. Remove from the pan and dry on paper towels. Keep warm.

Pan-Seared Loin of Venison, Carden's Folly

SERVES 4

There are two basic types of marinades; those that are raw and acid based, and those that are cooked. Each contributes its own special quality to flavoring or tenderizing the food marinated.

The juniper berry is a small blue-black berry of an evergreen shrub common in Ireland. The juniper berry is the principal flavoring agent used in gin.

PRESENTATION

PLACE SPINACH AND TOMATO ON A WARMED SERVING PLATE. ARRANGE VENISON SLICES ON TOP OF SPINACH. DRIZZLE THE SAUCE WITH MUSHROOM, SCALLION, AND HERB GARNISH AROUND.

MARINATION

2 tablespoons olive oil

1/2 onion, finely chopped

1 rib of celery, chopped fine

1 carrot, chopped

5 cloves garlic, crushed

6 juniper berries

6 sage leaves, chopped

4 bay leaves

2 sprigs thyme

1 sprig rosemary, chopped

2 sprigs parsley, roughly chopped

1 cup red wine

2 tablespoons balsamic vinegar

1 teaspoon freshly ground black pepper

VENISON

1 1/2 pounds boneless venison loin, cut in 1/4-inch-thick slices

1 1/2 tablespoon olive oil

8 scallions, white part only, finely diced

3 cloves garlic, crushed

1 1/2 cups oyster mushrooms, sliced thick

3 sprigs thyme, chopped fine

12 sage leaves, chopped fine

10 juniper berries, mashed and marinated in 2 tablespoons gin

1 1/2 tablespoon lemon juice

1 1/2 cups brown sauce or demi-glace

salt and freshly ground pepper

SPINACH

1½ cups spinach leaves, washed and stemmed

4 tablespoons melted butter

¼ teaspoon ground nutmeg

3 cloves garlic, crushed

4 tomatoes peeled, seeded, and cut into large chunks

salt and ground pepper, to taste

MARINATION

1. Heat oil in skillet. Add onion, celery, carrot, garlic, juniper berries, sage, bay leaves, thyme, and rosemary. Sauté until onion is transparent. Add parsley and sauté, 1 minute. Add wine, vinegar, and pepper. Cook until liquid is reduced by half.

2. Remove from heat and set aside to cool. Pour marination liquid over venison. Let stand, covered, in refrigerator, 4 hours.

VENISON

1. Heat olive oil in a heavy-bottomed skillet. Remove venison from marination. Place venison slices on the skillet and, over high heat, sear until browned on both sides. Remove from skillet and set aside. Keep warm.

2. Pour oil from the skillet. Add scallions, garlic, oyster mushrooms, thyme, and sage. Sauté, 10 seconds. Add the juniper berries (with gin) and lemon juice. Increase heat to high and ignite, away from the naked flame. Allow to burn off.

3. Add brown *demi-glace* and cook until reduced by half (about 30 seconds). Correct seasoning.

SPINACH AND TOMATO

1. Immerse spinach leaves in boiling salted water for 30 seconds. Drain. Shock in ice water.

2. Melt butter in a large sauté pan. Add drained spinach leaves, nutmeg, garlic, and tomato chunks. Toss until warm, about 20 seconds.

3. Correct seasoning.

Muckross Park Venison-and-Mushroom Pie with Basil and Jameson Irish Whiskey

Queen Victoria vacationed in the Great Southern Hotel in 1863. The accompanying photograph is taken at the scenic window table at which the venerable Victoria liked to dine during her stay in Killarney.

PRESENTATION

SERVE THE BAKED PIES IMMEDIATELY. PLACE ON A PLATE WITH A NAPKIN UNDERLINER. SERVE WITH IRISH BROWN BREAD AND A SIMPLE SALAD OF SEASONAL GREENS TOSSED IN VINAIGRETTE.

GUEST CHEF

**Paul O' Neill Chef,
Great Southern Hotel, Killarney,
Co. Kerry**

1¼ pounds venison loin, trimmed and cut into 1-inch cubes

1 tablespoon vegetable oil

1 tablespoon all-purpose flour

2 tablespoons Jameson Irish whiskey

1¼ cups beef stock

⅔ cup red wine

⅔ cup button mushrooms

1 tablespoon mild mustard

4 fresh basil leaves, chopped

1 each 8-ounce sheet prepared puff pastry

1 egg mixed with 1 tablespoon of milk

1. Preheat oven to 375°F.

2. In a skillet, over high heat, sear venison in vegetable oil and shallots on all sides. Add flour and reduce heat. Cook, 40 seconds, stirring all the time.

3. Add whiskey and carefully set alight, away from flame. When flame has subsided, stir in stock and red wine. Bring to a boil. Reduce heat and simmer, 3 minutes.

4. Add button mushrooms, mustard, and basil. Simmer, 45 minutes.

5. Place into individual pie dishes.

6. On a lightly floured surface, roll out the puff pastry to ¼-inch thickness. Cover the individual pies. Seal the edges and brush with egg wash.

7. Bake in preheated oven, approximately 10 minutes, until the pastry is fully baked, and is crisp and golden brown on top.

Braised Center Cut of Rabbit with Pearl Onions
in a Broth of Red Lentils

SERVES 1

The humble rabbit was once an important part of the Irish peasant's diet. Although commercially raised rabbit tastes quite good, it is not as flavorsome as the wild variety.

PRESENTATION

MOUND TURNIP PUREE IN THE CENTER OF A WARMED DEEP-DISH PLATE. REMOVE RABBIT FROM THE BRAISING DISH, CARVE, AND ARRANGE OVER TURNIPS. SPOON LENTILS AND COOKING LIQUID AROUND THE TURNIPS, AND PLACE PEARL ONIONS ON TOP OF THE LENTILS.

GUEST CHEF

**Gerard Costello,
Executive Chef, Adage Manor, Co.
Limerick**

RABBIT

1 center cut portion rabbit, trimmed

$1/8$ teaspoon salt

$1/4$ teaspoon ground pepper

1 tablespoon olive oil

$1/2$ cup white wine

1 clove garlic, crushed

$1/4$ teaspoon chopped thyme

1 cup chicken stock

6 pearl onions

TURNIPS

2 medium purple-top turnips, peeled and diced

1 tablespoon butter

LENTILS

1 tablespoon butter

1 shallot, diced fine

2 tablespoons red lentils

1 cup chicken stock

$1/8$ teaspoon finely chopped tarragon

$1/4$ teaspoon finely chopped chervil

$1/4$ teaspoon finely chopped parsley

RABBIT

1. Preheat oven to 350°F.

2. Sprinkle rabbit with salt and pepper. Over high heat, fry the rabbit in olive oil in an ovenproof skillet until the rabbit is browned.

3. Remove rabbit from skillet. Pour off fat. Deglaze with white wine.

4. Return rabbit to skillet. Add garlic, thyme, and chicken stock. Cover and braise in preheated oven, 30 minutes. Add pearl onions 15 minutes into the cooking time.

TURNIPS

1. Boil turnips in salted water, about 20 minutes, or until tender. Drain, dry, and mash. Melt butter.

LENTILS

1. Place butter in a small saucepan. Add shallot. Sauté over medium heat, about 30 seconds, without coloring.

2. Add lentils, cover with chicken stock. Stir and simmer, 12-15 minutes. Stir in tarragon, chervil, and parsley.

Roast Mount Juliet Pheasant with a Potato-and-Parsnip Puree and Apple-and-Grape Sauce

1 whole pheasant, trimmed (about 2 pounds)

2 slices bacon

1 tablespoon melted butter

1 medium all-purpose potato, peeled and cut into chunks

1 medium parsnip, peeled and cut into chunks

½ cup heavy cream

2 tablespoons butter

2 tablespoons diced scallion onion

salt and freshly ground black pepper, to taste

¼ cup apple juice

1 cup brown stock

1 Granny Smith apple, peeled, cored, and diced

¼ cup seedless red grapes

PHEASANT

1. Preheat oven to 425°F.

2. Remove the legs from the pheasant. Insert point of a knife into pheasant where the meaty part of leg meets the breast; slice through skin to hip joint to expose joint. Stick knife directly into the joint and sever leg. Repeat on other side. Trim the legs at the narrow end, and expose the drumstick bone.

3. Remove breast meat in one piece by inserting blade of knife flat along breastbone. Follow contour of the bone with knife, and breast will come away from frame. Repeat on other side. Pull skin from the pheasant breast and discard. Season the breasts with salt and pepper. Wrap the pheasant breasts in the bacon slices.

continued

If desired, pheasant breasts alone may be used in this dish. Many specialty stores stock pheasant. In the United States, pheasant are raised domestically.

Generally, farm-raised pheasants weigh about 1½ pounds and may be roasted whole. However, larger pheasant must have its legs removed and braised separately.

In Ireland, pheasant may only be hunted during the official season.

PRESENTATION

PLACE THE PARSNIP-AND-POTATO PUREE ON A WARMED PLATE. SLICE THE PHEASANT LEGS AND BREASTS AND PLACE ON THE POTATO-AND-PARSNIP PUREE. COAT WITH THE APPLE-AND-GRAPE SAUCE. CRANBERRIES OR RED CURRANTS TOSSED IN IRISH MIST MAY ALSO BE ADDED AS A GARNISH.

GUEST CHEF

Tina Walsh, Co. Kilkenny

4. Over high heat, sear the pheasant breasts and legs on an ovenproof skillet, place the pheasant in the preheated oven for 10 minutes, baste with melted butter and pan juices during the roasting process. Remove and keep warm.

POTATO-AND-PARSNIP PUREE

1. In a 3-quart saucepan, cook potatoes and parsnip until soft, about 20 minutes. Drain, let dry, and mash until smooth.

2. Place cream in a medium saucepan and over medium heat, bring to a boil. Add potato-and-parsnip puree. Add butter and scallion. Season to taste, stirring well.

SAUCE

1. Pour off fat from skillet. Deglaze with stock. Add apple juice and simmer gently over medium heat, 2 minutes.

2. Strain stock into a separate saucepan add cream and reduce to a thick consistency.

3. Add the apple and grapes and heat, 30 seconds.

Vegetable & Potato Dishes

~

A SIMPLE RULE TO REMEMBER WHILE COOKING VEGETABLES IS THAT THOSE GROWN ABOVE

the ground should be started in boiling salted water; those grown below the ground

should be started in cold salted water. The exception to this rule (a very important one

in Ireland) are new potatoes, which should be started in boiling salted water.

An important point: Leaving the peel on washed vegetables and fruits gives a

bonus of fiber and nutrition. Do not add baking soda to the water for green vegetables

like broccoli, spinach, cabbage, or green beans. Baking soda is an alkali and, therefore,

will kill the high concentration of ascorbic acid in those vegetables, which should be

cooked uncovered, and never with acidic ingredients such as lemon juice, vinegar, or wine. Keep blanched vegetables bright and crisp by cooking them *al dente* (to the tooth), draining off the water, and shocking them in ice water. Parboil dense vegetables like carrots, turnips, or parsnips. Parboiling partially cooks the vegetables, so that they will cook at the same pace as other less dense vegetables, such as mushrooms or squash.

In the early nineteenth century, potatoes offered the land-starved Irish peasantry an economic way to produce food that could sustain them all year round on a meager allotment of soil. Part of the potato's attraction for a rapidly expanding Irish population lay in its easy cultivation. This was for a nation of tenant farmers who often had little time to tend their crops.

During the period of the Great Potato Famine of 1845–47, one million Irish people perished from hunger and disease as a result of the failure of the potato crop. Approximately one quarter of Ireland's population emigrated.

Although it carries both blessings and curses for its role in Irish history, the potato still enjoys an honored place in Irish cuisine. The humble spuds also affectionately referred to as murphys or praties are still an important and essential part of the Irish diet. Indeed, most Irish people consider a meal without a potato incomplete.

Generally, most researchers agree that the potato first appeared in South America, but how the potato got to Ireland is a mystery. Many credit Sir Walter Raleigh with its introduction, but historians disagree. There is speculation that the potato arrived accidently as a result of a Spanish ship that foundered off the west coast of Ireland following the ill-fated Armada of 1588.

One way or another, the association of the potato with the Irish diet continues today. Irish cooks make them into soups, pancakes, pastry, and breads. Potatoes continue to appear at both the main meal in an Irish home and on the menus of elegant restaurants.

New potatoes are much anticipated by the Irish. These potatoes are cooked in boiling salted water, and are then served with fresh mint leaves and butter. Natives describe the delectable ideal of the new spuds as balls of flour.

Some of the most popular varieties of potatoes grown in Ireland are Records, Kerrs Pinks, Queens, Golden Wonders, and King Edwards.

Lemon Cauliflower and Broccoli

2 tablespoons canola oil

1 onion, diced fine

1 tablespoon peeled and diced ginger

1 teaspoon salt

3 cups bite-sized pieces cauliflower

3 cups bite-sized pieces broccoli

1 tablespoons lemon juice

1 tablespoon lemon zest, optional

1. Heat oil in a large skillet. Add onions, ginger, and salt. Over medium heat, sauté, 2–3 minutes.

2. Add 1 cup water and cauliflower. Cover, and steam vegetables, 2 minutes.

3. Add broccoli, cover, and steam, 2 minutes.

4. Add lemon juice to vegetables just before serving. Sprinkle with zest, if desired.

SERVES 4–6

Special care should be taken not to overcook this dish.

The dense white flower head gave cauliflower its old English name of coleflower or cabbage flower. Mark Twain dubbed it "cabbage with a college education."

PRESENTATION

SERVE IMMEDIATELY. FINELY CHOPPED CHIVES MAKE A COLORFUL ADDITION.

Pureed Rutabagas with Garlic

A food mill uses a rotary system to push cooked fruits, vegetables, and potatoes against a perforated disc. Like a sieve, it traps skin and seeds, creating a smooth puree—a filtering process food processors can do only with a special attachment, and which blenders can't do at all. The 3-quart is the most popular size food mill.

PRESENTATION

THIS DISH MAY BE SERVED AS AN ACCOMPANIMENT TO MANY ROAST DISHES. THE TURNIPS MAY BE PLACED IN THE CENTER OF THE PLATE WITH SLICED MEATS SERVED OVER IT.

2 pounds rutabagas, peeled and quartered

8 tablespoons butter, divided

8 cloves garlic, peeled

salt and ground pepper, to taste

1. Boil rutabagas 7 minutes, in salted water. Drain.

2. In a medium saucepan, over low heat, cook gently the turnips, garlic cloves in 4 tablespoons butter, until soft.

3. Place in a food mill and puree, or hand mash, with the remaining 4 tablespoons butter. Season to taste.

Minted White Turnips

1½ pounds purple-top white turnips, peeled and quartered

4 tablespoons butter

salt and ground pepper

1 tablespoon chopped fresh mint

1. Preheat oven to 350°F.

2. Boil turnips in salted water until soft, approximately 20–25 minutes.

3. Dry turnips on a sheet pan in preheated oven, 1 minute.

4. In a food processor fitted with a steel blade, blend the turnips to a puree.

5. Place puree in a medium saucepan over medium heat. Stir until all moisture has evaporated.

6. Stir in butter, salt, pepper, and mint. Serve immediately.

SERVES 4

Mint is considered a symbol of hospitality. Mint has been used for centuries in Ireland as an accompaniment to roast lamb, as well as to flavor new potatoes.

Braised White Cabbage

2 slices lean bacon, diced fine

1/4 cup sliced onions

2 pounds white cabbage, shredded into thin strips

1 tablespoon lemon juice

2 tablespoons sugar

salt and freshly ground black pepper, to taste

1. Heat a heavy-bottomed saucepan to high heat and add the diced bacon. Fry the bacon until crisp. Add onions and sauté until tender and slightly browned.

2. Add the cabbage, lemon juice, and sugar. Cover, and cook, 4 minutes, stirring occasionally.

3. Season cabbage with salt and milled peppercorns. Continue cooking until it is an even color and tender, about 6 minutes.

SERVES 5

Onions have a high sugar content; when sautéed, they caramelize and provide a golden color.

Green Beans with Roasted Red Bell Peppers

SERVES 6

The most widely available sweet pepper is the bell pepper, named for its shape. Green bell peppers are the most common, but red, yellow, and even purple bells are available. Most green peppers become red with age; red bell peppers are simply green bells that have been allowed to ripen on the vine. As a result, red bell peppers are sweeter. All bell peppers have a mild flavor and a crisp crunchy texture. Peppers are a rich source of vitamin C, superior even to citrus fruit, and contain as much vitamin A as carrots.

¼ cup finely diced onion

4 cloves garlic, crushed

½ cup chicken stock

1 large red bell pepper, roasted, julienned

1 teaspoon butter

1½ cups green beans, blanched

vegetable oil spray

1 small red bell pepper, julienned

salt and ground pepper, to taste

1. In a medium saucepan, over low heat, slowly cook onion and garlic in chicken stock until the liquid evaporates.

2. In a food processor fitted with a steel blade, puree the onion mixture, roasted bell pepper, and butter, about 30 seconds.

3. In a skillet sprayed with vegetable-oil spray, cook over medium heat the sliced (julienned) bell pepper for 2 minutes.

4. Add the green beans, along with the pureed mixture, to the skillet, sauté until beans are warmed through. Season with salt and pepper to taste.

Creamed Spinach with Garlic

ROASTED GARLIC

2 heads garlic

2 tablespoons olive oil

SPINACH

vegetable-oil spray

1 cup diced celery

1 tablespoon chopped walnuts

3 cups cooked spinach, drained and chopped

⅓ cup fat-free sour cream

1 teaspoon ground nutmeg

salt and freshly ground black pepper, to taste

ROASTED GARLIC

1. Preheat oven to 350°F.

2. Using sharp knife, cut about ½ inch off the top of the garlic heads. Trim roots even with the base of the heads. Remove some papery skin from the outside of the heads, but do not separate the cloves.

3. Arrange in shallow baking dish and drizzle oil evenly over the tops.

4. Bake, 45 to 60 minutes, or until soft, brushing often with oil.

SPINACH

1. In a skillet sprayed with vegetable-oil spray, over low heat, cook the celery and walnuts, 4 minutes.

2. Add the cooked and pressed spinach. Mix well, and warm through.

3. Stir in sour cream and mix well. Carefully warm mixture over low heat. Season with nutmeg, salt, and pepper.

4. Squeeze the garlic cloves to release from skin. Stir into spinach mixture.

As it bakes, garlic becomes sweet and buttery.

Spinach is grown in sand and can be very gritty. Wash well, in several changes of water if necessary, and remove tough stems.

Carrots in Orange Sauce

SERVES 4

Carrots and other root vegetables
have been eaten in Ireland since
prehistoric times. History records
they were part of St. Ciaran's
evening dinner.

½ cup orange juice

1 teaspoon orange zest

1 teaspoon lemon juice

1 teaspoon cornstarch

2 medium carrots, peeled and sliced

½ teaspoon salt

½ teaspoon granulated sugar

1. Place the orange juice in a medium saucepan. Bring to a boil. Add orange zest and lemon juice.

2. Dissolve cornstarch in a tablespoon of cold water. Add to orange juice mixture, stir until sauce thickens.

3. Gently boil carrots in water seasoned with salt and sugar until crisp-tender. Shock in ice water.

4. Mix carrots into sauce. Reheat. Serve hot.

Double-Baked Westmeath Potatoes with Shrimp and Scallions

SERVES 4

Crème fraíche is thinner and richer than sour cream. It has a tart, tangy flavor. Crème fraíche is available in most supermarkets.

4 large baking potatoes

3 tablespoons butter

½ cup finely diced onion

3 cloves garlic, crushed

½ cup finely chopped mushrooms

2 cups of cooked shrimp

3 scallions, chopped fine

salt and freshly ground black pepper, to taste

1 cup dry white vermouth

½ cup crème fraíche

½ cup grated cheddar cheese

1–2 tablespoons heavy cream

1. Preheat oven to 375°F.

2. Wash potatoes and pat dry. Set the potatoes on the middle rack of preheated oven. Bake, about 1 hour, or until potatoes are tender when pierced.

3. Increase oven temperature to 400°F.

4. Let potatoes cool slightly. Slice the top off the potato lengthwise, ½ inch from the top. Carefully, without tearing the skin, scoop out the potato pulp into a bowl. Hand mash the potatoes. Reserve the shells.

5. Melt butter in a small saucepan. Over medium heat, sauté chopped onion and garlic until soft and tender, about 3 minutes. Add mushrooms and sauté, 3 minutes. Stir in chopped shrimp and scallions. Season with salt and pepper, add vermouth, and bring to a boil. Stir frequently over high heat until all liquid has evaporated. Stir in crème fraíche and remove from heat.

6. Combine shrimp mixture with reserved mashed potato and ½ cup cheddar cheese. Correct seasoning. Add heavy cream.

7. Spoon or pipe the potato mixture into reserved skins. Sprinkle additional grated cheese on top. Place on sheet pan.

8. Return potatoes to oven and bake again, until potatoes are hot and cheese begins to bubble.

Parsnip Puree with Sesame Seed

1 pound parsnips, peeled and cut into 2-inch dice

1 tablespoon sesame seeds

1 tablespoon heavy cream

1 tablespoon butter

¼ teaspoon salt

½ teaspoon ground black pepper

1. Preheat oven to 350°F.

2. Place parsnips in cold salted water. Bring to boil and cook, approximately 25 minutes.

3. Drain, place on sheet pan with sesame seeds and dry in preheated oven, 3 minutes.

4. Place butter and parsnips in a food processor fitted with a steel blade. Blend, 30 seconds, until smooth.

SERVES 4

Sesame seeds are native to India. It is one of the world's oldest flavoring agents, and also provides oil.

Moore Street Vegetable Tart

Dublin's Moore Street is home to a colorful open market where a wide variety of vegetables, fruit and fish are sold.

A springform pan is generally used for cheesecake; however, springform pans can also be used for other dense items that need special handling to be unmolded. A clamp releases the sides from the base, ensuring that the item inside can be removed intact.

PRESENTATION

ALLOW TART TO COOL SLIGHTLY BEFORE REMOVING FROM SPRINGFORM PAN. THIS TART IS EQUALLY GOOD SERVED WARM, AT ROOM TEMPERATURE, OR COLD.

vegetable-oil spray

1 sprig fresh thyme

2 cups very thin carrots, slices, blanched

1 cup cooked spinach, pressed to remove excess liquid

2 cups sliced mushrooms

6 cloves garlic, crushed

1 onion, diced fine

1 cup nonfat cottage cheese

2 eggs, beaten

1/3 cup grated Parmesan cheese

1 tablespoon chopped thyme

1 teaspoon chopped oregano

1 teaspoon chopped basil

1–2 teaspoons ground black pepper

salt, to taste

1. Preheat oven to 375°F.

2. Spray a springform pan with vegetable-oil spray.

3. Place sprig of fresh thyme in the center of the pan. Line the bottom of pan with a layer of half the carrots.

4. Place the pressed spinach in a bowl and set aside.

5. Spray a heavy-bottomed skillet with vegetable-oil spray. Over medium heat, sauté mushrooms, 3 cloves garlic, and onion until moisture from mushroom evaporates.

6. Mix mushroom mixture with spinach.

7. In a food processor, blend the remaining 3 cloves garlic, cottage

cheese, eggs, Parmesan cheese, chopped thyme, oregano, basil, and remaining 3 cloves, pepper with a steel blade, 30 seconds.

8. Spoon the mixture on top of carrots and smooth. Cover top with remaining carrots.

9. Spray top with vegetable-oil spray. Bake in preheated oven until tart is semifirm, 30–35 minutes.

Bird Flanagan Potato Pancakes

SERVES 6

Once the ingredients have been combined for this dish, use immediately. Serve the potato pancakes while crisp. These pancakes were developed at Dublin's Gresham Hotel and were featured on the "Bird Flanagan" bar menu.

The "Bird" Flanagan was a celebrated Dublin character who once rode his horse into the lobby bar of Dublin's famous Gresham Hotel and requested a drink for the horse.

2 medium potatoes

1 whole egg

4 slices lean bacon Canadian bacon

1 tablespoon finely diced onion

1 teaspoon chopped parsley

¼ teaspoon ground pepper

2 tablespoons grated cheddar cheese

3 tablespoons vegetable oil

¼ teaspoon salt

1. Peel and grate raw potato; place in a bowl. Beat egg, and add to the potato.

2. Slice the raw lean bacon into thin strips (julienne). Add to the potato along with the diced onion, parsley, pepper, and cheddar. Combine thoroughly.

3. In a crêpe pan, heat oil over medium-high heat. Pour the mix onto the pan. Cook on both sides until golden brown.

Bella Cullen's Colcannon

8 medium all-purpose potatoes

1 head curly kale, chopped fine

1¼ cups milk

6 scallions, diced fine

1 tablespoon chopped parsley

½ teaspoon chopped fresh thyme

8 tablespoons butter, divided

1. Peel potatoes. In a saucepan, cover with cold salted water. Bring to a boil and cook, 20 minutes, or until done. Strain off water. Let potatoes dry, then hand mash.

2. In a 2-quart pot, boil the kale in salted water, until tender, about 25 minutes.

3. In a large saucepan, over low heat, heat the milk with scallions, parsley, and thyme.

4. Strain the chopped kale and add to milk. Simmer, 3 minutes. Add mashed potatoes to kale, stir in 4 tablespoons butter.

5. Mix to a smooth creamy consistency. Correct seasoning.

SERVES 8

My mother, Bella Cullen, would make this dish on Halloween and, in keeping with an ancient Irish custom, would wrap some coins in parchment paper and place them in the colcannon for us children to find.

PRESENTATION

PLACE INTO A SERVING DISH, MAKING A WELL IN THE CENTER. FILL THE WELL GENEROUSLY WITH REMAINING BUTTER AND SERVE.

Traditional Ulster Champ

Champ is a simple, warming Irish dish that is easy to prepare and very filling. There are numerous versions of this traditional Irish dish and, apart from the potatoes, ingredients vary from region to region. Key to the success of champ are the potatoes; they should be thoroughly cooked and allowed to dry before hand mashing or passing them through a food mill. Serve with a generous portion of butter melting on top. Each forkful of potato is dipped into the melting butter as it is eaten.

PRESENTATION

PLACE IN A SERVING DISH, FORMING A MOUND. MAKE A WELL IN THE CENTER AND FILL WITH REMAINING BUT-TER.

1½ pounds potatoes

1 cup milk

8 tablespoons butter, divided

8 scallions, finely chopped

salt and ground pepper, to taste

1. Peel potatoes and roughly cut into chunks. Place in a saucepan and cover with cold salted water.

2. Bring to a boil and simmer, 20–25 minutes, or until soft.

3. Drain and place over low heat for a few minutes to dry out.

4. Combine milk and 4 tablespoons of butter in a small saucepan. Bring to a boil.

5. Place scallions into the boiling mixture. Remove from the heat for a few minutes so that scallions can infuse their flavor.

6. Hand mash potatoes. Stir in milk mixture until smooth. Season with salt and pepper.

Roasted Dublin-Style Potatoes

3 large baking potatoes, peeled, quartered, and dried

oil, for greasing

3 cloves garlic, crushed

1 teaspoons chopped fresh rosemary

2 tablespoons olive oil

salt and ground pepper

1. Preheat oven to 370°F.

2. Quarter each potato into 4 wedges and arrange on greased shallow baking dish.

3. In a small bowl, combine garlic, rosemary, and olive oil and brush over potatoes.

4. Season to taste with salt and pepper. Bake 45 minutes to 1 hour, turning several times, until potatoes are crispy and browned all over. When fully roasted, remove excess fat from potatoes with paper towels prior to serving.

SERVES 4–6

Dublin, the capital city of Ireland, is home to 1 million people. The Gaelic name for Dublin is *Baile Atha Cliath*. The City of Dublin celebrated its millennium in 1988.

Linenhall Boxty

SERVES 4

Boxty is a traditional Irish dish found throughout Ireland. It enjoys its own street rhyme:

Boxty in the pan
Boxty on the griddle
If you don't get boxty
You'll never get a man

4 medium potatoes

1 medium onion, diced fine

1 whole egg

2 tablespoons all-purpose flour

salt and round pepper

2 tablespoons vegetable oil

1. Peel and grate potatoes. In a bowl, mix with onion.

2. Whisk the egg. Add to potatoes, along with flour, salt, and pepper. Mix well.

3. Heat oil in a heavy-bottomed skillet. Over medium heat, drop 2 tablespoon of the mixture onto the oil. Flatten slightly to form a round.

4. Fry until golden brown, turning once, 3–4 minutes per side.

Sligo Glazed Potatoes

SERVES 10–12

This potato dish is an ideal accompaniment to most roasted meat or fowl. It is rich with garlic flavor and, therefore, an ideal accompaniment to roast lamb.

1 cup milk

½ cup cream

2 pounds peeled and thinly sliced potatoes, rinsed well

1 cup cheddar cheese

3 cloves garlic, crushed

½ teaspoon salt

½ teaspoon freshly ground black pepper

1. Preheat oven to 350°F.

2. In a large saucepan, combine milk and cream. Bring to a boil. Add potatoes and simmer, 6 minutes.

3. Remove from heat. Add cheese, garlic, salt, and pepper.

4. Pour mixture into a 8 x 8 inch casserole dish.

5. Bake in preheated oven, 1 to 1½ hours, or until the potatoes are soft and casserole is browned on top.

Donegal Twice-Baked Potatoes

4 large baking potatoes, washed and dried

6 slices bacon, finely chopped (strip or Canadian bacon)

1 small onion, diced fine

½ cup heavy cream

4 tablespoons butter

6 scallions

salt and freshly ground black pepper, to taste

1. Preheat oven to 400°F.

2. Bake potatoes preheated oven on the center rack, approximately 45 minutes, or until is soft when pressed. Cool slightly.

3. In a skillet, over medium heat, fry bacon until crisp. Drain bacon fat from the skillet. Add onion, and sauté over low heat with the bacon until onion softens.

4. Slice ½" from top of each potato. Without tearing the skins, scoop out pulp into a bowl. Hand mash potatoes. Reserve shells.

5. In a saucepan, mix potato and bacon mixture with the cream, butter, and scallions. Warm gently and correct seasoning.

6. Pipe or spoon the mix into potato shells.

7. Place potatoes on a lightly greased sheet pan. Bake, 5 minutes, or until the top is golden brown.

SERVES 4

This dish is convenient because it can be prepared ahead, then rebaked when required, hence its name twice-baked. However, when baked for the second time, the potatoes should be served immediately.

Russet potatoes are the most appropriate for baking. The potatoes for this dish can also be cooked in a microwave oven. They should be pierced and pricked with a fork before cooking. Cook at 100% power (for 6–8 ounce baking potato allow 4–6 minutes). Touch potatoes at the end of cooking time. If they are very hard, cook for 1–2 minutes. Allow to stand 2 minutes before scooping out the flesh.

Breads, Cakes & Desserts

⌘

THE IRISH HAVE ALWAYS BEEN EXPERT BAKERS, SERVING FRESHLY BAKED BREAD AT EVERY

meal. Soda bread and whole-wheat brown bread are the most famous. Almost every

restaurant in Ireland has its own recipe for these breads, and many of these special

recipes are included in this chapter. For the most part, Irish bread making is an out-

growth of traditional griddle cooking, as the oven was late arriving in Ireland.

Indeed, the use of yeast in baking is relatively new to Ireland. Raising agents for

some breads, especially soda bread, was provided by buttermilk and, later on, baking soda.

Although the excellence of Irish baking is primarily associated with her breads, cakes, and

scones enjoy equal popularity and are important components of Irish traditional baking.

Breads can be divided into one of four basic categories: yeast breads, which are leavened with yeast and require kneading to stretch the flour's gluten; batter breads, which are yeast-leavened breads that are beaten instead of kneaded; quick breads, which use baking powder, baking soda, or eggs for leaveners, and require gentle mixing; and unleavened bread, like matzo or pita, which are flat because they have no leavening at all.

An important aspect of baking is the temperature of ingredients; these should be warm (room temperature) in both yeast and quick-bread mixtures. Having ingredients at room temperature prior to use speeds rising and baking times. Additionally, liquids such as milk, beer, and juice, should be at room temperature before adding to the other ingredients. Dry ingredients that have been refrigerated should also be brought to room temperature. This is also true for cake baking.

Liquids used to make bread bring their own characteristics to baking. For example, water creates a crisp crust and brings out the flour's wheat flavor. Potato water (the water in which potatoes have been boiled) adds flavor, and gives bread a smooth crumb. The added starch contained in the potato water also makes the dough rise slightly faster.

Dairy products such as milk, buttermilk, yogurt, and sour cream give bread a creamy beige color and produce a fine texture with a soft, brown crust. Eggs give bread and cakes a rich, moist crumb and a yellow tinge. Fruit and vegetables add flavor and body to bread. White liquid sweeteners such as molasses, honey, and maple syrup give a moist finish to bread. Fruits marinated in tea provide a rich, dark, crisp crust.

Try not to open the oven until the near the end of baking time, but *never* during the first 15 minutes. After this time the door should be opened gently; sudden movement or temperature changes can cause a cake to fall.

In addition to the great cake and bread recipes in this chapter, there are also wonderful easy-to-prepare recipes for a wide variety of desserts. They range from traditional pies and tarts to liqueur-flavored soufflés and mousses, cheesecakes, and bread-and-butter pudding to unusual fruit combinations and sauces. Also included are sorbets and an unusual recipe for brown-bread ice cream.

Flour provides the basic structure of bread, cakes, batters, and pastry. The structure is further dependent upon the type of flour and the raising agent. Bread flour must be aerated by yeast, although brown flour can be leavened by either yeast or baking soda. Bread flour also requires kneading to strengthen the gluten. The soft flour in cakes is raised by the dispersal of air or gas, by baking powder, and/or whisked eggs. Steam is released in oven-cooked batters by whisked eggs. Pastry owes its texture to the plasticity of fat, and steam released by water in the dough, depending on the type of pastry. Soft flours produce a softer, spongier texture—air cannot be beaten into bread flour, but soft flours are easily leavened by thorough beating which introduces air.

Whole-wheat flour: When the entire wheat berry (outer husk or bran; endosperm, containing most of the starch; and embryo) is milled, a brown flour rich in nutrients and protein is produced. In Ireland this flour is known as *wholemeal* flour. The brownness of the flour depends on the amount of bran included, and the amount of milling it receives affects its coarseness.

Cake flour: This is a soft-wheat flour; it has a low-protein, high-starch content. When moistened, it develops weak gluten, so the products made from soft-wheat flours are tender and crumbly. Consequently, soft-wheat flour is preferred for cakes and some pastries.

Bread flour: Also referred to as *strong* or *hard-wheat flour*, it is ground from wheat with a high-protein and low-starch content. The relatively high quantities of gluten make hard-wheat flour preferable for bread baking.

All-purpose flour: This is a blend of hard- and soft-wheat flours. Its medium protein and starch content makes it acceptable for most culinary purposes. All-purpose flour can be successfully used in both cake and bread recipes, although it will not produce the superior product that specialized flour will.

Almost all flours available to the home baker today have been sifted many times before packaging. Sifting does however, aerate flour, giving it greater volume. Because most recipes, especially older ones, are written under the assumption

Sifting Flour

that cooks have sifted the flour before measuring, it is a good idea to do so whenever a recipe calls for sifted flour. Sift, then measure as directed. The aeration provided by sifting is more important with delicate cakes that have little or no chemical leavening. Wherever sifting is not specifically suggested, it may be omitted.

A NOTE ON CAKE BAKING

If cake batter curdles? Each egg was not sufficiently mixed in before the next one was added, or the batter was beaten at too high a speed. If the batter begins to curdle, ignore it, or reduce the mixing machine speed to medium or low speed and add 1 tablespoon of flour per egg.

If cake falls in the middle? The batter was overbeaten, creating excess aeration that the cake was unable to contain. Alternately, too much sugar, baking powder, or liquid was added to the batter; the cake was overcooked; or the oven door was closed with much force.

If cakes peak in the center? A hard (high-gluten) flour was used instead of soft flour (cake flour), the batter was overbeaten after the flour was added, which overactivates the gluten in the flour, creating a tough cake, or the oven was too hot and the cake rose too quickly.

If cake is tough, flat, and heavy? The cake batter was underbeaten, causing insufficient aeration, or not enough sugar or baking powder was added.

Bunratty Brown Treacle Bread

2½ cups whole-wheat flour

½ cup bran

¼ cup all-purpose flour

1 teaspoon sugar

1½ teaspoons baking soda

1 large egg, beaten

2 cups buttermilk

4 tablespoons molasses

1. Preheat oven to 400°F.

2. Sift all dry ingredients into a bowl. Mix.

3. Make a well in the center of the flour. Add egg, buttermilk, and molasses. Knead gently until a slightly wet dough forms.

4. Shape into a round and turn out onto lightly greased and floured baking sheet.

5. Bake in preheated oven, 10 minutes. Reduce temperature to 325°F. Bake, 1½ hours.

6. To test for doneness, turn the bread over and tap underneath. If the bread sounds hollow, it is fully cooked. Allow to cool.

Treacle, known in America as molasses, is a by-product of sugar making. Golden syrup is a clarified residue of molasses.

Cream-and-Honey Whole-Wheat Bread

MAKES 3 LOAVES

Milk and milk products were the essential sources of food in early and medieval Ireland and, to this day, the Irish remain great consumers of milk products. Not surprisingly, many traditional Irish bread recipes include soured milk or buttermilk.

1½ tablespoons dry yeast

½ cup warm water

½ teaspoon honey or sugar

1 cup heavy cream, at room temperature

⅓–½ cup honey, to taste

2 large eggs

2 teaspoons salt

5 cups whole-wheat flour, divided

1. Preheat oven to 350°F.

2. In a large mixing bowl, dissolve yeast in water with the ½ teaspoon honey or sugar, and let stand in a warm environment (105–110°F) until the yeast is activated and frothing.

3. Add cream, honey, eggs, and salt in yeast. Mix well.

4. Add 2 cups of the sifted flour and mix in a standing mixer, 2 minutes. Cover the bowl and let the dough sit in a warm, draft-free area for 1–2 hours, until doubled in bulk.

5. Stir it down; the dough will sink in volume. Gradually add more flour, until the dough pulls away from the sides of the bowl.

6. Turn the dough out onto a floured surface and knead until smooth and elastic, sprinkling with a little more flour if it is too sticky. Expect this dough to remain somewhat clingy, even after it is at the elastic stage. Do not add too much flour or the loaf will become too dry.

7. Place the dough into a buttered bowl and turn over, or brush the top with melted butter. Cover with a damp towel and allow it to rise until doubled in volume.

8. Punch the dough down, and turn it out onto a flat surface. Knead a

few times to press out the air bubbles. Cut in half, cover with the towel and allow to rest, 10–15 minutes.

9. Grease 2 8 x 4 inch loaf pans. Shape the dough into loaves and put in the pans. Brush the tops with melted butter. Cover and allow to rise again until almost double in size.

10. Bake, about 30 minutes, in the preheated oven, until fully baked or until the bottom of the bread sound hollow when tapped. For a tender crust, brush the tops with melted butter when you take them from the oven. Cool on a rack.

King Sitric Brown Bread

3 cups coarse whole-wheat flour

½ cup all-purpose flour

1 teaspoon baking soda

1 teaspoon salt

2 teaspoons sugar

3 cups buttermilk

2 tablespoons melted butter

MAKES 2 LOAVES

The Irish bread *par excellence* is the brown soda, although this variety of bread only appeared in Ireland in the nineteenth century, when bread soda was introduced.

The King Sitric Restaurant's version of brown bread is quite famous; what sets this recipe apart from others is the use of melted butter and the slow bake.

1. Preheat oven to 400°F.

2. Sift and mix the flours, soda, salt, and sugar in a large mixing bowl. Add the buttermilk and mix thoroughly, until all ingredients are moistened.

3. Mix in the melted butter. Turn into a warmed 2 x 8 x 4 inch loaf pans. Cover, and bake, 1 hour in preheated oven. Remove the cover for the last 10 minutes to allow the top of the bread to brown. Aluminum foil can be used to cover these pans; however, place parchment paper between foil and dough. The entire dough may be baked in a large 2-quart casserole dish.

4. When baked, remove from oven and turn the bread onto a rack. Wrap in a clean kitchen towel and allow to cool before slicing.

GUEST CHEF

**Aiden Mc Manus,
Chef/Proprietor, King Sitric
Restaurant, Howth, Co. Dublin**

Traditional Irish Soda Bread

MAKES I LOAF

While there are many variations of Irish soda bread, this one is the most traditional; this recipe has been passed from generation to generation. Irish soda breads containing raisins are a distinct category of their own. In some areas of Ireland this variety is known as Spotted Dog.

Cut in means to mix solid fats, such as shortening or butter, with dry ingredients, such as flour. Pastry blenders, which resemble two curved knives, are used for this purpose. This process cuts the shortening into tiny bits, so that when the pastry or soda bread is placed into a hot oven the fat will melt and, being encased in flour, form pockets. These tiny pockets are what make pastry or soda bread flaky and tender.

4 cups all-purpose flour

1 teaspoon baking powder

1 teaspoon baking soda

1 teaspoon salt

1 teaspoon grated orange zest

2 tablespoons caraway seeds

¼ cup butter, softened

1 cup dried currants

1 to 1¼ cups buttermilk or sour milk, at room temperature

1 egg beaten with 2 tablespoons milk, for glaze

1 teaspoon of honey

1. Preheat oven to 325°F.

2. Generously grease with butter 2 x 8 inch round cake or pie pans.

3. In a large bowl, sift and combine flour, baking powder, and baking soda. Add salt, orange zest, and caraway seeds.

4. Use a pastry cutter or fingers, cut in or blend butter and sugar into flour mixture until the dough resembles coarse crumbs. Stir in the currants. Set aside.

5. In a medium bowl, combine honey with 1¼ cups buttermilk.

6. Stir into flour mixture until dry ingredients are moistened. Turn out onto a floured surface (dough will be sticky).

7. Knead, 1 minute. Cut dough in half. Shape each piece into a round loaf. Place on a greased and flour-dusted baking sheet. Dip a sharp knife into flour and cut across ½ inch deep, across top of each loaf.

8. Brush loaves with egg-and-milk glaze. Let stand for 10 minutes before baking. Bake in preheated oven, 65–75 minutes. To test for doneness, turn the bread over and tap underneath. If the bread sounds hollow, it is fully cooked. Let cool on racks before slicing. Slice thin or cut in wedges.

Killarney Cream Scones

2¼ cups cake flour, sifted

¼ cup sugar

½ teaspoon salt

2 teaspoons baking powder

2 tablespoons unsalted butter, chilled and cut into small pieces

⅓ cup dried currants

grated zest of 1 medium orange

1 cup heavy cream, plus 1 tablespoon for brushing tops

1. Preheat oven to 400°F. Position a rack in the middle of the oven.

2. In a bowl, combine flour, sugar, salt, and baking powder. Stir until well blended. Cut in the butter pieces into the flour and mix until crumbly. Add currants.

3. Combine the orange zest with the cup of cream. Using a spatula, stir the cream into the flour mixture.

4. With floured fingers, knead gently, and form into a soft ball. Transfer to a lightly floured flat surface.

5. Roll the dough into a square (2 inches), approximately to ½ inch thickness. Using a sharp knife, cut the square into 3 strips (about 3 inches). Cut each strip into 5 triangles. Place on a lightly flour-dusted sheet pan. Brush the tops of the scones with the remaining cream.

6. Bake, 20–25 minutes in preheated oven, until golden brown on top.

MAKES 15 SCONES

You can leave Killarney behind you, walk along the road with the grey wall that hides the beauties of Muckross on your right hand, and the moving shoulder of Torc above you on the left, up and up until everything touristed and ticketed is below in the deep valley, until you feel the color of the mountains, soaking into your eyes, your hair, the fragile fabric of skin, until the silence of the high places has seeped into your soul.—BENEDICT KIELY

PRESENTATION

SERVE WARM AT TEA TIME, WITH LEMON CURD OR ORANGE MARMALADE.

Buttermilk Tea Scones

MAKES 18 SCONES

Irish scones are rich cousins of the ordinary American biscuit. Smothered in fresh butter and jam, scones are the ubiquitous accompaniment to Irish tea. They have been part of the Irish afternoon tea for decades.

PRESENTATION

ALLOW TO COOL SLIGHTLY. SERVE WITH BUTTER AND STRAWBERRY JAM.

3½ cups cake flour

4 teaspoons baking powder

½ cup sugar

8 tablespoons butter chilled

3 medium eggs, lightly beaten

⅔ cup buttermilk

½ cup raisins

1. Preheat oven to 425°F.

2. Sift, and mix together, flour, baking powder, and sugar.

3. Cut in butter, knead until the texture resembles breadcrumbs. Reserve 2 tablespoons beaten egg for glazing. Add remaining egg to flour.

4. Add buttermilk and raisins to flour. (Dough will be sticky.)

5. Knead lightly on a flat floured surface. Flatten to ½-inch rectangle.

6. Cut into 18 squares. Separate, and place on a greased flour-dusted sheet pan.

7. Brush with reserved egg and bake in the oven, 30 minutes, or until golden brown.

Soda Farls

1 cup all-purpose flour

1 cup cake flour

2 teaspoons baking soda

1 teaspoon salt

1 cup buttermilk

4 tablespoons butter

1. In a large bowl, mix all dry ingredients. Add the buttermilk and stir.

2. When combined, turn dough out onto a lightly floured surface. Knead gently.

3. Using a rolling pin, roll the dough to a 10–12-inch round. Cut into 6 wedges. Set aside.

4. In a heavy-bottomed skillet, over medium heat, melt butter. Place the soda farls into the butter and cook, for 4–5 minutes on each side, until browned.

MAKES 6 SCONES

Soda farls, native to Ulster, were traditionally cooked on flat iron-griddle pans that were suspended over open-turf fires.

PRESENTATION

WHILE SODA FARLS ARE USUALLY SERVED WITH THE TRADITIONAL IRISH BREAKFAST, THEY MAY ALSO BE SPLIT AND SERVED WARM WITH BUTTER OR JAM.

Paddy Irish-Whiskey Cake

MAKES 1 CAKE

Cream means to beat fat—butter or solid vegetable shortening— and sugar until soft, smooth, and light. This process traps air, which expands in the oven to help create a baked product with more volume. Creaming is especially important for butter cakes, which depend on this step for all their leavening. To incorporate the most air, butter should be at warm room temperature (75–79°F).

Paddy Irish Whiskey is produced in Middleton, County Cork.

PRESENTATION

SERVE WARM WITH WHIPPED HEAVY CREAM AND, OF COURSE, A CUP OF TEA.

1 tablespoon grated orange zest

1 cup golden raisins

4 tablespoon Irish whiskey, preferably Paddy

12 tablespoons butter

3/4 cup sugar

2 medium eggs

2 cups all-purpose flour

1/8 teaspoon salt

3/4 teaspoon baking powder

1. Preheat oven to 350°F.

2. Soak orange zest and raisins in whiskey, 30 minutes.

3. In a medium bowl, cream butter and sugar. Add eggs one at a time and beat well.

4. Sift together flour, salt, and baking powder. Add to egg mixture. Beat well and fold in zest, raisins, and whiskey.

5. Pour into greased 9 x 9 inch square cake pan. Bake, 40 minutes in preheated oven.

Biddy Mulligan's Dublin Cake

½ pound butter

1 cup brown sugar

4 large eggs

2 cups cake flour

½ teaspoon salt

1 teaspoon baking soda

1 teaspoon allspice

¼ cup Guinness stout

2 cups sultanas (golden raisins)

1 cup dried currants

½ cup chopped candied fruits

¼ cup Irish whiskey

1. Preheat oven to 350°F.

2. In a standing mixer fitted with a paddle, cream butter and sugar until light and fluffy.

3. Add eggs, one at a time, with a teaspoon of flour each time. Mix well after each addition.

4. Sift remaining flour with salt, soda, and spice. Fold into egg mixture.

5. Add Guinness stout and stir in fruit and candied fruit.

6. Place in a greased 9-inch round cake pan, lightly greased and lined with parchment paper.

7. Bake in oven, 2 hours. Reduce temperature to 300 F for the last ½ hour.

8. Remove from oven and cool completely. Pierce the cakes with a wooden skewer or a fork. Remove from cake pan and, when fully cooled, pour over the Irish whiskey. Wrap in parchment paper and store in a cool dry area. Let mature for 2 days.

Biddy Mulligan, a Dublin street character, is immortalized in this popular Irish ballad:

You may travel from Clare to the County Kildare, from Dublin back to Macroom.
But no where (sic) you'll find a fine woman like me—Biddy Mulligan the pride of the Coombe.

Dicey Reilly's Apple Cake

SERVES 6–8

This cake gets its name from a famed Dublin street character immortalized in popular ballad:

Poor old Dicey Reilly she has taken to the sup,
Poor old Dicey Reilly she will never give it up.

½ pound unsalted butter

1 cup sugar

4 large eggs

1¼ cups cake flour

1 teaspoon baking powder

3 apples, peeled and sliced thin

2 teaspoons sugar

1½ teaspoons cinnamon

4 tablespoons Irish whiskey, optional

1. Preheat oven to 350°F.

2. In a large bowl, cream butter and sugar until light and fluffy.

3. Add eggs, one at a time, beating well after each addition.

4. Combine flour and baking powder. Fold into egg mixture, combining thoroughly.

5. Pour half the batter into a greased 9–10-inch springform pan.

6. Arrange ⅔ of the apples over batter. Sprinkle with sugar and cinnamon.

7. Cover with remaining batter.

8. Place remaining apples on top of cake and sprinkle with sugar.

9. Bake on the middle of preheated oven, 50 minutes.

10. Remove from oven, let cool and sprinkle with Irish whiskey.

Chocolate Steamed Pudding, Clontarf

9 ounces bittersweet chocolate

¾ cup unsalted butter

6 medium eggs, separated

1 cup sugar, divided

¼ cup all-purpose flour

1. Preheat oven to 325°F.

2. Combine chocolate and butter in upper bowl of a double boiler. Melt slowly over simmering water. When melted, thoroughly combine. Remove from heat.

3. In a standing mixer, beat egg whites at high speed until foamy. Add ½ cup sugar. Continue to beat, until soft peaks form and hold. Remove from mixing bowl and set aside.

4. Place egg yolks into cleaned mixing bowl and beat at high speed, gradually adding remaining sugar. Continue to beat until the mixture triples in volume, the color is light yellow, and all sugar has dissolved. Add the chocolate-butter mixture and beat until thoroughly blended.

5. Add flour and beat at low speed, 10 seconds. While the mixer machine is running, add egg whites. When thoroughly combined, detach the bowl and scrape along the sides and bottom to ensure all the mixture is fully blended.

6. Pour the mixture into a 9 x 1 inch cake pan. Fill to the rim and level the top. Place the cake pan into a deeper dish or roasting pan. Pour boiling water into the deeper pan until it reaches halfway up the cake pan. Cover the deep pan with aluminum foil, allowing 2 inches above the cake pan for rising.

7. Place in preheated oven and bake, 45 minutes. The cake will swell and expand 1–2 inches above the cake pan, and deflate upon cooling.

SERVES 6

This is an old-fashioned method of baking cakes common in Ireland. The results are a dense, rich, and moist cake.

The Battle of Clontarf took place in 1014. This battle marked the end of the Viking wars, dashing their hopes of domination in Ireland. Brian Boru, the High King of Ireland, died at the moment of victory. The loss of such a hero, reputedly slain in his tent while kneeling in a prayer of thanksgiving, was considered a great tragedy.

PRESENTATION

LOOSEN THE CAKE AROUND THE EDGE WITH A KNIFE, AND INVERT ONTO A PLATE FOR SERVING. SERVE WITH VANILLA ICE CREAM AND YOUR FAVORITE CHOCOLATE SAUCE.

Dowling's Irish Mist Iced Soufflé

SERVES 6-8

Irish Mist is a blend of four whiskeys, along with honey, heather, clover, and essences of more than a dozen herbs.

To prepare this dish in a soufflé mold, fold a sheet of parchment paper in half and wrap around the top of an individual soufflé dish, forming a *collar*. Tie securely with string or a rubber band. Freeze the dish for 1 hour before lightly spooning mixture inside. Fill to 1/2 inch above the level of the dish and freeze overnight.

PRESENTATION

PIPE A ROSETTE OF CREAM ON TOP OF EACH SERVING. GARNISH WITH GRATED CHOCOLATE AND MINT LEAVES.

GUEST CHEF

Matt Dowling,
Chef Instructor, CERT, Dublin

5 egg yolks

3/4 cup sugar

2 cups lightly whipped heavy cream

2 tablespoons Irish Mist

8 mint leaves

1/2 cup grated hard chocolate

1. In a standing mixer, fitted with a whisk attachment, whisk the egg yolks at high speed, until they thicken slightly.

2. In a medium saucepan, boil sugar with 2/3 cup water, 4 minutes.

3. Over high speed, in the mixer, slowly pour the warm syrup into the egg mixture. Continue beating until the mixture becomes creamy and cold.

4. Fold whipped cream into the egg yolks.

5. Add the Irish Mist and pour mixture into wine goblets.

6. Freeze immediately, at least 6 hours.

7. Thaw 5 minutes at room temperature before serving.

Banshee Caramelized Pear with Mango Fool

CARAMELIZED PEAR

4 pears

6 tablespoons sugar

1 cup water

4 tablespoons peeled, chopped hazelnuts

1 teaspoon Poire William liqueur

MANGO FOOL

2 tablespoons sugar

½ teaspoon lemon juice

1 large ripe mango

1 cup cream, whipped

BRANDY SNAPS

4 tablespoons butter

6 tablespoons sugar

4 tablespoons honey

1 teaspoon brandy

4 tablespoons all-purpose flour

CARAMELIZED PEARS

1. Peel pears and cut into 8 pieces.

2. Place sugar and ½ cup water in a medium saucepan, heat. Add pears and cook until sugar starts to turn brown. 2–3 minutes.

3. Add ½ cup water and liqueur along with the chopped hazelnuts.

4. Let cool at room temperature.

MANGO FOOL

1. In a medium saucepan over high heat, boil sugar, 2 tablespoons water, and lemon juice until sugar dissolves. Cool completely.

2. Peel mango and puree in a food processor fitted with a steel blade.

continued

The word *banshee* means female spirit. The banshee, according to popular Irish folklore, wasn't just a fairy woman. Her wailing was the harbinger of impending doom. She was featured in traditional stories as a white-clothed figure. The banshee is now often incorporated into ghost stories.

Once considered exotic, mangos are quite common in Ireland, and may be found regularly in the Dublin fruit markets.

PRESENTATION

PLACE 8 SLICES OF PEAR ALONG WITH THE CARAMEL SAUCE AND HAZELNUTS ON ONE SIDE OF EACH PLATE. PLACE SHAPED BRANDY SNAPS ON OTHER SIDE OF PLATE. FILL WITH MANGO FOOL.

GUEST CHEF

Sandra Earl, Chef, Ernie's Restaurant, Dublin

3. Blend sugar syrup with mango puree in food processor.

4. Refrigerate. Fold cold whipped cream into mango mixture.

BRANDY SNAPS

1. Preheat oven to 350°F.

2. In a saucepan, melt butter, sugar and honey. Bring to a boil.

3. Add brandy and flour.

4. Place 4 spoonsful of the mixture onto parchment paper. Smooth out with a spatula.

5. Bake in preheated oven, 4–5 minutes, until golden brown.

6. Let cool briefly. Mold into a cone.

Eugene's Hot Chocolate Tart

$^2/_3$ cup dark chocolate, minimum 70% cocoa content

12 tablespoons unsalted butter

$^1/_4$ cup unsweetened cocoa powder

1 cup sugar, divided

5 medium eggs, separated

confectioners' sugar

1. Preheat oven to 400°F.

2. In upper bowl of a double boiler bowl, melt chocolate with butter and cocoa over hot water bath. Stir until completely combined.

3. In a separate bowl, whisk egg yolks with ½ cup sugar until light and fluffy. Fold into chocolate-and-butter mixture.

4. In a separate bowl, whisk egg whites with remaining sugar until they form firm peaks.

5. Using a spatula, gently fold whites into chocolate, in thirds. Pour into 8 3-inch buttered tartlet molds.

6. Chill, at least 3 hours.

7. Bake, 15 minutes in preheated oven.

8. Cool, 5 minutes.

SERVES 8

Cocoa powder is the crushed residue of the cocoa bean. Cocoa butter is the fat found in cocoa beans; it is used in fine chocolate.

PRESENTATION

TURN OUT TARTLET ONTO PLATE. DUST WITH CONFECTIONERS' SUGAR. SERVE WITH CUSTARD SAUCE AND CHOCOLATE-CHIP ICE CREAM.

GUEST CHEF

Eugene McSweeney, Proprietor, Lacken House Restaurant, Kilkenny

Driscoll's Irish Summer Pudding

SERVES 6

Leaf or sheet gelatin is more commonly used in Ireland. If available substitute 4 leaves of gelatin for the powdered variety. Dissolve them in cold water.

PRESENTATION

TURN OUT PUDDING, SLICE, AND SERVE WITH FRESH FRUIT AND WHIPPED CREAM.

8–10 slices white bread, crusts removed

6 tablespoons sugar

1 teaspoon lemon juice

1 cinnamon stick

½ cup strawberries

½ cup raspberries

½ cup blackberries

1 teaspoon gelatin powder, dissolved in cold water for 5 minutes enough to cover

1 cup heavy cream

1. Cut slices of bread to fit the interior of a deep 1-quart bowl.

2. Boil ½ cup water with sugar, cinnamon, and lemon juice, a few seconds. Divide into three medium saucepans.

3. Place each of the fruits (strawberries, raspberries, and blackberries) separately in each of saucepans. Bring to a boil.

4. Simmer each, approximately 1 minute. Let cool in liquid.

5. Add ⅓ dissolved gelatin to each saucepan.

6. Arrange a layer of fruit alternately with a slice of bread in the pudding dish.

7. Pour the remaining liquid from each pot into the middle and cover with slices of bread. Press down gently with a weight. Let rest, about 12 hours, in the refrigerator.

Colin's Fresh Fruit in a Paper Bag

HAZELNUT COOKIES

½ pound plus 2 tablespoons unsalted butter

2 cups brown sugar

2 eggs

2 teaspoons baking soda

6 tablespoons chopped hazelnuts

1 cup whipped cream, for serving

FRUIT

4 tablespoons butter

1 pear, cored, peeled, and quartered

2 bananas, peeled and halved

2 plums, cut in quarters

8 strawberries

1 orange, segmented, juice reserved

½ melon, peeled, seeded, and quartered

8 sprigs fresh mint

¼ teaspoon honey

4 teaspoons Irish Mist

HAZELNUT COOKIES

1. Preheat oven to 350°F.

2. Cream together butter and sugar.

3. Add eggs, one at a time.

4. Fold in dry baking soda and chopped hazelnuts

5. Drop spoonfuls of the mixture onto a lightly greased sheet pan.

6. Bake in a preheated oven at 350°F for 10 minutes.

SERVES 4

In this recipe, parchment paper is used to encase the delicate fruit, assuring flavor by sealing in the natural juices.

PRESENTATION

PLACE ON HOT PLATE AND CUT OPEN FROM THE TOP. GARNISH WITH FRESH MINT, AND SERVE WITH WHIPPED CREAM AND HAZELNUT COOKIES.

GUEST CHEF

**Colin O'Daly,
Chef, Roly's Bistro, Dublin**

continued

FRUIT

1. Preheat oven to 400°F.

2. Cut 4 sheets parchment paper into 4 x 12 inch circles. Butter edges of paper circles. Divide fruit among the four circles, placing on one side of the circle. Place sprig of mint on top of the fruit.

3. Mix honey, Irish Mist, and orange juice. Sprinkle over the fruit.

4. Fold paper in half, crimping edges.

5. Bake in preheated oven, 5–10 minutes, until well risen. (The parchment paper will puff up.)

Bread-and-Butter Pudding with Bushmills Whiskey Sauce

PUDDING

6 tablespoons sultanas (golden raisins)

8 tablespoons butter, plus additional for greasing

1 pound white bread, sliced

1 cup milk

1 cup cream

1 vanilla bean

3/4 cup sugar

3 eggs, beaten

WHISKEY SAUCE

1 cup cold milk

3 tablespoons sugar

2 egg yolks

1/4 cup Bushmills whiskey

PUDDING

1. Preheat oven to 350°F.

2. Soak sultanas in hot water, 10 minutes. Drain.

3. Butter the bread. Remove crusts and cut into triangles. Arrange in a greased deep dish, (6 x 6 x 2 inch casserole dish).

4. In a saucepan, bring milk, cream, vanilla bean, and sugar to just below a boil. Remove the vanilla bean. Add milk mixture to the eggs.

5. Through a strainer, pour the egg and milk mixture onto the bread. Leave to soak.

6. Cover with aluminum foil and cook in a water bath in preheated oven, approximately 55 minutes. Remove foil and bake, 5 minutes to allow top to crisp.

Bushmills, located on the dramatic northern coast of Ireland in scenic County Antrim, is the world's oldest distillery. Bushmills was granted its license to distill in 1608. It is often described as Ulster's Glory.

Irish whiskey is made using the pot still method. This involves the familiar copper coil or *worm*. Copper is the only metal known not to leave its taste on the final product.

In Ireland, *whiskey* is spelled with an e before the y, while in Scotland, it is spelled *whisky*.

continued

WHISKEY SAUCE

1. Boil milk, remove from heat.

2. In a separate saucepan, mix sugar and egg yolks.

3. Add egg mixture to milk and return to heat. Cook gently over low heat, stirring constantly, until sauce thickens slightly.

4. Add whiskey.

Orange-and-Irish-Mist-Flavored Strawberries with Sabayon

SERVES 4

The sabayon may be served alone or as a sauce or a topping. *Zabaglione* is Italian for sabayon.

PRESENTATION

SPOON *SABAYON* EVENLY ONTO 4 INDIVIDUAL SERVING DISHES. ARRANGE STRAWBERRIES, STEM SIDE DOWN, IN THE CENTER OF EACH DISH. PLACE UNDER BROILER, 3 MINUTES, OR UNTIL THE STRAWBERRIES ARE LIGHTLY BROWNED. DECORATE WITH JULIENNE OF ORANGE ZEST AND MINT LEAVES.

FRUIT
2 pints strawberries, hulled
2 tablespoons Irish Mist
2 oranges
10 leaves fresh mint, for garnish

SABAYON
4 egg yolks
¼ cup sugar
¼ cup Marsala
½ cup heavy cream

FRUIT

1. Place strawberries in a bowl, toss gently in Irish Mist.

2. Peel oranges and cut zest into julienne strips. Set strips aside.

3. Cut oranges in half, squeeze over strawberries. Refrigerate strawberries.

SABAYON

1. In upper bowl of a double boiler, beat egg yolks, sugar, and Marsala over simmering water. Beating until mixture thickens and triples in volume.

2. Remove from heat. Continue beating until mixture is cool.

3. Whisk heavy cream in separate bowl to peak stage.

4. Fold whipped cream into the cooled egg mixture.

Apple Charlotte with Custard Sauce

APPLE CHARLOTTE

1 pound bread, sliced ½ inch thick, crusts removed

8 tablespoons butter

1 pound Granny Smith apples, peeled, cored, and sliced thick

¼ cup sugar

1 teaspoon cinnamon

¼ cup fresh white breadcrumbs

confectioners' sugar, for serving

CUSTARD SAUCE

3 egg yolks

2 tablespoons sugar

2–3 drops vanilla extract or 1 vanilla bean

1½ cups milk

APPLE CHARLOTTE

1. Preheat oven to 425°F.

2. Using a cookie cutter cut enough circles of bread to fit the base and the top of the mold. Use either a charlotte mold, a deep ovenproof dish, or 4 dariole molds.

3. Cut the remaining bread slices into 1-inch fingers. Butter mold and place circle of bread onto base. Overlap bread fingers around edges, making sure not to leave any gaps.

4. In a medium saucepan, over medium heat, melt butter.

5. Add apples, cinnamon, and sugar to butter.

6. Cover. Simmer over moderate heat until apples soften.

7. Add breadcrumbs to apples. Remove from heat and set aside.

8. Fill the molds with cooked apples. Cover with remaining bread.

9. Bake in preheated oven, 30–40 minutes.

continued

SERVES 4

The original Apple Charlotte was created during the eighteenth century, and named for the wife of King George of England. It consisted of an apple compote baked in a round mold, lined with toast slices. Later, this dish found its way to Ireland, and was often featured on the menus of the Irish aristocracy.

All custards require slow cooking and gentle heat in order to prevent curdling. Don't try to hurry stirred custards by raising the heat. Most custards take at least 10 minutes to cook. Custard sauce is also called *English sauce* in Ireland.

PRESENTATION

UNMOLD THE APPLE CHARLOTTE VERY CAREFULLY ONTO A SERVING PLATTER. CUT INTO 4 PORTIONS. POUR CUSTARD SAUCE ONTO A WARMED SERVING PLATE. PLACE A WEDGE OF APPLE CHARLOTTE ON TOP. DUST WITH CONFECTIONERS' SUGAR.

CUSTARD SAUCE

1. Mix egg yolks, sugar, and vanilla extract in a bowl (if using a vanilla pot, add to milk).

2. In a medium heavy-bottomed saucepan, over medium heat, bring milk to a boil. Add to egg mixture, whisking constantly.

3. Return the egg-and-milk mixture to the saucepan. Cook slowly over low heat (8–10 minutes) stirring constantly. Do not boil. Sauce is cooked when it coats the back of a spoon. Remove vanilla bean, if used.

Bailey's Irish Cream Caramel

SERVES 5

Cream caramel, also known as *crème caramel,* is a custard baked over a layer of caramelized sugar, then inverted to service. What makes this recipe different is the addition of Bailey's. The sweetness and flavor of Bailey's Irish Cream make it appropriate for many desserts.

PRESENTATION

UNMOLD THE CREAM CARAMEL ONTO A CHILLED DESSERT PLATE, INCLUDING THE CARAMEL SAUCE. PIPE A ROSETTE OF CREAM ON TOP OF EACH CREAM CARAMEL, AND TOP WITH A CHERRY.

CREAM CARAMEL

$1\frac{1}{2}$ cups milk

$\frac{1}{2}$ cup heavy cream

4 eggs

6 tablespoons sugar

$\frac{1}{8}$ teaspoon salt

3 tablespoons Bailey's Irish Cream Liqueur

$\frac{1}{2}$ cup whipped cream, for serving

5 cherries, for garnish

$\frac{1}{8}$ teaspoon of vanilla essence

2-3 drops vanilla extract / 1 vanilla pod

CARAMEL SAUCE

$\frac{1}{2}$ cup sugar

Cream caramel

1. In a heavy-bottomed saucepan, over medium heat, bring the milk and cream and vanilla to boil.

2. In a separate bowl, beat the eggs. Add sugar and salt. Mix thoroughly.

3. Add the hot milk to the egg mixture, stirring constantly. Add the Bailey's Irish Cream.

CARAMEL SAUCE

1. Preheat oven to 350°F.

2. Boil sugar with ½ cup water. Simmer until the mixture is golden brown. Add ½ cup water, taking care not to get splashed with hot liquid. Incorporate water to form smooth caramel by rotating pot over moderate heat. Pour immediately into 5 individual molds.

3. Pour custard into molds. Place in a deep pan. Place pan in the oven, then pour boiling water halfway up the sides of mold.

4. Bake in preheated oven, 30–45 minutes, or until the center of the custard is no longer liquid.

5. Remove from oven. Let cool and refrigerate.

Tipsy Pudding with Mulled Wine

TIPSY PUDDING
butter, for greasing ramekins

3/4 cup fresh white fine breadcrumbs

4 eggs, separated

12 tablespoons granulated sugar, divided

grated zest of 1 lemon

MULLED WINE
3 cups red wine

juice and zest of 1 lemon

juice and zest of 1 orange

1/2 cup sugar

1 cinnamon stick

4 cloves

TIPSY PUDDING

1. Preheat oven to 350°F.

2. Sprinkle 8 buttered ramekin molds with 2 tablespoons breadcrumbs (total).

3. In a bowl, beat the egg yolks with 6 tablespoons sugar and lemon zest, until the mix becomes frothy.

4. In a separate bowl, whisk egg whites until stiff, gradually adding remaining sugar.

5. Fold a quarter of the egg white mixture into the yolk mixture. Gently combine.

6. Fold remaining breadcrumbs and egg whites into egg-yolk mixture.

7. Fill molds and bake in preheated oven, 25 minutes.

MULLED WINE

1. In a medium saucepan, over high heat, bring all ingredients to a boil. Stir to dissolve sugar. Allow to mull for a few minutes before pouring over the puddings.

2. Remove cinnamon stick and cloves.

Individual Cinnamon-and-Raisin Apple Pie with a Mint Custard

PASTRY

1 cup cake flour

8 tablespoons margarine, plus additional for greasing

2 ounces sugar

1 egg, beaten

1 egg beaten with 1 tablespoon of milk, for egg wash

1 tablespoon confectioners' sugar, for serving

APPLE FILLING

1 pound tart apples

2 tablespoons butter

¼ cup sugar

¼ teaspoon cinnamon

1 tablespoon raisins

MINT CUSTARD

3 ounces sugar

5 egg yolks

1 cup milk

1 cup cream

1 teaspoon chopped fresh mint

GARNISH

Blackberries, blueberries, physalis, strawberries, nectarine

Melted chocolate, for decorating plate

PASTRY

1. Sift flour into a bowl. Cut in the margarine until it crumbles. Add sugar and egg. Add a little cold water to the pastry until it forms a moist paste. Let stand, 30 minutes, before using.

2. On a lightly floured surface, roll out the pastry to ¼-inch thickness.

continued

SERVES 4

Physalis are also known as *cape gooseberries.* These rather unusual fruits are each surrounded by a beige, ballooning, parchmentlike husk called a *calyx.* The seedy yellow berry inside is about the size of a cherry, and has a sweet orange flavor, but with more acidity.

To keep apples from browning, toss in lemon juice or grapefruit juice, or dip in 1 quart cold water mixed with 3 tablespoons lemon juice. Choose well-colored apples with a fresh, not musty, fragrance. The skins should be tight, smooth, and free of bruises and punctures.

PRESENTATION

USING MELTED CHOCOLATE, PIPE A LARGE APPLE OUTLINE ONTO A LARGE PLATE. POUR THE COOLED MINT-CUSTARD SAUCE INTO THE APPLE OUTLINE. LAY THE APPLE TART ON TOP AND GARNISH WITH THE FRUITS. STRAWBERRY JAM MAY BE PIPED INTO THE TOP OF THE APPLE FOR ADDED COLOR.

Place into lightly greased individual 3-inch tartlet molds. Cut 3-inch pastry tops for the tartlet molds. Set aside.

APPLE FILLING

1. Preheat oven to 350°F.

2. Peel and core the apples. Cut into wedges.

3. Melt butter in a medium saucepan over low heat. Add sugar, cinnamon, raisins, and apples. Sauté, 2 minutes.

4. Place apple filling into the tartlet shells. Cover with the pastry tops. Seal the edges and brush with egg wash.

5. Bake in preheated oven, approximately 20 minutes, or until fully baked.

6. Let cool. Dust with confectioners' sugar.

MINT CUSTARD

1. In top bowl of a double boiler, combine sugar and egg yolks over simmering water. Whisk until slightly thickened.

2. In a separate saucepan, bring milk and cream to a boil.

3. Add milk and cream to the egg yolks slowly, over a period of 3 minutes, whisking constantly.

4. When cooked and thickened, add mint.

Ardtara's Toasted Oatmeal and Bushmills Whiskey Pudding

Oatmeal is made from ground or rolled oats, after the grain has been cleaned and the husks removed. Oats thrive in cool, high altitudes, where they invade and supplant wheat. Oats are one of the earliest cultivated grains in Ireland; they were an important food in pre-potato-dependent Ireland.

PRESENTATION

DUST THE PUDDINGS WITH CONFECTIONERS' SUGAR. CLEAN SIDES OF THE BOWLS AND PLACE UNDER HOT BROILER UNTIL PUDDINGS BROWN SLIGHTLY. PLACE ON INDIVIDUAL PLATES; WITH A RAMEKIN OF BERRIES ON THE SIDE.

GUEST CHEF

Patrick Mc Larnon, Chef, Ardtara House Hotel, Upperlands, Co Derry.

1 ounce oatmeal

1 tablespoon Bushmills Whiskey

5 egg yolks

½ cup sugar

1 pint cream

¼ cup confectioners' sugar, for serving

8 ounces hulled strawberries, raspberries, or other seasonal berries, for garnish

1. Preheat oven to 375°F.

2. Place oatmeal in a shallow ovenproof dish. Bake until color turns brown and oatmeal smells nutty. Remove from oven and pour whiskey over oatmeal. The heat should evaporate the alcohol.

3. Reduce oven temperature to 325°F.

4. Place egg yolks into a bowl. Stir in sugar until dissolved.

5. Add cream and oatmeal.

6. Divide mixture evenly between four ovenproof serving dishes.

7. Place the ramekins in a deep pan and add enough warm water to come halfway up sides of the dishes. Place in the oven and bake, approximately 45 minutes, until the pudding has set.

8. Remove from the oven. Let cool. Remove the bowls from the pan, cover with plastic wrap, and refrigerate before serving.

Blackberry and Apple Tartlet with Rose-Scented Creamed Rice

PASTRY

8 tablespoons butter, softened

1/4 cup confectioners' sugar

1 egg yolk

2/3 cup cake flour, sifted

FILLING

2 medium apples, peeled cored and cut into wedges

2 ounces sugar

1 1/2 pounds blackberries

ROSE-SCENTED CREAMED RICE

2 cups arborio rice

4 cups milk

2 cups rosewater

1 cup cream

1/4 cup sugar

PASTRY

1. Preheat oven to 350°F.

2. Place butter into a bowl and with a spatula, blend in sugar.

3. Add egg yolk and mix lightly.

4. Add flour to egg yolk, butter, and sugar mixture. Beat lightly until mixture comes together. Take care not to overwork it.

5. Roll the pastry into a ball and pat gently. Wrap in plastic wrap and refrigerate, 2 hours.

6. Divide the pastry into 8 even pieces. On a lightly floured surface roll out pastry to 1/4-inch thickness. Line 8 4-inch individual pastry pans with the

continued

SERVES 8

Choose plump, glossy, deep-colored berries without hulls. If the hulls are still attached, the berries are immature and were picked too early–they will be tart. Fresh blackberries can be refrigerated for up to two days. Blackberries have lots of seeds, which you may want to strain out of sauces. One pint of blackberries yields 1 1/2 to 2 cups berries.

In Ireland, short grained rice is generally called *pearl* rice. In the United States, it is commonly referred to as *arborio* rice.

PRESENTATION

PLACE TARTLET IN CENTER OF PLATE. SHAPE THE RICE IN A ROUND RAMEKIN MOLD. UNMOLD RICE TO ONE SIDE OF THE TARTLET. GARNISH WITH A LITTLE SYRUP WITH CREAM AND CANDIED ORANGE WITH A LEAF OF MINT.

GUEST CHEF

Patrick McLarnon Chef, Ardtara House Hotel, Upperlands, Co. Derry

pastry. Trim off any excess. Cover each with parchment paper, and fill with baking beans or rice. Chill, 20 minutes.

7. Bake tartlets in preheated oven, 10 minutes. Remove parchment paper and beans and bake, 5–7 minutes, until light golden brown.

8. Remove from oven. Let cool.

FILLING

1. Place apple, sugar, and 1 tablespoon water into shallow saucepan. Simmer gently.

2. When apples are semi-soft, add blackberries. Simmer until soft.

3. Place a sieve over a bowl. Pour in apples and berries. Strain.

4. Return juices to pan and reduce to syrup.

5. Combine fruit and syrup in a bowl.

ROSE-SCENTED CREAMED RICE

1. Wash rice. Place in a saucepan with the liquids and sugar.

2. Bring to a boil. Simmer gently, 30 minutes, stirring frequently.

Irish Coffee

Alex Levine humorously observed that only Irish coffee provides in a single glass all four essential food groups—alcohol, caffeine, sugar, and fat.

When serving the finished Irish coffee, a teaspoon should not be provided, as the coffee is best sipped through the cream while it is still floating on top of the coffee.

In many countries, coffee is the most popular hot beverage. It is prepared in various forms, from the simplest to the complex. A variety of tastes and flavors are added to coffee according to national, regional, or local tastes. The most popular specialty coffee (those flavored especially with alcohol) in the world is Irish (or Gaelic Coffee). This method of serving coffee was popularized in the early 1940s in Ireland's Shannon Airport.

As World War II was drawing to a close, civilian air travel began to increase. Shannon Airport, located on Ireland's west coast, was strategically located to be an important part of this expanded method of travel. As with most airports in those years, airline arrivals and departures were not always on schedule. Passengers were sometimes delayed, so extra meals, snacks, or beverages had to be made available for these travelers. By far the most popular of these offerings was Irish coffee.

Irish coffee, well made, consists of hot strong black coffee, sugar to taste, with a measure of Irish whiskey, all topped with cold, fresh, heavy cream.

1. **Coffee.** Your favorite brand is perfectly adequate; but freshly ground, freshly made coffee will produce the best results. Use 5–6 ounces per glass. Make coffee 25 percent stronger than usual.

2. **Sugar.** Traditionally, Demerara brown sugar has been served with Irish coffee. Any type of sugar will suffice, but Irish brown sugar is best. Originally, 2 teaspoons were used in each glass, and many believe this is essential but, if the other ingredients, particularly the cream are of sufficient quality, Irish coffee can be made without sugar.

3. **Cream.** Ireland is a producer of first-class dairy products. Top-grade heavy cream should be used. It should not be whipped. Approximately $\frac{1}{4}$ cup per glass should be poured over the back of a spoon, and gently floated on top of the hot coffee. This has best effect if the cream is cool, straight from the refrigerator.

4. **Whiskey.** Only real Irish whiskey, made in Ireland, should be used. Other whiskeys taste the same. The main brands of Irish whiskey are Jameson, Paddy, Power, and Tullamore Dew. A small (Irish) measure should be used per portion.

Basic Preparations, Stocks & Sauces

GOOD STOCK IS THE MOST IMPORTANT LIQUID USED IN THE PREPARATION OF MANY

recipes, including soups, sauces, stews, and braised dishes. Stocks and sauces are the

foundations of all great cooking and, when correctly made using fresh ingredients,

good stock will enhance the quality of any dish. Conversely, poorly prepared stock

made from inferior ingredients will ruin a dish. While the quality of stock cubes or

soup-base mixes may be very good, nothing surpasses the freshly made variety.

Good stocks are also economical to produce, as their ingredients (such as bones

and vegetables) are generally by-products of other preparations, or may be purchased

cheaply. In this chapter five basic types of stocks are described: chicken, veal, beef, vegetable, and fish stock. The principle elements in producing a quality stock are meat and bone; fish bones and trimmings; vegetables; aromatics; spices and herbs; and water, wine, or consomme. In most cases, salt should not be used in stock (in small amounts salt can serve to extract proteins from fish and meat, giving the final sauce or soup shine and flavor because it becomes too concentrated as the stock reduces).

Always begin with cold liquid when making stock. Hot liquid has a tendency to seal the flavor-releasing capabilities of the ingredients. Stocks must be skimmed regularly during the simmering process; fat and scum should be skimmed off as it rises to the surface. If not skimmed, regularly stocks become cloudy and bitter.

In preparing stock, timing is critical. Some think that the longer a stock is simmered, the greater its flavor. While it is true that certain stocks, once cooked and strained, are further reduced to concentrate flavor, initial cooking times, if not strictly observed, can ruin a stock. For example, if fish stock is cooked beyond the initial 20 minutes, it becomes bitter. When, instead, it is strained and reduced, the flavor is much improved.

This chapter includes sauces that are most used in Irish cooking, and are also easy to prepare; they are also the mother sauces from which other sauces throughout this book are made.

Contrary to what most people believe, the word *sauce* does not always imply a thickened flavored liquid; sauces may be thick or thin. The thickening agents most commonly used are *roux*, cornstarch, egg yolks, or puree. Sauces should have a definite recognizable consistency or body, and should coat food. They should not be runny or watery.

GENERAL GUIDELINES FOR SAUCE

Delicate and light colored foods are usually served with the lighter sauces, made with light stock, wine, milk, or cream. Darker meats, such as beef and game, are complemented by brown sauces.

The process of boiling down stocks or sauces is called as *reduction*.

Reduction is very important, because, it helps develop a velvety and delicate texture, and gives each ingredient in the saucepan an opportunity to release its flavor. The finished sauce should have a well-blended flavor, the product of a mixture that has been slowly reduced and concentrated.

Regardless of the liquid used, sauce is always improved by the addition of roasting juices, or the brown bits left in the pan in which meat was sautéed. Both are ways of carrying the flavor of a food into its sauce and, in many instances, form the best sauces.

It is not necessary to use vintage wine in sauce making. The choice of a suitable wine depends upon how it is going to be used. If, for example, it is to be reduced to almost nothing in the pan with shallots, it can be a less expensive wine. On the other hand, if the recipe calls for reduction by half, you should use a better wine. Sometimes fortified wines such as sherry or Madeira are added just before serving.

It is very easy to oversalt a sauce, so, only correct the seasoning near the end. (Most of the recipes in this book ground milled peppercorns; the flavor of freshly milled peppercorns is much fuller and richer.) Onions can be substituted for shallots, even though shallots have a better flavor. Shallots, butter, and wine are a combination of an unusual savoriness.

Roux: The most common method of thickening a sauce is with a *roux*. A roux is a carefully cooked mixture of equal amounts of fat and flour. Usually butter is used. There are three types of roux: blanc, blond, and brown, that is, white, golden, or brown. The longer the mixture cooks the darker it gets. Obviously a white roux is for the whiter sauces, a brown for the dark. Roux should be cooked over low heat, so that the starch grains can expand, and should be stirred constantly. Rapid cooking shrivels the starch grain and produces a grainy, less smooth sauce. Neglecting to stir results in uneven cooking and, in the case of a brown roux, produces a spotty browning, often with burned specks which affect flavor, texture, and appearance. A shortcut to a darker, more richly flavored roux is to cook the flour, stirring often, in a dry skillet or saucepan over medium heat until well browned. Add the fat and cook, 3–4 more minutes.

A sauce thickened with a roux is started by melting the butter, adding the flour, and cooking the two together. The liquid, which should be hot, is then added. As cooking continues, the mixture must be stirred constantly until it thickens. After frequent stirring, during slow, gentle cooking, the sauce reduces to the proper thickness.

Beurre manie: *Beurre manie,* an uncooked paste of equal amounts of butter and flour, is used to build up sauces that are too thin. To make beurre manie, knead butter and flour together with fingers, or mash with a fork or spoon. For soup, use 1 tablespoon flour and 1 tablespoon butter. For sauce, use 2 tablespoons flour and 2 tablespoons butter to thicken 1 cup liquid.

Purees: These are generally vegetable purees, used in place of roux. They provide a unique taste. Vegetable purees add bulk, so that another thickener is usually not required. However, cream is often added to a vegetable-puree-based soup for added richness. Vegetables suitable for pureeing and adding to soups include beans, tomato, carrot, cucumber, potato, and leek. The quantity of puree needed to thicken a soup varies with the vegetable; add in small amounts until the desired consistency is reached.

Egg yolks and cream: When combined, egg yolks and cream act as both thickener and enrichment. For a prepared sauce that is already thick, mix 1 egg with 2–3 tablespoons whipping cream per 1 cup sauce. If the sauce is quite thin, 2–3 yolks may be needed to thicken sufficiently. Pour a little of the hot sauce into the combined yolk and cream, and whisk to blend. Pour this mixture back into the sauce and gently heat. Do not allow it to boil, or it will curdle. To thicken 6 cups of soup, use 2 egg yolks and ¼ cup heavy cream.

Cornstarch: A sauce thickened with cornstarch is glossy and translucent. Cornstarch is often used to thicken dessert sauces and glazes. To avoid lumping, always add cornstarch mixed with liquid, in paste form. To thicken 1 cup liquid, mix 1 tablespoon cornstarch with 2 tablespoons water.

Fish Stock

4 tablespoons of butter

½ cup sliced onions

½ cup sliced leeks

¼ cup sliced celery

1 sprig parsley

1 bay leaf

4 white peppercorns

3 pounds fish bones, rinsed

juice of 1 lemon

1 cup white wine

1. Heat butter in a 2-quart saucepan.

2. Place onion, leek, celery, parsley, and bay leaf in pan and cook, over low heat, without browning. Approximately 2–3 minutes.

3. Lay fish bones on top. Add lemon juice and white wine.

4. Cover surface with parchment paper. Sweat until wine is almost evaporated.

5. Remove paper. Cover bones with cold water.

6. Bring to a simmer. Cook no longer than 20 minutes.

7. Strain stock through a sieve. Cool and refrigerate.

MAKES 2 QUARTS

Generally, all stocks should be cooled as quickly as possible. The most common method for chilling stock is to place the strained stock in a clean metal container and place it in an ice bath to speed chill. The stock can then be divided into appropriate containers and frozen for later use.

The bones of white fish are the most suitable for stock. It is important to wash and remove the gills from fish prior to making stock. The flavor of this fish stock is not improved by longer cooking.

To sweat means to cook food in a pan (usually covered) without browning, over low heat until the food softens and releases moisture. Sweating allows the food to release flavor more quickly when cooked with other foods.

Chicken Stock

Chicken bones can be saved and placed in the freezer until needed.

The principle stock seasonings are peppercorns, bay leaves, thyme, and parsley stems, and, optionally, garlic. These seasonings generally can be left whole. A stock (other than fish stock) is cooked long enough for all its flavors to be extracted.

To defat stock, place ice in a strainer and pour the warm stock over the ice. Any fat still present in the stock will adhere to the ice as it passes through.

4 pounds chicken bones

½ cup diced onions

¼ cup diced celery

¼ cup diced carrots

¼ cup diced leeks

1 bay leaf

2 teaspoons black peppercorns

1 sprig parsley

1 sprig thyme

1. Chop the chicken bones into small pieces with a heavy knife.

2. Place in a 3-quart stock pot and cover with 3 quarts cold water.

3. Bring to a simmer; do not boil.

4. Skim fat and protein matter from top of stock as it rises to the surface.

5. Add vegetables, herbs, and seasonings.

6. Simmer, 2–4 hours.

7. Strain. Cool and refrigerate.

Vegetable Stock

2 medium carrots, chopped

5 medium onions, chopped

1 bulb fennel, chopped

2 medium leeks, chopped

1 rib celery, chopped

4 tablespoons butter

6 cloves garlic, crushed

8 peppercorns, coarsely ground or crushed

6 tablespoons roughly chopped fresh herbs (parsley, thyme, chervil, rosemary, and sage), or 2 tablespoons dried herbs

1. Cook vegetables in a stock pot in butter with peppercorns and garlic, 3 minutes, stirring constantly. Do not brown.

2. Cover with 3 quarts cold water and bring to a boil.

3. Reduce to a simmer, skim, and cook, 30 minutes.

4. Add herbs and simmer, 1 further minute.

5. Strain. Cool and refrigerate or freeze.

MAKES 3 QUARTS

This simple-to-make vegetable stock is an excellent base for soups and sauces, and also for poaching fish and vegetables.

If salt is added to stock when reduced or extended, it concentrates the salt.

Beef Stock (Brown Stock)

MAKES 4 QUARTS

A *mirepoix* is a coarsely chopped mixture of onions, carrots, leeks, and celery used to flavor stocks and stews and other foods. Generally, it is a mixture of 40 percent onions and 20 percent each of leeks, celery, and carrots by weight.

The principle steps in producing a quality beef stock are: start with a cold liquid, skim carefully and simmer, do not boil vigorously. Cloudy stock is normally the result of stock being boiled too long and fast over high heat.

4 pounds beef bones (shin bones are best)

1½ pounds mirepoix (roughly chopped vegetables, including onions, celery, carrots, and leeks)

1 bunch tied mixed herbs: sprigs of thyme, parsley, bay leaf, and peppercorns tied together in cheesecloth

6 cloves chopped garlic

½ cup mushroom trimmings

2 cups tomatoes, diced, peeled, and seeded

1 bottle dry red wine

bouquet garni (peppercorns, bay leaf, thyme, parsley stalks, wrapped in cheesecloth)

1. Preheat oven to 400°F.

2. Trim all fat from bones. Place bones in shallow roasting pan.

3. Set the bones to roast in a preheated oven. For approximately 30–40 minutes.

4. Place the bones in a stock pot and fill with 5 quarts cold water.

5. Bring to a boil. Skim.

6. In a pan, brown vegetables. Add to stock. Add *bouquet garni*, the mushroom, tomatoes, and garlic.

7. In a separate pot, reduce the red wine by half. Add to stock.

8. Leave pot uncovered and reduce by simmering, 4–6 hours.

Veal Stock

2 pounds veal bones, knuckles or breast

2 ounces tomato paste

4 ounces onions, chopped ½ cup

3 ounces carrots, chopped ⅓ cup

3 ounce leeks, chopped ⅓ cup

2 ounces mushrooms or mushroom trimmings, ¼ cup

3 ounces celery, chopped ⅓ cup

1 bunch tied mixed herbs: sprigs of thyme, parsley, bay leaf, and peppercorns tied together in cheese cloth

1. Preheat oven to 400°F.

2. Chop the bones.

3. In a roasting pan, roast the bones with tomato paste in oven preheated about 30 minutes. Remove any excess fat. Deglaze with 2 cups water.

4. Place the roasted bones and deglazed liquid from the roasting pan into a large stock pot (about 1 gallon size) with onions, carrots, leeks, mushrooms, celery and herbs. Add 2 quarts cold water.

5. Bring to a boil, skim, and simmer, uncovered, 6–8 hours.

6. Skim off all fat, lift the bones out of the stock with a tongs. Strain. Cool. Refrigerate.

Demi-Glace (Brown Sauce)

MAKES 2 QUARTS

Demi-glace is a well-flavored brown stock reduced by half. It is one of the most important mother sauces, from which many other sauces, stews, and braised dishes are made. Add sherry only after the sauce has been reduced. A little butter may be whisked into sauce immediately prior to serving—it will impart a desirable sheen to the sauce.

4 pounds beef bones (shin bones are best)

½ cup tomato paste

2 onions, diced

2 carrots, diced

1 leek, diced

1 bunch celery, diced

1 bunch tied mixed herbs: sprigs of thyme, parsley, tarragon, bay leaf, and peppercorns tied together in cheese cloth

6 sprigs parsley

3 sprigs thyme

½ cup all-purpose flour

4 quarts brown stock or water

salt and pepper

1 cup sherry

1. Preheat oven to 350°F.

2. Chop bones into small pieces and place into roasting pan with vegetables and herbs.

3. Roast in preheated oven, 2 hours.

4. Mix tomato paste into bones and cook, 20 minutes.

5. Mix all-purpose flour with the fat in the pan. Return to the oven. Cook until it browns slightly.

6. Add beef stock or water. Stir and cook, at least 4 hours.

7. Strain. Reduce volume by half by simmering gently over a moderate heat.

8. Add sherry. Cool and refrigerate.

Simple Brown Sauce

4 tablespoons butter ½ cup

4 ounces of all-purpose flour ½ cup

1 tablespoon tomato paste

3 tablespoons beef base

⅛ cup sherry

brown coloring

salt and pepper

1. Melt butter in a saucepan.

2. Using a spatula, add flour to butter and combine to the consistency of wet sand. Cook over low heat, about 1 minute.

3. Add tomato paste to flour mixture.

4. Add beef base to water. Stir until combined. Bring to a boil.

5. Slowly add the boiling stock to the flour-and-butter *roux*. Stir well, so as to achieve a smooth sauce. Add sherry. Correct color and seasoning. Cool and refrigerate.

MAKES 2 QUARTS

This basic and simple sauce may be used in many recipes which call for a demi-glace.

Bechamel Sauce

Bechamel is considered a mother sauce. Double-thick bechamel can be used as a binding agent for combining foods or, with the addition of other ingredients such as cheese, parsley, or capers, can become standalone sauces. (Double thickness can be obtained by cutting the liquid in half, while using the same amount of roux.)

A properly made bechamel is rich, creamy, and absolutely smooth, with no hint of graininess The flavors of the onion and clove used to season it should be apparent, but not overwhelm the sauce's clean, milky taste. The finished sauce should have a light velvety texture with a white appearance.

4 tablespoons butter

⅓ cup all-purpose flour

1 quart hot milk

1 small onion studded with cloves

salt to taste

⅛ teaspoon ground white pepper

⅛ teaspoon nutmeg

1. Make a *blond roux* by melting butter in a saucepan and adding flour. Cook 1–3 minutes, being careful not to brown.

2. Bring milk to a boil. Place onion in the hot milk.

3. Remove onion. Stir milk, in thirds, into roux, whisking vigorously, until a smooth, velvety sauce is formed.

4. Simmer, 20 minutes, over moderate heat, stirring frequently.

5. Adjust seasoning. Strain through a fine-mesh sieve.

Lemon Butter Sauce

1 shallot, diced fine

1 tablespoon white-wine vinegar

1 tablespoon lemon juice

¼ cup white wine

6 white peppercorns

2 tablespoons heavy cream

12 tablespoons unsalted butter, cut into cubes

salt and ground pepper, to taste

1. Place shallot into a saucepan and add vinegar, lemon juice, white wine, and peppercorns.

2. Reduce the liquid over medium heat to a syrup (about 2 tablespoons) about 1 minute.

3. Add cream and 2–3 drops of cold water.

4. Reboil. Remove from heat.

5. Gradually whisk in butter, piece by piece, away from heat. Return briefly to heat between additions. Return to gentle heat for 1 or 2 minutes.

6. Correct seasoning.

7. Pass through a fine-mesh sieve. Keep in a warm area until needed.

MAKES ABOUT 3 CUPS

This is a basic lemon butter sauce and can be adapted for use either with meat, fish, or vegetable dishes by adding fresh herbs or wines. Special care should be taken so as not to break the sauce by overheating it once the butter has been added.

One simple method to fix the sauce if it breaks is to heat 2 tablespoons water in a separate pot. Remove from heat. Gently drizzle the broken sauce into the water until it reconstitutes.

Tomato Sauce

MAKES 1 ½ QUARTS

This basic tomato sauce has many uses. It may be extended by adding other cooked ingredients, depending on its eventual use, or what it will accompany. When serving with pasta, for example, the sauce need not be strained.

2 ounces bacon, chopped

2 tablespoons butter

½ cup diced onion

¼ cup diced carrot

2 cups diced tomatoes, peeled and seeded

¼ cup all-purpose flour

1 cup tomato paste

1 quart chicken stock

3 cloves crushed garlic

1 teaspoon chopped fresh oregano

3 sprigs thyme

1 bay leaf

salt and pepper

1 teaspoon sugar added just before serving

1 teaspoon of chopped fresh basil

1. Cook bacon over medium heat in a saucepan with butter and vegetables.

2. Stir in flour. Mix over low heat until ingredients resemble wet sand.

3. Add tomato paste and combine. Cook for several minutes, stirring frequently.

4. Whisk in the chicken stock.

5. Add the garlic, oregano, thyme, bay leaf, and seasoning.

6. Simmer over low heat, 90 minutes.

7. Adjust consistency, if required, with a little stock. Strain.

8. Stir in basil.

Fresh Tomato Relish (Coulis)

²/₃ cup chicken stock, reduced to about 2 tablespoons, cold

1 tablespoon tomato paste

½ cup peeled, seeded, and diced tomatoes

4 tablespoons red-wine vinegar

juice of ½ lemon

1 teaspoon sugar

4 tablespoons olive oil

salt, to taste

⅛ teaspoon ground black pepper

1. Combine cold chicken stock with tomato paste.

2. Place fresh tomato into a food processor and puree. Add chicken stock-tomato paste mixture, vinegar, lemon juice and sugar. Blend in food processor, about 30 seconds.

3. With the processor motor running, gradually add oil until desired consistency is obtained. Season with salt and pepper.

The flavor and color of a *coulis* should be that of the main ingredients. The flavors of herbs, spices, and other ingredients should only complement and not dominate the relish, which may be served hot or cold.

Lobster Sauce

A lobster's roe is called the *coral*; it adds great flavor to the sauce. Shrimp shells may be substituted to make a shrimp sauce. This basic sauce may be thinned slightly with fish stock. With the addition of lobster meat, cream, and brandy, it can become a lobster bisque.

1 cup lobster shells (including cooked coral, if possible)

2 tablespoons butter

1 tablespoon diced carrot

1 tablespoon diced onion

1 sprig thyme

3 parsley sprigs

1 ounce diced bacon

2 tablespoons all-purpose flour

½ cup peeled, seeded, and diced tomatoes

2 tablespoon tomato paste

2 cups fish stock

½ cup dry white wine

4 peppercorns

½ teaspoon salt

1 tablespoon brandy

1. Crush lobster shells and coral. A food processor can be used, or pound the shells in a saucepan until they are crushed.

2. Place the pounded shells in a heavy-bottomed saucepan with butter, carrot, onion, thyme, parsley, and diced bacon. Sweat until vegetables are soft.

3. Stir in flour. Continue cooking, 1 minute without allowing the flour to color.

4. Add tomato, tomato paste, fish stock, and white wine, stirring continuously to achieve a smooth consistency.

5. Bring to a boil. Skim off any fat. Add peppercorns. Simmer gently 1 hour, reducing volume by ⅓.

6. Skim as necessary. Strain through a strainer or sieve. Correct seasoning. Add brandy.

Hollandaise Sauce (food-processor method)

3 tablespoons malt vinegar

1 teaspoon finely diced shallots

1 bay leaf

½ teaspoon crushed black peppercorns

3 egg yolks

3 tablespoon of water

1 cup clarified butter, hot

juice of ½ lemon

⅛ teaspoon cayenne pepper

1. In a medium saucepan, over high heat, reduce vinegar with shallots, bay leaf, and peppercorns to approximately 1 tablespoon liquid.

2. When reduced, add 3 tablespoons water. Strain, reserving the liquid.

3. In a food processor fitted with a steel blade, combine the warm reduction and egg yolks. Blend, 15 seconds, at high speed, or until the mixture thickens slightly.

4. While the food processor is running, pour in the hot clarified butter over a 15-second period, in a thin stream. Butter must be hot (120°F) to cook the egg yolks. Use an instant-read thermometer. If the butter is too hot, egg yolks may curdle.

5. Add lemon juice and cayenne.

Hollandaise is an emulsified sauce. Egg yolks, which contain large amounts of lecithin, a natural emulsifier, are used to emulsify warm butter and a small amount of water, lemon juice, or vinegar. By vigorously whipping the egg yolks with the liquid, and slowly adding the warm butter, the lecithin coats the individual oil droplets and holds them in suspension.

Hollandaise sauce will curdle at 180°F. A properly made hollandaise is smooth, buttery, pale lemon-yellow, and very rich.

Hollandaise sauce should be used as soon as possible after preparation. This sauce particularly enhances poached salmon, broccoli, and asparagus spears.

If hollandaise sauce separates, whisk 1 tablespoon separated sauce with 1 tablespoon cold water until the mixture is smooth. Gradually whisk in the separated sauce. If this does not work, start again by whisking 1 egg yolk and 1 tablespoon water in a small, heavy-bottomed saucepan over low heat. until thick. Very gradually whisk in the remaining separated sauce.

Index